FREEMASONRY

A HISTORY

FREEMASONRY
A HISTORY

ANGEL MILLAR

THUNDER BAY
P·R·E·S·S

San Diego, California

Thunder Bay Press
An imprint of the Advantage Publishers Group
5880 Oberlin Drive, San Diego, CA 92121-4794
www.thunderbaybooks.com

Produced by PRC Publishing Limited
The Chrysalis Building
Bramley Road, London W10 6SP, United Kingdom

An imprint of **Chrysalis** Books Group plc

ISBN-13: 978-1-59223-409-7
ISBN-10: 1-59223-409-7

Printed and bound in Malaysia

1 2 3 4 5 09 08 07 06 05

For Gene, my friend and Brother.

Contents

Introduction

The term "free mason" can be found as far back as the thirteenth century and refers to the stonemasons who carved freestone (a type of stone, such as limestone, that would not fracture when chiseled).

In time, it came to signify a stonemason who was free to ply his trade without restriction from the builders' guild or trade union. It seems likely that these free masons traveled from one location to another, joining local groups of builders as required. By the late seventeenth century in Britain, there is evidence that these stonemasons were demonstrating their professional qualifications with specific signs and words that were kept secret within the industry.

The work of early stonemasons was very different from that of modern builders, and their lives and the rules governing their vocation differed from those of their modern counterparts. A master stonemason might share in menial tasks, but he was, for all intents and purposes, the architect of the guild. He knew geometry, designed buildings, and drew architectural plans—though these were far less technical than those produced today and sometimes only gave an artistic impression of the building. In fact, the word "architect," from Greek words, *arche* (premier) and *tektōn* (builder or craftsman), did not enter the English language until fairly late in the sixteenth century.[1] The Christian Church, which, over time, has probably been the greatest patron of the building arts, originally reserved the word as a title for God, the "Architect" of Creation.[2] Freemasonry still refers to God as "the Great Architect," though the fraternity holds all religions in equally high esteem.

The term "free mason" gained popularity among the stonemasons or builders of the seventeenth and early eighteenth century, and it is from here that we derive the contemporary name "Freemason." At that time the term "accepted mason" also came into use and applied to those intellectuals (or at least men not employed in the building profession) who had joined, or rather were accepted by, a masons' lodge. These two terms were later employed together, and today, for example in America, "Free and Accepted Masons" is used as a more official term for a body of Freemasons.

It is also worth noting that in the early medieval period, a lodge was a hut or temporary building in which preparatory building work, such as hewing stones or making some sort of plan, was carried out. By the fourteenth century, stonemasons began forming themselves into guilds or unions around one master mason, and the word "lodge" began to also refer to a

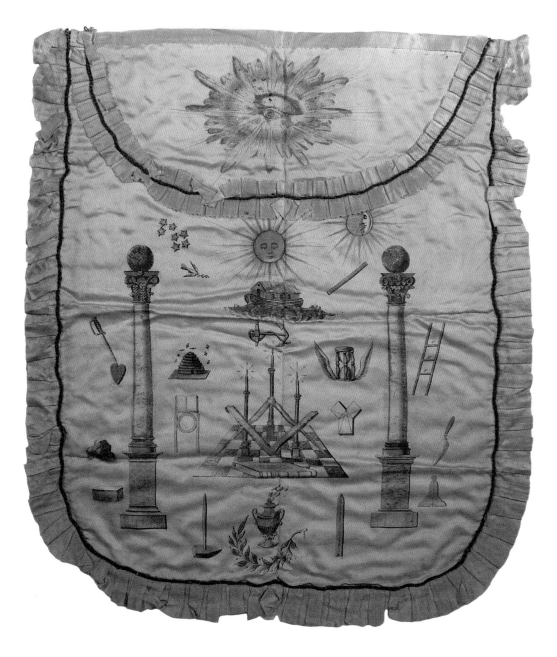

ABOVE: *The lodge is seen at the center with the mosaic pavement, three tapers, the square and compasses, and the Sacred Book. Traditionally, the Sacred Book is also placed on the highest point of the circle in that symbol made up of the point, circle, and parallel lines. This symbol may have related to the architectural plan of the lodge and the positioning of the Sacred Book, the altar, and other materials.*

ABOVE: *This dinner plate from 1833 shows the All-Seeing Eye of God at the center of the square and compasses. The foliage appears to be purely decorative.*

or Freemasonry and Masonry, and all of these terms are employed throughout the book. The lowercase word "mason," however, has been specifically used to refer to a member of a lodge or a guild prior to 1717, when it is not clear whether the primary interest was in building or what might loosely be termed "philosophy." "Mason" has been used when referring to intellectuals initiated into lodges before and after the official establishment of Freemasonry.

Although it is customary among Freemasons to refer to actual builders as "operative masons," the more common terms, "stonemason" or, as we move closer to our own time, "builder," have been used in this book. For significantly, this book is not concerned with the technical or practical (operative) element of building, but is rather concerned with the mythology and rituals (the non-operative elements) of stonemasonry, because it is here that we find the basis of Freemasonry. Finally, since it arose from the craft of stonemasonry, Freemasonry is sometimes simply called the "Craft," and the rituals in which its first three degrees—entered apprentice, fellowcraft, and master mason—are bestowed are sometimes called "Craft Masonry."

Perhaps the most widespread idea of Freemasonry is that its members use secret handshakes. Strictly speaking, Freemasonry has no handshakes

group of stonemasons. These two meanings are retained in Freemasonry today, but it is perhaps more common for the lodge to be a group of Freemasons rather than the place where they meet. There is no practical difference between Freemasons and Masons, whatsoever. What is incorrectly being referred to are the Mason's "token," or "tokens." Superficially, these may look like a handshake as they are usually, though not always, made by two Freemasons gripping each other's hand. However, if we consider that the old meaning of the word "token" was proof, clue, or symbol, we shall see that the Masonic gripping of hands is more complex. On the most basic level, one might think of the token as being "proof of," or at least "a clue to," membership in Freemasonry, though the token is rarely employed outside the lodge room and as such is not often the test of membership in the fraternity (just like other societies, the Freemasons now have membership cards for that purpose). Tokens are used during Masonic rituals, at specific points where they might represent a certain idea or element of mythology. Some tokens represent, for example, the actions or stories of various Biblical characters. Thus the most important and revealing definition of "token" is "symbol." Freemasonry is a philosophy embodied in a language of symbols; for this reason, it is sometimes called "Symbolic Masonry" and the Freemason a "Symbolic Mason."

Today, it is perhaps difficult for many people to understand why Freemasonry is explained through various rituals and symbols. While most of this book seeks to explain this from a historical perspective, we

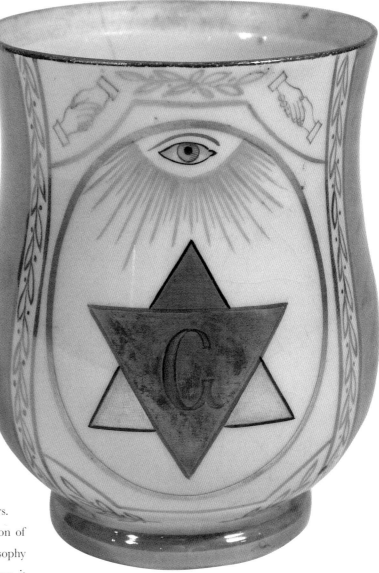

ABOVE: *This Plymouth Masonic mug from the mid-1800s is adorned with the later hexagram type of Blazing Star. A letter "G" representing geometry is at the center. Above is the All-Seeing Eye of God.*

may turn back to the notion of proof (token) and consider it in its higher or truer meaning in regard to Masonic symbolism. The symbols that Freemasonry employs usually demonstrate, or prove, the ideas put forth by Freemasonry, showing that the mysteries of the Craft have an actual basis or existence in the world through nature or society. For example, the Masonic symbol of the beehive (now generally only found in American and some East Asian lodges) illustrates cooperation or the benefits of society. This, of course, is because bees work together to make their honeycombs. So, a society based on cooperation is not then merely an idea, but is something fundamental to our world, or, if one prefers, to the innermost nature of living beings. Using another example, Freemasonry points out the practical or mundane use of the hammer and chisel among stonemasons but redefines or elevates their meaning, putting them in intellectual or spiritual terms. Builders use hammers and chisels to smooth the surface of stones; Freemasonry uses this as an example of how the process of refinement is integral to the world as a whole. The importance of this process primarily concerns the initiate himself; the hammer and chisel symbolize the process of smoothing out the Mason's own rough edges.

While the ritual gives the initiate an actual experience, a sense of participating fully in the mysteries, it also gives the symbols a historical or mythological context and language that draws the many different symbols together into a coherent whole. The Masonic ritual evolves through the story of the life of the head builder of Solomon's Temple, Hiram Abiff. It is through this narrative that the initiate understands that the beehive, as much as the trowel, is also a symbol of building. Indeed, the lecture and ritual act as a dictionary through which the initiate finds his world redefined and elevated. There is no sudden or magic transformation in Freemasonry. Transformation occurs primarily through an intellectual process, because if Freemasonry does not represent one clearly defined intellectual tradition, then it at least represents an intelligent tradition.

Nevertheless, there has been a tendency to perceive Freemasonry in black or white terms. On the one hand, its store of rituals and symbols have seemed to many as somehow occult, though if we look at the symbols themselves we find that they do not really strike us as such. There is nothing very occult about a beehive, for example, and even less so about a hammer and chisel. On the other hand, Freemasonry is often regarded as a social club, a perspective from which it becomes very difficult to explain why such symbols exist. It should be noted that in the same century in which Freemasonry began to be formed, mathematics was much more mystical or religious than it is today. The eminent German mathematician and astronomer Johannes Kepler spoke of the Architect—God—as designing the universe through mathematical formulas, and, for example, teaching bees how to build hexagonal honeycombs. While this might strike us as bizarre, if not occult, neither Kepler nor the scientific world viewed it as such—Kepler himself condemned occultism. England's Sir Isaac Newton studied alchemy and, although he ultimately rejected it, he

ABOVE: *Apron used for the 30th degree of the Ancient and Accepted Scottish Rite, known as the Knight Kadosh.*

took it very seriously. As with Kepler, Newton's scientific findings began to usher in a greater regard for rational thinking, both men's approach to the sciences being one of observation and calculation about the observed.

It has long been suspected that Newton influenced Freemasonry, directly or indirectly, and there is every reason to believe that the beehive in Freemasonry was derived from Kepler's ideas. As such, it would be true to suggest that Freemasonry was born from an anti-occult tradition, though one that was, and is, both rational and mystical (or esoteric) in essence. It is a tradition that has been largely forgotten, to the detriment of a complete understanding of Western

ABOVE: This Masonic apron (early twentieth century) is similar to those traditionally worn by Knight Templar Masons in America.

history and esoteric philosophy. Certainly, it is against this backdrop, and partly in this forgotten intellectual and mystical tradition, that we need to consider Freemasonry, because it was in this environment that this unique society was crafted.

While it was certainly rooted in the guilds of stonemasons, as we shall see, there is no doubt that Freemasonry, or Speculative Masonry, as it is sometimes called, was crafted in the discussions and speculation of the members of these lodges and later codified or preserved in its elaborate rituals.[3] This opens up a number of possibilities, for in the seventeenth century intellectuals began joining masons' lodges, and it was largely as a result of this phenomenon that Freemasonry became independent from the builders' trade. Certainly, some of the intellectuals who joined masons' or builders' lodges were interested in alchemy and, more specifically, in the secret mystical

ABOVE: American Craft certificate (mid-1800s). Charity, represented by a female figure in the center, is flanked on either side by two Freemasons with plain white aprons.

ABOVE: This Liverpool ware pitcher is decorated with a stanza from the "Entered Apprentices Song" by Matthew Birkhead, originally printed in Anderson's Constitutions.

society known as the Rosicrucians; some of the first references to Freemasonry tie it to this society.

Freemasonry continued to develop in the eighteenth century. Most notably, pictorial symbolism took over from a symbolism of geometry, on which much of the former was based. This naturally changed the emphasis of the Masonic lodge, which was only then really beginning to define what Speculative Masonry might be. Moreover, discussions about Freemasonry did not stop here, and as Freemasonry found its way to the European continent from Britain, debate raged as to the meaning of the symbols and the very origin of the society. Although some of the Masonic symbols were comparatively new at that time, they were regarded as clues to the antiquity of Freemasonry. Consequently, while three rituals or degrees (known collectively as the Masonic Ritual) had been established as the structure of a Freemason's spiritual ascent in the lodge, numerous origins for the society were proposed, and new rituals or degrees were devised in order to explain or supposedly prove various theories. Each newly devised ritual had to be older, more interesting, and more exotic than the last. Such rituals were frequently claimed to be the most ancient of all, and newer Masonic bodies often referred to themselves as "Ancient," while previously existing Masonic groups were not infrequently dubbed as "Modern."

To a large extent, the development of Freemasonry into so-called higher degrees was largely owing to various personalities and the human need to rein-terpret tradition. This may seem to invalidate these rituals, but it should not. For in this way they differ very little from some of the greatest poems, paintings, liter-ary works, and sculptures. Indeed, the higher degrees have a certain affinity to works of art since, like them, the rituals were meant to create an impression on one who contemplates them. Most important, the authors of these degrees drew on broader and richer aspects of Western and sometimes Eastern society, and inter-preted the secrets of Freemasonry by them. In a sense, it is here that Freemasonry comes closest to philosophy, mysticism, or pure intellectual speculation. This has not always drawn admiration, especially from Masonic bodies in the English-speaking world, mainly because the narratives of the rituals largely omit the history of Freemasonry as emerging through stonemasonry and the first masonic lodges of Britain.

The most prominent themes that appear in the European reinterpretations of the original Masonic rit-uals are alchemy, or Hermeticism, Kabbalah, and the secret society of the Rosicrucians, or Rosicrucianism, and knighthood, especially the Knights Templar. During this period, "Freemasonry" became a generic term for anything "mystic," and it was common for mystical societies to call themselves "Masonic," even if they had no legitimate link to the Masonic fraternity as descended through stonemasonry. Even these groups have had their spin-offs. In Germany, for example, from 1750 onward was a self-proclaimed Masonic group known as the Clerks Templar. They alleged that it was not the knights but rather their clerks that were in pos-session of all sorts of fabulous wisdom, which by some

miracle they, the Clerks Templar, had inherited. Toward the latter half of the eighteenth century, an unrelated Knights Templar degree also appeared in America. This grew so popular that newspapers reported thousands of Knights Templar Masons parad-ing along main streets during certain celebrations.

Despite its popularity, the Knights Templar degree, and the Knights Templar theory, have been the most criticized in the published writings of prominent and historically inclined Freemasons, though the the-ory is the one best known to non-Masons. Likewise, while this Knights Templar degree still exists, the gov-erning bodies of America make no claim to be either related to, or derived from, the original Knights Templar, but see themselves as bestowing the lessons of chivalry within a Masonic framework.[4]

One of the immediate problems when consider-ing these orders, from a historical perspective, is whether they are to be regarded as Masonic or simply pseudo-Masonic. The Strict Observance, for example, was one of the most powerful so-called Masonic bod-ies existing on the European continent for at least part of the eighteenth century, though it had little, if any, legitimate links to the fraternity that emerged from the building trade at the beginning of the eighteenth cen-tury. In consideration of this problem, as the phenomenon of the development of the higher degrees can, and shall, be viewed as the "second wave" of Masonry, this book refers to these orders as neo-Masonic.

The reinterpretation of Freemasonry has not been confined to the production of various rituals, but has also taken the form of literary and scholarly studies, particularly in the English-speaking world. While much Masonic scholarship—especially in recent years—has been of an extremely high standard, it is worth pointing out that the same sort of errors that have filled many of the higher degrees have also been propagated through such intellectual reinterpretation. One error, which illustrates how the ritual has been occasionally removed from its origin in stonemasonry and recolored according to the proclivities of the individual Freemason through entirely incorrect assumptions, is that the Masonic ritual warns the Freemason to be on his guard against "cowans" so that the secrets of Freemasonry might not be overheard. As the Masonic historian A. E. Waite has pointed out, this term has been variously considered as derived from Hebrew, Syriac, Arabic, and Greek, in the latter case from *kuon*, the Greek word for "dog."[5] A moment's reflection should have been enough to realize that Freemasons would not have cared if their secrets were overheard by dogs, cats, or any other animal for that matter, though this interpretation continues to enjoy some acceptance. *Cowan* is actually an old Scottish word meaning a person who is able to make walls only by piling stones or rocks, lacking the knowledge of how to make mortar, which of course was a trade secret of the stonemasons. In a Masonic sense, this term refers to those who are ignorant of the secrets of Freemasonry.

During the medieval period, secrecy was chiefly a practical matter of guarding the secrets of the building trade from nonbuilders. In the eighteenth century, it largely served to keep the many exotic teachings, symbols, and theories of history within a specific group, one that was competing with a number of others. Ironically, as we shall see, Freemasonry has continually influenced artists and playwrights, and by the latter half of the nineteenth century most, if not all, of the secrets were published. Some of the published materials were exposés, or simple reproductions of the rituals and symbols, produced for a quick profit, and some were clear distortions. Nevertheless, in inspiring artists, writers, and composers, Masonry reached a very broad section of people and became, arguably, the major cultural influence of the eighteenth century. By the latter half of that century, Freemasonry had saturated the arts in Europe. In America, at a time when that nation did not really possess much of an iconography that could express its ethics, the symbols of the Craft were often used in the designs of folk arts, such as quilting, embroidery, or woodwork. Notably, many of the early American revolutionary leaders, such as George Washington, Benjamin Franklin, and Paul Revere, were Masons, and the idea naturally took root that the ethics of Freemasonry were essentially the same as those of newly independent America, especially after Washington had made a public display of his membership in the fraternity.

Although Freemasonry is not, and does not consider itself, a secret society today, it does claim that it has secrets. These are, of course, the symbols and rituals of the society, although, as we have said, they have been published numerous times and are likewise to be found in classical literature and both high and low art. However, in a sense, the real secrets are the insights of the individual Freemason, gleaned both from his personal involvement in as well as the study of the Craft. The symbols, rituals, and the history itself are only clues. In this regard, Freemasonry is exactly the same as any art or science that remains of value to the human soul. Science also has secrets, as does painting and poetry. Like the Masonic secrets, the secrets of painting, for example, have been written down and are freely available, but merely reading them will not, and cannot make anyone a painter. Indeed, the peculiar recipes of making paint by mixing egg white and pigments derived from metal, for example, would be surely arcane and superfluous, if not ridiculous, to someone who only reads about them. Yet to the painter they might provide enormous help in his practices, and through them he might gain invaluable insights. The nonpainter must view the finished painting to understand art, for here the techniques, the exact brushstrokes, and colors used are in evidence.

Similarly, while all of the so-called Masonic secrets have been written down, they would not enable the non-Mason to understand the essential aspects of Freemasonry.

In a sense, the Mason, like the painter, is one who is not only engaged in but also attempting to know the secrets of his art through the practice of it. What the artist and scientist share with the world are their "results"—the new painting, the new understanding of physics. In this work we also share the results of that art and science called Freemasonry. It is an experiment that has lasted hundreds of years. Freemasons may not have made gold, but they have sometimes made history, and more important they have often succeeded in making good men better. Regardless, one point should be made clear: Freemasonry cannot enlighten man. Rather it is man who might enlighten himself through Freemasonry.

Chapter 1: The Legend of the Craft

Like other medieval trade guilds, the British stonemasons' lodge demanded fair treatment for and from its members. It also expected the stonemason to respect the directions of the master mason, to obey the civil law, and to attend church regularly.

However, the lodge was held together not only by social and practical concerns relating to wages, labor, and skill, but also by much more profound issues. Stonemasons had developed a complex mythology that not only supposed the roots of the craft to lie in the lands of the Bible, but showed it being brought to the West in a winding and magnificent journey, patronized along the way by kings, princes, Biblical figures, and the most learned names of history. Just as important, the stonemason viewed the code of conduct that had been laid down by his lodge as extending from Biblical figures through all of the lodges that had existed before his own.

The stonemasons' mythology and codes of ethics were recorded throughout the centuries in various texts known today as the "Old Charges." In the early eighteenth century, when the fraternity of Freemasonry was especially conscious of its roots in the building industry, these texts were used to establish much of its own mythology and ethical, fraternal doctrine. Here it is important to note that medieval architectural design was based on geometry; for example, the designs of the great churches were based on the square or triangle.[1] As a consequence, the Old Charges place a great deal of emphasis on the history of geometry, which is commonly portrayed as identical to stonemasonry. Taking its cue from the stonemasons, when Freemasonry finally emerged some centuries later it would view geometry as synonymous with Freemasonry.

The oldest of the British Old Charges in existence is known as the Regius Manuscript (Regius MS), or the *Halliwell Poem*, after James Orchard Halliwell, who first published the text in 1840 in his *Early History of Freemasonry* in England. The *Halliwell Poem* is thought to have been written around 1390, although the Masonic scholar Albert Mackey proposes the possibility of it having been drafted as early as 1300 and suggests that its content was derived from the mythologies of the stonemasons of Germany.[2] Whether or not this claim is justifiable, there were comparable trade lodges on the European continent, some of which had a similar mythology to that of their English counterparts, and British stonemasonry almost certainly adopted some of its major ideas and mythological motifs from abroad. Nevertheless, the *Halliwell Poem* is thought to have been copied from one or more earlier British texts that are no longer in existence.

The Cooke Manuscript (Cooke MS), dated to between 1410 and 1490, is generally considered to be the next oldest of the Old Charges. It is written in a distinctly less archaic style than the *Halliwell Poem*. Curiously, the *Halliwell Poem* is somewhat different in content than all the other Old Charges, which closely resemble one another both in structure and content. As such, the Cooke MS may represent the start of a divergence of thought or myth in the medieval building trade. Most important, this text contains the very first reference to the Temple of Solomon in any known Old Charge. The Temple would not only remain a constant in these builders' texts, but would become, arguably, the main motif of Freemasonry by the eighteenth century and would penetrate into the general sciences as a matter of serious consideration even before this.

With the exception of the Regius MS, which does not mention the Temple, the stonemasons' mythological writings agree on essential points. They tell us, for example, the importance of the seven classical sciences of medieval education, better known as the Seven Liberal Arts. Likewise, they give a history of geometry as developing in Egypt, propagated by the famous geometer Euclid, and they discuss Hermes and the twin pillars, most of which has found its way into the rituals and symbolism of Freemasonry. Except for

ABOVE: A Masonic Craft certificate from 1876. In the oval frame are various masonic symbols, many drawn from stonemasonry.

a few obvious gaps in the journey of stonemasonry, it describes how the Craft came from the Biblical lands to Britain. The importance of a direct line of descent is of equal significance for Freemasonry today as it had

ABOVE: This Masonic Craft apron shows many of the symbols of the first three degrees. Like many other Masonic symbols, the trowel, plumb line, and level (left) are derived from stonemasonry. Strangely, the letter "G" is suspended from a ribbon, held by a figure.

OPPOSITE: Detail of a master Mason's apron, early nineteenth century. The lamb and the cock are rarely seen on Masonic aprons. The lamb represents innocence, as well as the Mason's apron, and here may also allude to Christ. Beneath the lamb is a Calvary cross with the traditional Roman letters, I.N.R.I. (signifying Iesus Nazarenus Rex Iudaeorum, "Jesus, King of the Jews"). The cock represents courage. The crossed keys are generally an emblem of the lodge treasurer, to whom this apron may have belonged.

been for Freemasonry and the guilds of stonemasonry in the past. Today, for example, Masonic lodges must be licensed, or chartered, by a governing or grand lodge that is recognized as having a legitimate history, and must adhere to the principles of Masonry.

The other most critical point of similarity among the texts is that they open with a prayer to God the Creator and, in manuscripts later than the Cooke MS, to the Christian Trinity. The Grand Lodge MS (1583), for example, opens with "the might of the Father of Heaven and the wisdom of the glorious Son through the grace and the goodness of the Holy Ghost that is three persons and one God."[3] The Cooke MS reads:

> Thanks be to God
> Our glorious Father and founder and former
> of heaven and earth
> And of all things that in him that he would
> vouchsafe
> Of His glorious Godhead to make so many
> things
> Of diverse virtue for mankind.

Because at this time Roman Catholicism was the religion of the British people and monarch, Mackey defines the Christian content of the *Halliwell Poem* as Catholic and suggests that some sections of the text were authored by a priest or cleric.[4] However, since the texts reveal a broad mythology, the term "Roman Catholic" may be somewhat naïve, though it is certainly true that a substantial portion of the *Halliwell Poem* is concerned with Church ritual. It is true also

that stonemasons in Britain were Christian, but this would hardly have singled them out as in any way different from most of society. The explicit references to church ritual, however, would appear to have been added to the main text later on, almost certainly by a cleric, as Mackey suggests, and we should not underestimate the importance of such references. Thus, for example, we read in regard to the Eucharistic ritual:

> And when you hear the [church] bell ring
> To that holy consecration
> Kneel most, both young and old,
> And both hands fair uphold
> And say then in this manner
> Fair and soft, without noise
> "Lord Jesus welcome, thou
> In the form of the [Eucharistic] bread, as I
> thee see,
> Now Jesus for thy holy name
> Shield me from sin and shame."

Churches often took several decades to build, and the stonemasons' lodges became permanently established and connected to churches and cathedrals for the period of construction, even when work was temporarily halted due to lack of funding—in the records of York, from 1344, it is reported that, as there was little work to do, the masons of one lodge had begun to squabble among themselves, apparently through boredom.[5] Given that that there was sometimes a permanent connection between the stonemasons' lodge and the Church, we might ask whether their

ABOVE: An angel shows a weary traveler the way to the Temple. In the top left is the square and compasses, and in the top right are two hands gripping.

Holy Church and all Saints, and his master
and fellows as his own brethren.

The Old Charges assert that stonemasonry was brought to England in the reign of King Athelstan, when Saint Alban patronized it. Though there have been several British kings named Athelstan, it is most likely that the Old Charges refer to the one whose coronation took place in 925. In later texts, the entrance of stonemasonry into Britain was both elaborated and somewhat corrupted. Thus, in the Cooke MS, for example, we read simply that Athelstan's son patronized masonry, while in later texts he is named Edwin, though the historical Athelstan did not have a son by this name. According to the later stonemasons' myth, Edwin held an assembly of masons at York, granting them their "charges," or rules of conduct or ethics, and in some cases founding a lodge or grand lodge of stonemasons from the assembly.[6]

In the Cooke MS, we read the bare bones of this later mythology:

relationship was not one of employer and employee, but rather one of clergy and acolyte, particularly in regard to the master mason of the lodge. That is to say, we might ask whether any religious scholarship had passed from the Church to the builder and, moreover, whether this affected his particular mythology. Most interestingly, we read in the Cooke MS:

This council is made by diverse lords and
masters of diverse provinces and diverse congregations of masonry. And it is that [he] who
covets to come to the state of the aforesaid art
he is behoved principally to love God and the

[Then] came Saint Adhabelle in to England
and he converted Saint Alban to Christendom.
And Saint Alban loved masons well and he
gave them first their charges and manners in
England. And he ordained convenient [wages]
to pay for their travail. And after that was a
worthy king in England that was called
Athelstan, and his youngest son loved well the
science of Geometry. And he knew well that
[no] handcraft had the science of Geometry so

ABOVE: *French pitcher, early nineteenth century. This pitcher shows two figures between two pillars surmounted by the celestial and terrestrial globes found in Freemasonry.*

may have been the cause of some confusion to the original author, before the myth was replicated in later texts. There was a King Edwin in Northumbria from 617 until his death in 633. He is almost certainly of significance as he introduced Christianity to his kingdom and patronized the bishop of York. The foundations of York Cathedral, or Minster, were also laid during his reign. It is possible that Edwin was joined with Athelstan, who lived some centuries after him, as both were Christian kings for whom Northumbria and York were of significance. Mackey has suggested that the connection is a more literal one, namely, that Edwin promoted architecture and building, and Athelstan reestablished it later on, it having fallen into decline after Edwin.[7] Nevertheless, it is difficult to disassociate stonemasonry from the religion, and perhaps even the politics, of Christianity in Britain at that time or before—the building of places of worship distinguished the Christians from pagans.

According to the *Halliwell Poem*, the origin of stonemasonry lies in the building of the Tower of Babel. The Cooke MS, however, not only apparently introduces the Temple of Solomon for the first time in the builders' myth, but also strongly suggests that it is the origin of what might be called "real masonry." Some Freemasons repeat this theme later on, in part to show the beginning of Freemasonry, rather than the building trade. Certainly the shift from the Tower to the Temple is, psychologically, a dramatic one and suggests, perhaps, that the builders' guild had begun to see themselves as participating in a religious voca-

well as masons, so he drew them to council, and learned the practice of that science of his speculations. For of the speculative he was a master, and he loved well masonry and masons. And he became a mason himself.

If Athelstan did not have a son named Edwin, he did have a brother by this name and, although unlikely, this

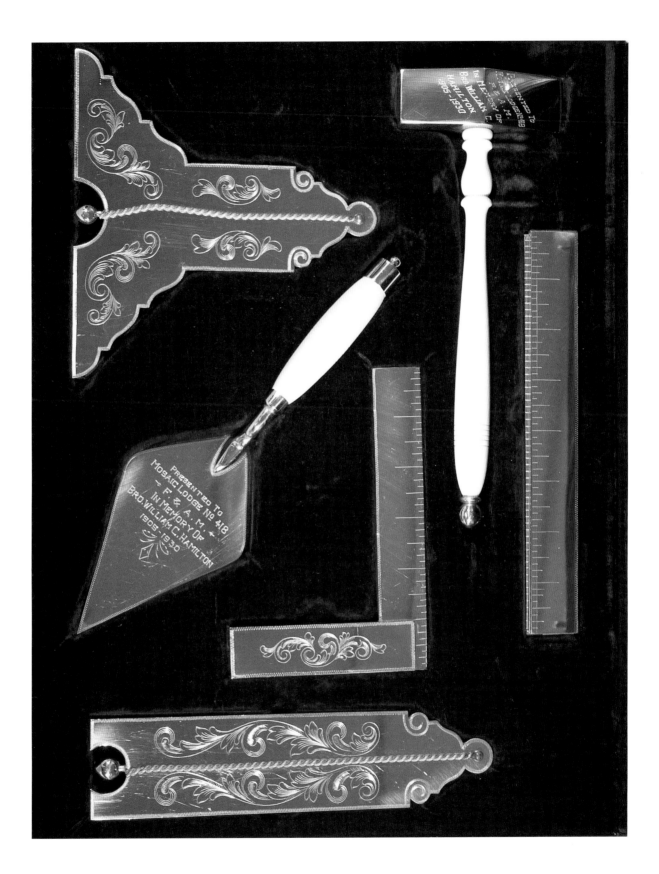

ABOVE: A box containing the "working tools," dated 1930. It contains the 24-inch gauge, the gavel, the level, trowel, square, and plumb line.

ABOVE: *Certificate from the Grand Lodge of Scotland, 1889.*

tion, that is to say not simply constructing churches, but actually being a continuation of a tradition stemming from the first church—the Temple. Indeed, according to the Old Testament, the Tower of Babel was not only built in defiance of God but also ended in a shambles, and it is very likely that the medieval British builders simply accepted this tale as historical fact. Interestingly, the Temple's history exactly opposes that of the Tower because, according to the Old Testament, God laid down the plans for the construction of the Temple. Nevertheless, the building of

the Tower is recorded in the later Old Charges. The Cook MS states:

> And this same Cam began the tower of Babylon and he taught to his workmen the craft of masonry and he had with him many masons, more than xl thousand.
> And he loved and cherished them well.

Also according to the Cooke MS:

> [At] that time the children of Israel dwelled in Egypt they learned the craft of masonry. And afterward they were driven out of Egypt they came to the land of their behest, which is now called Jerusalem, and it was occupied [by them] and charges held. And the making of king Solomon's Temple that king David began. King David loved well masons and he gave them first [their charges] right, not as they are now. And at the making of the Temple in Solomon's time as it is said in the Bible . . . that Solomon had iiii score thousand masons at his work. And the king of Tyre was his Master Mason. And in other chronicles it is said and in old books of masonry that Solomon confirmed the charges that David his father had given to masons. And Solomon himself taught them their manners [that are] but little different from the manners that now are used.

ABOVE: *This silk case has very unusual symbolism depicted on it. It is decorated with a central symbol that appears to be an incense burner. The sphinx does not form a part of Masonic symbolism, though it has sometimes been used as a decorative device.*

There appears to be a literary or scriptural background to the Cooke MS that extends beyond the Bible. Thus, we hear of "other chronicles" and of the "old books of masonry," the latter being most likely some Old Charges that are now lost to us.

The Cooke MS also mentions the work of the Venerable Bede, the monk and historian who has left us much information on King Edwin of Northumbria and Saint Alban. All of these literary influences, and others besides them, naturally created a mythology unique to the stonemasons.

On the north porch of Chartres Cathedral, France, there are several Biblical figures that represent the fathers of the various crafts. For example, we find Adam, the First Man, representing agriculture, Jubal representing music, and Tubal Cain representing metallurgy. Moreover, we find on a twelfth-century arch of the cathedral the Seven Liberal Arts represented both by individual female figures (typically in the West the sciences and virtues are represented as feminine) and various classical thinkers.[8] Thus the Seven Liberal Arts and their patrons are:

Dialectic:	Aristotle
Rhetoric:	Cicero
Geometry:	Euclid
Arithmetic:	Boethius
Astronomy:	Ptolemy
Grammar:	Priscian or Donatus
Music:	Pythagoras

Not only these Liberal Arts, but Jubal, Tubal Cain, Noah, and other Biblical characters also entered the stonemasons' mythology. Yet, it is the introduction of Tubal Cain, the Bible's own blacksmith, to the Old Charges that is particularly interesting. Certainly in the Biblical account of Solomon's Temple, metalwork is of importance, its two great pillars, for example, being cast in brass. However, Tubal Cain, being a far more ancient personage, did not work on the Temple and is naturally entirely distinguished from it in both Biblical and building texts. In pre-Christian, northwestern Europe, the various trades had become a part of the mythologies of the numerous deities, with the exception of stonemasonry, as this had not been developed in that region. To some extent, the inclusion of Jubal, Tubal Cain, and other Biblical characters in the Old Charges might stem from a deliberate attempt by the

ABOVE: *This mark master s jewel shows the square, beneath which is a capstone. The ritual of the mark master degree focuses on the use of trade marks by stonemasons.*

stonemasons to recast the trades in a Biblical light. Distinct from the other arts of northwestern Europe, as linked specifically to Christianity, stonemasonry might well have been considered the capstone of the trades in this new era.

In pre-Christian Europe, blacksmiths participated in religious rites, where they often performed in an official and semipriestly or magical capacity. Many ancient religions gave special attention to fire as a symbol of the Divine, and the smith was the person most adept at controlling fire, albeit in a literal sense. Smiths also developed a symbolism of their own tools (e.g., the smith hammer), as they did of metal and, more interestingly, stone, which was not regarded as entirely different or even distinct from metal. While today we make a definite distinction between the two, we also tend to forget that some types of stone act in ways not entirely unlike metal. Marble burns, and sparks can be procured from flint, which was commonly used to start fires. Also, like metal, stones are mined. Myths and rites surrounding mines were probably once the privilege of blacksmiths (in Europe these rites were still performed at mines until the end of the medieval period[9]). As Christianity spread and established itself throughout Europe, however, such quarries became the temporary property of stonemasons as they excavated stone to be shaped into building blocks for churches.

As the references to the Biblical smith in the Old Charges and to metalworking at the construction sites of the Temple might imply, smiths and stonemasons had certainly come into contact professionally, though smiths played a much subordinate role in the building trade. For example, in the massive expansion of fortifications in Britain at the end of the thirteenth century, 227 stonemasons and 30 smiths were employed at Harlech.[10] If stonemasons in Britain were only beginning to construct a mythology of their craft at this

BELOW: This Masonic mug from the early 1900s is decorated with the two pillars and a letter "G," representing geometry.

ABOVE: A Masonic jewel with two pillars, the square and compasses (center), and a dove (above).

point, blacksmiths were probably barely still clinging to theirs. However, it can hardly be overlooked that just as mining rites continued to be performed, so blacksmiths seem to have continued to participate in initiations of male members of society.[11]

It is also certain that other trade groups had and continued to practice their own guild rituals, at least on the Continent, if not in Britain. As such, stonemasonry in Britain was well placed to adopt some of the initiatory aspects of the smith's craft, or the ritualistic practices of other guilds with which it had contact. The same is undoubtedly true of the building guilds of continental Europe, and it would not have been impossible for such an influence to spread to Britain.

We have considered the influence of both trade guilds and Christianity on the mythology of the stonemasons, but another possible influence on the development of the stonemasons' mythology should also be taken into account, namely the Kabbalah. Despite the fact that it is sometimes regarded as beginning with Adam or Moses, historically speaking, the Jewish forms of mysticism, known as Kabbalah, first emerged in the South of France in the twelfth century, and from there spread to Spain and beyond.[12] According to Arthur Versluis, contact between Freemasonry and Kabbalah was probably first made during this period, due to the relationships that existed at this time between the Jewish, Islamic, and Christian communities of these areas.[13] While we should not confuse the myths and ritual practices of stonemasonry with Freemasonry proper, it would appear that the early British stonemasons' myth was influenced by a European tradition that in turn had been shaped by Jewish traditions that might very loosely be considered Kabbalistic.

According to one Jewish tradition, the Middle Eastern prophet Zoroaster had been taught the arts of magic and astronomy by Abraham, who, in turn, learned them from the Egyptians.[14] Moreover, Zoroaster had recorded the Seven Liberal Arts on fourteen columns, half being made of brick, and half of brass. Similarly, we are told by the Old Charges that all the sciences that man had learned—music, metallurgy, weaving, building, geometry, etc.—as well as the Seven Liberal Arts, were written upon two pillars. The Old Charges assert that God would wreak havoc on the earth, specifically for the sins of the people there. This, of course, was realized in the form of the great flood. In the builders' texts, though, we are told that it was not known whether God would send his wrath by water or fire, so the two pillars were each crafted from different types of stone, one of marble and one of brick, in the hope that at least one of the pillars would survive. Oddly enough, the Cooke and other such manuscripts appear to mix up the qualities of these two materials, claiming that marble would not burn and that brick would not sink in water. In fact, marble does burn (it was burned by stonemasons in order to make lime—the primary ingredient in mortar), and brick certainly does not float in water.

There are several versions in the Old Charges of how geometry came to be invented. In the Cook MS, for example, more than one origin is ascribed. In one version, Jabal invents geometry and becomes the master mason at the building of the first city, Enoch. In other versions, Euclid or Abraham is held to have been the inventor, and in the latter case, Abraham is held to have taught Euclid, who then taught the ancient Egyptians. In one other version, the Egyptians are said to have invented geometry themselves.

ABOVE: *This early-nineteenth-century master Mason s apron shows the pillars, the square and compasses, sun, moon and stars, and triangle.*

Several years after the flood, the two pillars were discovered. Thus, the Cooke MS reads:

> And after this flood—many years as the
> chronicle says—these ii pillars were found
> and . . . a great scholar called Pythagoras
> found one and Hermes the philosopher found
> the other. And they taught the sciences they
> found there written.

With regard to the identity of Hermes, there have been several, perhaps partly historical, figures who bore that name. These have sometimes been linked together in various ways. Hermes is equated with the Egyptian god Thoth and also with the Roman god Mercury; he became the son of Zeus and Maia in Greek mythology, while in some of the Old Charges he has been transformed into Euclid, who takes over his mythology.[15] Just as Hermes was also considered the inventor of so many arts, particularly agriculture, geometry, astronomy, and music, as well as those pertaining to alphabets, numbers, and weights, Euclid also becomes a cultivator of the land.[16] Geometry, as the Cooke MS points out, literally means earth *(Gê)*, measurement *(metron)*:

Euclid was one of the first founders of
Geometry, and he gave it its name. For in his
time there was water in that land of Egypt
that is called the Nile. And it flowed so far into
the land that men might not dwell therein.
Then this worthy cleric Euclid taught them to
make great walls and ditches to hold out the
water. And by Geometry he measured the
land and partitioned it into diverse parts.

Given his appendage as "philosopher," the Hermes of the Cooke MS seems to be equated with Hermes Trismegistus ("thrice greatest"), the father of alchemy. According to the alchemical, or Hermetic, tradition, he wrote the laws of this art on an emerald stone or tablet, while in parallel traditions an earlier Hermes recorded the various sciences on either stone tablets or pillars that were later recovered by Hermes the philosopher, or Hermes Trismegistus.[17] Notably,

medieval Christians also adopted Hermes, as the inventor of various arts, into their tradition, while Hermes the father of alchemy remained of importance in the alchemical tradition of Europe, which again found many of its patrons among Christian intellectuals of the Middle Ages and later.

The notion of an earlier and later Hermes brings us back to the idea of the "son" in stonemasonry. For example, we read in the Old Charges of the lineage of which Tubal Cain was part, of the sons of Noah, of the Egyptian desire to find a vocation for their sons, and that King Athelstan also had a son who had proved significant for the building trade. Yet, most provocatively, according to the Cooke MS, King David began the construction of the Temple and gave the stonemasons their charges or rules, but the Temple was merely completed by his son, King Solomon—this, of course, contradicts Biblical testament that says David was forbidden by God to construct the Temple. It is not unlikely that, given the emphasis on the son, or sons, in the Old Charges—to the point of historical and Biblical inaccuracy—that it perhaps points to a hereditary aspect of the stonemasons' tradition: that it was largely passed from father to son and that this had, in part, affected the choice of myth and their interpretation of it. Even today, the son is still accorded symbolic significance in Masonry, though to a far lesser extent. The son of a Freemason is referred to as a "lewis," after the type of clamp that is used to help raise building blocks from the ground.[18]

Most important, for the later Freemasonic mythology, we frequently read in the Old Charges,

ABOVE: *Triangular box, mid-1800s. This small box once contained a miniature set of working tools. The lid is decorated with a painting of a plumb, symbolic of the upright man and Mason.*

ABOVE: *The trowel is specifically a symbolic tool of the master Mason and represents the cementing of friendship and fraternal love.*

And King Solomon sent and fetched Hiram out of Tyre. He was a widow's son of the tribe of Naphtali, and his father was a man of Tyre, a worker in brass: and he was filled with wisdom, and understanding, and cunning to work all works in brass. And he came to king Solomon, and wrought all his work.

such as the Cooke MS, that the master mason at the construction of King Solomon's Temple was the son of Hiram, king of Tyre. According to the Bible (2 Chron. 2:13), King Hiram had written a letter to King Solomon stating, "And now I have sent a cunning man endued with understanding of Huram [Hiram] my father's." This master mason, Hiram, or Hiram Abiff as he is more generally referred to in Freemasonry, has been identified with the son spoken of in the Old Charges.[19] Again, according to the Bible (2 Chron. 2:14), Hiram was "skillful to work in gold, and in silver, in brass, in iron, in stone, and in timber, in purple, in blue, and in fine linen, and in crimson." According to 1 Kings 7:13–14:

While stone and linen are mentioned in Chronicles, the emphasis is clearly on Hiram's ability as a smith, while in Kings his work is exclusively that of a metalworker, not a stoneworker. Nevertheless, despite a rather modest place afforded King Hiram's son in the Old Charges, in the early eighteenth century Hiram Abiff was elevated to the central figure of the Masonic ritual, where he is held as the master stonemason of Solomon's Temple. Nevertheless, the historical situation for stonemasonry is enriched when we realize that Hiram Abiff, the alleged son of Hiram, king of Tyre, had, according to Biblical testament, made two pillars in brass that stood before the entrance to the Temple of Solomon. The two different pillars in the Old Charges, already mentioned, were merged in Freemasonry with the Biblical pillars. At Würzburg Cathedral in Germany there are two columns carved by the stonemasons *(Steinmetzen)* of the medieval period and identified with the two pillars of the Temple.[20] At the tops of the Würzburg columns are the traditional names of the pillars, Jachim and Boaz, signifying respectively, "he will establish" and "in strength" (per-

ABOVE: Painting on the theme of the broken column, associated with the death of Hiram Abiff, originally printed in the magazine American Masonic Outlook, *by Paul Orban, 1950s.*

haps meaning, "in strength shall my house be established").[21] This could suggest the notion that Hiram Abiff was important to stonemasonry, at least on the European continent, and was contemporary with the idea propagated in British stonemasons' lodges that the son of Hiram, king of Tyre, was the builder of the Temple. These pillars are also important in that they suggest that the stonemasons identified the Church, or churches, with the Temple of Solomon. In early Masonic rituals we find the Temple, Church, and lodge regarded in accord with each other.

The British stonemasons had some at least occasional link to the guilds of Europe, and there can be no question that myths of the British stonemasons were to some extent imported from the trade guilds of the Continent. Most notably, the *Halliwell Poem* speaks of the Ars Quatour Coronatorum (Four Crowned Ones) who were heralded as something like the patron saints of various trade groups in parts of Europe—a memorial niche was built by a Florentine guild of stonemasons and smiths in the fifteenth century.[22] The *Halliwell Poem*, in essence, offers them as examples of the stonemason ideal. Simply put, these figures were four Roman stonemasons who, refusing to denounce their Christian faith, were executed by the Roman emperor.

While the Old Charges should not be considered as factually correct, it is interesting to note that most of these texts speak of stonemasonry coming to England from France, while British and French stonemasons both claimed King Charles Martel (Charles the second) of France as one of their early patrons.[23] For example, the Cooke MS states, "And this same King Charles was a mason before he was king. And, afterward when he was king he loved masons and cherished them, and gave them charges and manners."

The trade organization that is most often compared to the Freemasonic fraternity, and which arguably bore the greatest resemblance to the stonemasons' lodges of Britain, is the Companionage, or "Companions," which acted as an umbrella organization for the various stonemasons and related groups of France. Like their British counterparts, the Companions practiced an initiation ritual and possessed a mythology of their guild. In one of the most recent of the Old Charges, the Carmick MS (dated 1727), we are told rather simplistically that the master mason, or head of the assembly, took a Bible in his right hand while the aspiring mason also laid his hand on it. An oath was read aloud by the master mason, apparently from an Old Charge manuscript, and the initiate kissed the Bible at the completion of the recitation, signaling his intent to conform to the rules of the lodge. This ceremony, which appears to have been common practice among the stonemasons' lodges, is undoubtedly the root of the later Freemasonic ritualism and has remained part of the rituals of the three degrees. However, in addition to these simple actions, the mythology of the Old Charges may also have constituted some part of the British stonemasons' ritual, as such bringing it closer to the later, mythologically influenced Freemasonic ritual.

The French Companions were divided into three different groups or types of trades, each of which possessed a legend linking it to a mythical founder. Calling themselves "sons" or "children," the three groups are known as the Sons of Solomon, Sons of Maître Jacques, and the Sons of Maître Soubise, with the stonemasons being the original group calling itself the Sons of Solomon.[24] According to their myth, Maître Jacques traveled to Jerusalem, via Egypt, in order to work for King Solomon. There he was asked by the master of the work to carve two columns. He did this and was received as a master of the work by Solomon and Hiram. Having left Jerusalem with Maître Soubise, Jacques was set upon by the devotees of his companion, as Soubise had grown increasingly jealous of Jacques' success during the construction of the Temple. Maître Jacques escaped into a reedy swamp, where his disciples rescued him. Unfortunately, he was betrayed and killed by the followers of Soubise. His sons then divided his clothes among the various guilds; his hat was given to the hatters, his belt to the carpenters, and his tunic to the stonemasons.[25]

Chapter 2: An Exchange of Secrets

Society changed dramatically over the three hundred years or so that separated the writing of the first known of the stonemason's Old Charges in the late fourteenth century and the founding of the first grand lodge of Freemasons in the early eighteenth century.

Of particular importance was the invention of moveable type and the printing press in Europe in the fifteenth century. The Old Charges continued to be written, manuscripts continued to be circulated among the few, and the first Rosicrucian texts published in the seventeenth century were written out as almost pious exercises. Nevertheless, after the fifteenth century, and the first appearance of printing on the European continent, the roots that would later inform the intellectual content of Freemasonry can be found as much in the printed book as in handwritten documents. Although the audience intended by authors for their works undoubtedly consisted of educated specialists, the mass production, distribution, and the relative inexpensiveness of the printed book enabled more people to access information. Printing allowed for a greater exchange of established knowledge and new ideas throughout Europe among groups that were not defined by location but rather, broadly speaking, by a shared philosophy.

The influence and expansion of the printing press was rapid. By the sixteenth century the works of the second-century Greek astronomer Ptolemy and the ancient Greek mathematician Euclid (circa 325–250 BC) had been published. The eternally indiscriminate printing press not only was available to the rational sciences but also availed itself to the explicitly esoteric thinker—the Kabbalist, the alchemist, and the magician. The academic and the esoteric were not quite as distinct as they are regarded today, and they were often linked by a similarity of perception regarding the world, the universe or heavens, and even history (in which Biblical history was included). This does not mean, of course, that the academic did not view the magician with contempt; he often did. The sciences tended to deal with what might be called "principles," and geometry, or the principles of geometry, were seen to underlie most, if not all, of the disciplines, from architecture to astronomy. We should not exclude mysticism and Kabbalah from the domains of thought in which geometry played a fundamental role. Nor was religion uninfluenced by geometry. Indeed, religion and geometry were often fused, and the vocabulary related to one gave way to the other. Thus, the Christian theologian considered God as the Architect par excellence. To some extent, a rather mystical type of Christian theology (and perhaps even Christianized Kabbalah) entered the sciences, while the sciences, for their part, influenced Christian interpretations of Kabbalah.

God, the Architect, became a theme not only of the theologian but also of the mathematician. In the seventeenth century, the German astronomer Johannes Kepler (1571–1630) composed and published *The Six-Cornered Snowflake*, a treatise on geometry, the language of which touches on the religious. Similarly, one of Germany's greatest artists, Albrecht Dürer (1471–1528), who was also connected to the mystical, wrote a mathematical textbook. It is only with the English physicist Isaac Newton (1642–1727) that we really start to find a line being drawn clearly between the scientific and the mystical, though even Newton had studied alchemy with some seriousness.

If printing paved the ground for the growth of intellectual argument, it also, somewhat antithetically, contributed to the growth of pictorial symbolism itself. An image only really becomes a symbol when it is seen repeated, and until its replication by others it really remains a personal, rather than a universal, expression. The printing press provided a proliferation of imagery. Illustrations generally and the frontispiece (the illustrated, decorative page facing a book's title page) in particular were made to represent the prevailing intellectual culture of the written word. Like fine art

ABOVE: This ornament shows the compasses suspended by a ribbon, as well as the square, rule, gavel, and plumb.

ABOVE: Detail of the frontispiece to the first English translation of Euclid's Elements, *1570. Geometry is represented by a female figure holding a rule, square, and compasses.*

painters, the illustrators of frontispieces borrowed whole compositional arrangements from previous works. Consequently, the composition of frontispieces became all but standardized, even as the content of publications themselves varied dramatically. Similarly, a particular motif that appeared within the composition of one important text would be borrowed for another and another, each replication probably referencing the previous book or books—this established the tradition of which the author was both a part and, temporarily, the culmination. One of the most frequently appearing compositions was that of a scene between two pillars, though these cannot be viewed as the origin of those that are represented in the Masonic lodge today, because these are derived from the two columns included in the myths of the British stonemasons.

Printing was important, however, in that it helped to fuse the intellectual, scientific culture of the sixteenth and seventeenth centuries with that of the stonemasons' culture and practice. The artist and the intellectual were increasingly encroaching on the world of the master mason (or architect, as he was then known) as perspective and proportion became of greater importance to the artist, while geometry was similarly becoming of greater consequence to the developing sciences. Although the square and compasses were sometimes found in representations of stonemasonry (e.g., in manuscripts, or as sculptures adorning churches) they had not yet become stylized in the form that Freemasonry would eventually adopt and make their most visible symbol. It is in printing that we find the now Masonic symbol par excellence, though even here it was originally set forth as a symbol of intellectual culture based on geometry.

In regard to the frontispiece, the historian Frances A. Yates (1899–1991) has highlighted the intellectual, astrologer, and sometimes alchemist John Dee. Yates pointed out, for example, that depicted in the frontispiece to Dee's *Monas Hieroglyphica* (printed in Antwerp in 1564 and reprinted in Frankfurt in 1591) is the Monas symbol stationed between two pillars, and that this symbol would later appear on the front page of one of the manifestos of the Rosicrucians of Germany, a society that has often been compared to, or considered to be historically connected to, the Masonic fraternity. Yates herself insinuates a pinnacle role for Dee in the creation of the Masonic fraternity and also makes the familiar comparison of the German and English fraternities. Perhaps most interesting of all in regard to Freemasonry, in 1570, Dee wrote the preface to the first English-language edition of the most influential of all geometrical works, Euclid's *Elements*. Discreetly, the Monas symbol also appeared in the decorative, first capital letter of the first word of the preface. Composed of circle, arcs, and straight lines, Dee's Monas symbol appears to owe much to Euclidean geometry, though Dee regards it as symbolizing, or embodying, knowledge of the Divine.

In histories of British culture, John Dee is an obscure and largely forgotten figure whose existence, let alone influence, is usually neglected. Conversely, in histories of Western European esoteric movements, he is often overplayed, and Yates, in this regard, is more culpable than most. Dee was a complex figure. He entered St. John's College, Cambridge, at the age of fifteen, where his natural ability in mathematics was cultivated. He traveled in Europe for the first time in 1547, where he struck up relationships with various scholars, though most especially with mathematicians. During this same period, Dee began writing on the subject of logic, but throughout his life he also made serious investigations into Kabbalistic philosophy and the art of alchemy, and, with his associate Edward Kelly, he attempted to converse with angels. Similarly,

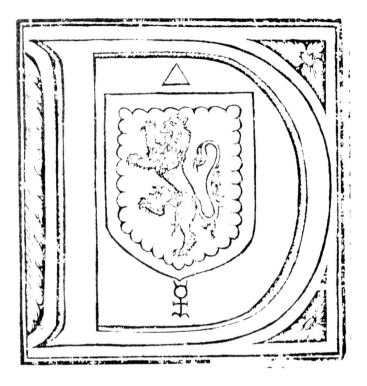

ABOVE: *A decorative letter, beginning the first word of Dee's preface to* Euclid's Elements. *Beneath the shield is Dee's Monas symbol.*

he was employed as astrologer to the British monarch Elizabeth I. Not surprisingly, Dee began to be regarded as a conjurer and black magician, which, in later life, lost him the royal patronage that had supported him.[1] In the preface to the *Elements*, Dee defends mathematics, and himself, against such accusations. After describing the possible applications of mathematics—for example, the production at Nuremberg of an "artificial eagle" that could fly—Dee states, "And for these, and such like miraculous acts and feats, naturally mathematically and mechanically wrought and contrived, ought any student, and modest Christian philosopher, be counted and called a conjurer? Shall the folly of idiots, and the malice of the scornful, so much prevail?" Unfortunately for Dee, the answer was "Yes."

While the first English translation of Euclid's *Elements* was published in the latter half of the sixteenth century, the stonemasons of Britain had included him in their mythology since at least the late fourteenth century. Euclid was considered the father of geometry by the stonemasons of Britain, while geometry was, in turn, regarded as synonymous with masonry. It was an idea that persisted and remained integral to the builders' mythology; it later entered Freemasonry as the fraternity adopted the Old Charges. Dee's authorship of the preface is central to Yates's argument, which suggests an essential role for Dee in Freemasonry—though there is no convincing evidence for such a role. Yates even goes so far as to suggest that Dee's "omission" from Freemasonry's first Constitutions printed in the eighteenth century[2] leaves a "curious gap in Masonic history."[3] However, little, if any, real change in the stonemasons' mythology or practices occurred either at the point of the writing of the preface by Dee, the publication of the *Elements*, or soon after.

Just over a century after the publication of the *Elements*, the stonemasons' rituals appear to have become more elaborate than the simple procedure of swearing an oath over a Bible that had been practiced by the medieval stonemason. It is possible that the ritual of the stonemasons was more elaborate than this procedure even as early as the fifteenth century and may have included the mythology itself in some manner. However, the builders' rituals of even the late seventeenth century were still extraordinarily simple when compared to those of the Freemasons a few decades later, even if these earlier procedures did provide the basis for this fraternity's Ritual. Again, there does not appear to be anything in the lodge ritual of the later seventeenth century, or in the symbolism, ritual, or philosophy of Freemasonry a little later that seems to hint at Dee's handiwork—we do not, for example, find his famous Monas. Freemasonry's first *Constitutions* were neither original works nor even pieces of historical or mythological investigation, but simply compilations of the Old Charges. These builders' texts did in fact continue to be written long after the death of Dee, but neither his name nor his philosophy or symbols are to be found anywhere in them. His name is not associated with Freemasonry in the first half of the eighteenth century, even though several alchemists and magicians were sometimes championed as earlier influences on the fraternity, though such assertions are baseless.

Yet, while not introducing anything foreign to the stonemasons in terms of additional symbolism, as the author of the preface to the *Elements*, Dee recontextualized Euclid's geometry, placing it in the developing intellectual and esoteric traditions, which saw geometry as exemplifying the Divine. Indeed, Dee clearly sees, and encourages, the reader through further study to see geometry as related to, or expressive of, God, who Dee also refers to as the "Architect." Interestingly, Dee also exhorts the reader to construct a geometrical figure that is to be regarded in an esoteric sense. It is close to his own Monas yet also strikingly close to and employing the language of alchemy. It is one of the first examples of the transformation of alchemy into geometry, which will be considered later as we regard alchemy and Freemasonry. In essence, Dee directs the reader to construct a figure of two intersecting lines forming a cross (each arm of equal length), with a circle at its center. He then writes,

> At the ends of the lines, write the names of the 4 principal elemental qualities, [i.e.,] hot and cold, one against the other, and likewise moist and dry, one against the other. And in the circle write temperate . . . temperature, has a good latitude, as appears by the complexion of a man.

Such an influence may, moreover, have been exerted for a long period afterward and may have only begun to take effect in the seventeenth century, where we see the emergence of Rosicrucianism. The English translation of *Euclid's Elements*, including Dee's preface, was reissued again in 1651 and 1661, while, less than a decade before the middle of the seventeenth century, the first intellectuals join what were ostensibly stonemasons' lodges. But why? Perhaps the builders' guild, with its rituals and mythology, was seen as implicitly mystical, or possibly even Kabbalistic. Or perhaps it was not the ritual per se but the mere fact that building, as a geometrical as well as architectural art, was essential to an understanding of the prevailing intellectual climate, though this does not necessarily mean Kabbalistic or occult. If Dee did influence the developing doctrines that were taken up by the Freemasons of the eighteenth century, then it is most likely that his influence was derived from the preface to *Euclid's Elements* alone.

As the eighteenth century progressed, Freemasonry became increasingly diversified, as it became interpreted and expanded through alchemical and Kabbalistic, as well as chivalric, symbolism. Such an expansion, however, was not drawn out of Freemasonry, but was rather impressed upon it. Some, possibly adulterated, Jewish mythology had entered the mythology of British stonemasonry, in regard to the marble and stone pillars. Yet, if there is any presence of Kabbalah in the Old Charges, it is extremely diluted. Nonetheless, a connection between Freemasonry and Kabbalah was asserted early in the eighteenth century. In *A Letter to a Friend Concerning the Society of Free-Masons* (1725), written by one undoubtedly pseudonymous Verus Commodus (Latin for the "True Advantageous One"), we read:

> They assume to themselves the August title of
> Kabalists; or rather, as I submissively conjecture, Cabal-ists: i.e., a Knot of whimsical,
> delirious Wretches, who are caballing together,
> to extirpate all manner of Science, Reason,
> and religion out of the World.[4]

In 1756, Laurence Dermott, an Irishman living in Britain, made an invaluable contribution to the history of Freemasonry, in part by publishing his strangely titled book, *Ahiman Rezon*. Its relevance here is that Dermott's remarks on the name of Freemasonry is not unlike that of Commodus, though Dermott was by that time a highly respected and prominent, though no less a controversial, Freemason. Although part of *Ahiman Rezon* is taken up with a Masonic "history," like most histories of Freemasonry, it is rather incredible and was probably meant to be. Dermott reports that as he began his task of writing a history of the Craft, he fell asleep and was visited in a dream by four Biblical persons. One of these was, we can surmise by his dress, a high priest of Solomon's Temple, while another one was named, rather tellingly, Ahiman. In Dermott's account of his dream, the high priest clearly differentiates between building and Masonry, saying that, neither "Nimrod, nor any of his Bricklayers, knew any Thing of the matter [of Freemasonry]," because, as the speaker being a high priest would imply, Freemasonry is spiritual rather than material.[5] The high priest figure of Dermott's dream continues,

> There were but very few Masters of the Art
> (even) at Solomon's Temple: Whereby it
> plainly appears, that the whole Mystery was
> communicated to very few at that Time; that
> at Solomon's temple (and not before) it
> received the Name of Free-Masonry, because
> the Masons at Jerusalem and Tyre were the
> greatest Cabalists then in the World; that the
> Mystery has been, for the most part, practiced
> among Builders since Solomon's Time.[6]

ABOVE: (Detail) A master Mason holding a square in his right hand, with a compass and a representation of Euclid's 47th Proposition placed on his desk. The floor is the mosaic pavement, in the center of which is the Blazing Star with a letter "G" for geometry. Beneath the figure are three steps, alluding to his position as master of the lodge, and what appears to a be a past master's emblem behind the right pillar.

ABOVE: A page from Ptolemy's Geographia. Note the interlinking square and compasses at the base of the left column. The letter "G" probably stands for geometry. In America, the letter "G" is frequently seen in conjunction with this Masonic symbol.

In his preface to *Euclid's Elements*, John Dee recommends the work of the famous German magician Cornelius Agrippa (1486–1535) as well as that of the

German artist Albrecht Dürer. Architecture and geometry had become increasingly significant in the interpretation of the Kabbalah, particularly as it centered on the supposed symbolic, and therefore potentially revelatory, proportions of Solomon's Temple. In his *Three Books of Occult Philosophy*, Agrippa comments on the mystical interpretation of proportion. Such concepts were far from alien to Dürer, who knew Agrippa's work. Besides painting and engraving, Dürer had studied architecture, mathematics, and, essential to the artist, proportion—inadvertently carving out, through his studies in perspective, the then new discipline of descriptive geometry.[8] He is also known to have referred to himself as a Mathematicus, or mathematician,[9] and with justification, for he wrote the first mathematics textbook in the German language, *Unterweisung der Messung mit Zirkel und Richtscheit (Instructions on Measuring with a Compass and Ruler)*, published in the first half of the sixteenth century.[10]

Albrecht Dürer was also enormously influenced by Agrippa, particularly by his *Three Books of Occult Philosophy*, which Dürer is thought to have owned in the form of a privately circulated manuscript for some time prior to its official publication (Dee highlights this text in his preface to the *Elements*).[11] This in itself would seem to suggest that Dürer, Agrippa, and the circle that had sprung up around the latter were close. Dürer himself, Yates has suggested, was particularly influenced by the Kabbalistic content of the magician's work, though she does not give him a role in the development of Freemasonry as she does with Dee. Nevertheless, Dürer has won some very minor attention by Freemasons over the last century. For example, in 1911 W. B. Tuckerman, writing in the *American Freemason*, suggested that Dürer had been a part of the Masonic fraternity at Nuremberg. While this is highly unlikely, given Dürer's dates, it is quite possible that Dürer at least helped the intellectual movement of his time and slightly later to move in a direction that was eventually taken up, in part, by Freemasonry.

Although the square and compasses appeared both in manuscripts and on stone reliefs of various churches, representing the stonemasons' trade, they were often pictured more as tools than symbols and are generally seen being used in the masons' craft, sometimes with the plumb line and level. Similarly, the square and compasses are not spoken of in the earliest of the Old Charges. It would seem that they first appeared in their familiar Masonic form in an illustration of Ptolemy's *Geographia*, reissued in 1522 in Strasburg by the printer Hans Rheinhard (otherwise known as Grüninger or Greininger, after his birthplace, Grüningen).[12] At the end of the seventeenth century, they are mentioned as a part of the stonemasons' ritual, though it is probable that they were being used earlier in the century. Ptolemy's *Geographia* had been previously published in 1513 and 1520, though the illustrations in these editions were confined to maps. Rheinhard, being a strong believer in the printed image, made sure to include various vignettes in the new edition. Three other persons besides the printer were also involved in the 1522 edition: Albrecht Dürer, Hans Koberger (who would act as editor), and Dürer's most intimate friend, supporter, and patron,

Willibald Pirckheimer. Although other scientific instruments—sometimes pertaining to astronomy or building—are presented among the vignettes in the *Geographia*, the now familiar square and compasses sign appears prominently in a vignette of twin pillars and cherubs, enigmatically enclosing a letter "G."

The 1522 edition was filled with illustrations. It would seem that Dürer and Pirckheimer had given instructions for at least some of them, possibly including the square and compasses image, though to what extent Dürer was involved is uncertain. After the publication, Dürer bewailed the artistic merit, or lack thereof, of the engravings, and with good reason; they were hardly up to Dürer's own standard. Despite a mediocrity of draftsmanship, however, the square and compasses symbol would soon become a prominent and frequently recurring emblem for intellectual culture, especially that of the sixteenth and early seventeenth centuries, before their adoption by the Masonic fraternity in the eighteenth century.

It is enormously beneficial to consider Dürer's *Melancholia I*, however, in regard to the later Masonic symbol, not least of all because we find the compasses at the very center of its symbolism. Dürer, as we have said, was strongly influenced by the philosophy of Agrippa, and it certainly seems that the German magician provided the main literary influence of Dürer's *Melancholia I*.[13] It is also certain that, on his journey to Bologna, Dürer became acquainted with the ideas of the architect Leon Battista Alberti (1404–1472), who Dee also mentions in his preface, and the then "secret" art of proportion and perspective. This art was based

on the conception of microcosm (Man) and macrocosm (God), with its laws of proportion established by the Deity as Architect. Dürer was to become the main promoter of the art in Germany,[14] while Agrippa was similarly concerned with proportion and its potential to link the macrocosm with the microcosm, that is to say to link God and Man, in an idealized or "Divine" proportion.

Dürer began to draft portraits for painting, not according to the anatomy of the sitter, but according to such notions of proportion, for example making the brow or nose longer or shorter. The mystical implication of proportion had already been laid down in writing in the first century BC by the Roman architect Marcus Vitruvius Pollio in his *Ten Books of Architecture*. In the third book, Vitruvius relates the perfect proportions of the human figure and likens them to the proportions of the Roman temple. Needless to say, this book influenced European thought enormously, and it is certain that Dee, Dürer, and Agrippa were conversant with the Roman architect's theories.

In his preface to *Euclid's Elements*, John Dee exhorts his reader to look specifically at chapters 27 and 28 of the second book of Agrippa's *Three Books of Occult Philosophy*. These chapters describe the human body, soul, or personality in terms of geometry. They explain that the human body contains numbers,

ABOVE: A male figure demonstrates the Golden Ratio, important in architectural theory. Unusually, this Vitruvian figure, from Agrippa's Three Books of Occult Philosophy, *is enveloped by astrological symbols.*

OPPOSITE: Dürer's Melancholia I *(detail) has elements of Freemason symbolism. The angel holds compasses in his hand, suggesting geometry, and the tools of the carpenter or builder are spread on the ground.*

weights, elements, and so forth, yet having been created by God, and in His image, they are perfectly harmonized.

Moreover, the various parts of the body of Man are held by Agrippa to correspond to the stars, or Divine or Kabbalistic names. Agrippa also explains the supposed mathematical relationships between various parts of the body, for example, the measurement from the breast to the crown of the skull. It is an idealized type of anatomy, though it is one ultimately very close, if not identical, to the art of proportion that Dürer was practicing for a time as a painter. Similarly, Dee states in the preface to *Elements* that "Anthropology is the description of the number, measure, weight, figure, situation, and color of every diverse thing, contained in the perfect body of MAN, with certain knowledge of symmetry, figure, weight, characterization, and due local motion."

Agrippa claims that the most perfect geometry of the body frames the most perfect type of personality or soul, naturally giving it the greatest fortunes. While certainly not confined to either this period or to the occult tradition, the pervasiveness of proportion is illustrated in book 2, chapter 28 of the *Three Books of Occult Philosophy*, where Agrippa turns his attention to

ABOVE LEFT: The compasses represent living moderately and responsibly. Within the compasses, a Freemason standing next to two beehives (emblematic of the work of Masonry) holds the Sacred Book in his right hand.

ABOVE RIGHT: This plate shows the symbolic lodge with the square and compasses, the sun and moon, the gavel, and the trowel.

the more invisible ratios of musical scales, which in turn lead us to the soul. Agrippa connects various, seemingly defected, personality traits to different ancient Greek musical scales and notes and says that the Ancients used music both to ward away evil spirits and as a medicine for the body, restoring its implicit celestial form.[15] However, in chapter 40 of Book One, Agrippa claims that it is the melancholic that most naturally receives impressions of the celestial and therefore impressions of the soul and of spirits and even of God Himself, for the planets or stars form the midpoint, and indeed constitute the invisibly connecting thread, between God and Man. Agrippa states explicitly that melancholy causes the inspiration of poets and prophets alike, although in this regard he does not differ greatly from Plato, who, in his *Phaedrus*, likens madness to prophecy, and asserts that it also gives rise to lyric and poetry. Indeed, Plato says that this type of madness "is the special gift of heaven."[16] In this tradition, then, the melancholic is, in some sense, Divine.

In Dürer's *Melancholia I* (1514), an angel sits amid the scattered and discarded tools of the builder. At the angel's feet rests a saw atop a wooden plank; some nails, a carpentry plane, and a hammer lie beside a polyhedron at the foot of a ladder. The angel is holding, and using, only one instrument, and it is not the tool of a lowly builder but of the master mason, or architect: the compasses (the top of which is almost the exact center point and therefore, by implication, the most important motif of the composition). The most striking feature of the composition is the "magic square" almost directly over the angel's head. Such numerical symbols represent the supposed powers of the planets as well as the various spirits associated with them. The magic square in this engraving is the magic square of Jupiter with its numerical arrangement only slightly altered, so that the middle two squares of the bottom line read the date that Dürer completed the work (1514). In his lifetime, Dee attempted, and believed himself to have succeeded, to evoke or conjure angels through similar methods, though it was this that eventually caused his reputation to suffer.

Panofsky has tended to concentrate on the supposed negative aspect of the angel of *Melancholia I*, whose face he sees as blackened by melancholy and whose wings are collapsed around him. True, he is not the typical flying angel, and the scene is not one of angelic joy. Nor is the cherub who sits writing on a slate by the Angel's shoulder very cherublike, with youthful cheeks swollen in exaggerated innocence, but instead appears stocky, a little dwarfish, and wizened by age. The mood is indeed bleak, and even the dog in the corner of the picture appears to be contemplating the world's problems. However, for all the image's concentrated despair, a rainbow bends across the horizon and a mystical arrow of light is let loose in the sky, surely intimating a Divine presence. The cherub and angel are both busy at work. Like a good pupil, the former is writing, or recording, while the angel, resting on a book and holding compasses, immerses himself in an undoubtedly metaphysical or metaphoric work of the "compass and ruler."

ABOVE: This handmade master Mason's apron shows three pillars, one of which is broken, suggestive of the third degree. To the left of the square and compasses is the Blazing Star in the shape of a pentagram, and on the flap we also see a Blazing Star in sequins.

OPPOSITE: St. Jerome in his Study *by Albrecht Dürer, 1514.*

The dog is, of course, excused from such work, though he also serves a part in the symbolism of the etching—even half asleep, he is a controversial character. While Panofsky sees the skinny dog in the corner of

the etching as a sign of the negative aspect of melancholia, and Yates sees it as the sleeping dog of the senses, there may be yet another interpretation. In 1505, *The Hieroglyphics of Horapollo*, a dictionary of symbols supposedly written by Horapollo Niciacus (an Egyptian magus of the fourth century), was translated into Greek. The text became an instant success, and thirty more editions followed. More important, despite the spuriousness of the document, the *Hieroglyphics* had an enormous impact on the understanding and interpretation of symbols for the next three centuries, affecting art, poetry, and philosophy. Notably, Pirckheimer gave the Holy Roman Emperor Maximilian a copy of the book illustrated by Dürer.[17]

According to the *Hieroglyphics*, a dog represents, among other things, a sacred scribe, a prophet, an embalmer, and the spleen. The angel of *Melancholia I* may certainly be seen in terms of a sacred scribe, and perhaps even as a prophet. The interpretation of the dog as a spleen is of great importance, since this part of the body had traditionally been considered to be the physical base of the affliction of melancholy. Dürer would certainly have been aware of this, as he thought of himself as a melancholic. Somewhere between 1512 and 1513, Dürer even drew a self-portrait—apparently for a doctor—in which he points to the area of the spleen on his naked body, claiming that that it "hurt." It would seem then that the dog-as-spleen symbol represents both the melancholic and divinely inspired.

There is one more symbol that the *Hieroglyphics* helps to identify. In the top left of the composition, a bat is seen soaring in the sky with the name of the work

ABOVE: *The alchemical hermaphrodite, Rebis, holds a square and compasses in his hands.*

emblazoned across his outstretched wings. According to the *Hieroglyphics*, the bat represents the weak but rash man. The weak man might, of course, refer to the melancholic, but it is not so much the definition of the symbol as the reasoning behind the definition that is important. Like a weak man who acts despite his sickness—or the melancholic who engages himself in the

art of the compass and ruler, despite his melancholia—the bat, we are told, flies even though it has no feathers. As such, it is the direct opposite of the cherub and angel. It may also mean that, like the ladder, there is another way to ascend spiritually, other than the accepted religious one that is symbolized by the wings of the angel. The ladder might well represent the Kabbalistic tree, with its pathways and hierarchy of angels, cherubs, and seraphs, or the stairway seen in Jacob's vision, as told in Genesis.

As well as the compasses, the ladder (often regarded as Jacob's Ladder), the polyhedron, and building tools (seen in the etching, *Melancholia I*) eventually became Masonic emblems. Polyhedrons, for example, formed a part of the Royal Arch degree of Freemasonry, while the elements of the engraving found their way into the first three degrees. W. B. Tuckerman has sought to connect Dürer and his *Melancholia I* to Freemasonry. He claims that this engraving shows the "ethical doctrines of Freemasonry." It is difficult to see what ethics Dürer meant to impress upon the viewer in this engraving, however, and it seems more likely that Tuckerman meant the "philosophical doctrines" of the Masonic fraternity. While there is a strong similarity between Dürer's *Melancholia I* and the symbols of Freemasonry, and while the philosophies both have points of contact, it is certain that neither could have influenced the other directly. Yet Dürer, and particularly *Melancholia I*, did have an affect on the cultural climate of Western Europe that eventually became a part of Freemasonry.

Both Panofsky and Yates link *Melancholia I* to another of Dürer's etchings, *Saint Jerome*, also executed in 1514. Notably, the dog of melancholia lies in approximately the same lower left section of the composition as *Melancholia I*, and an hourglass is also to be found in both works. Like the angel of *Melancholia I*, Saint Jerome is seated and engaged in intellectual study. Saint Jerome is famous for removing a splinter from a lion's paw, which accounts for the lion beside the dog of melancholia and prophecy. Significantly, Yates asserts a Kabbalistic connection with the saint, claiming that he was, in a sense, the adopted patron saint of the Christian Kabbalists. As the Hebrew scholar of the Church Fathers, Saint Jerome associated the originally Aramaic name of Jesus *(YHShVH)* with the Hebrew name of God *(YHVH)*, later used to legitimize Christian Kabbalism—Kabbalah developed and emphasized theories of the underlying or secret, numerical meaning of individual Hebrew words and the similitude of different words based, for example, on this numerology.

Returning to the square and compasses, although they would increasingly appear in frontispieces and other illustrations where they were used to represent the art of geometry, nearly a century after Dürer had executed *Melancholia I* these emblems were also adopted into the more mystical world of alchemy. They appeared in *Aureliae Occulta Philosophorum Partes Duo*, printed in the second edition of the alchemical anthology *Theatrum Chemicum* (1613). In an etching contained in this work, the square is seen held in the left hand and the compasses in the right hand of the hermaphrodite alchemical figure Rebis. Earlier versions of Rebis had portrayed the figure differently; for example, in the *Rosarium Philosophorum* (Basel, 1593), Rebis appears naked and holding in one hand a cup containing three snakes and in the other a single snake. It is probably because of this earlier Rebis that the Masonic historian Albert Mackey asserts that the alchemical square and compasses are meant as "phallic" emblems, and he uses his definition to differentiate the art of alchemy from that of Freemasonry.[18] The square and compasses, however, are not sexual symbols. When Rebis appears with what would later become the identifying emblem of Freemasonry, he is fully clothed, the snakes have disappeared, and a more modest Rebis is surrounded by astronomical, or astrological, as well as geometrical or architectural symbols, none of which would seem to hint of anything sexual or phallic.[19]

The image of Rebis with a square and compasses would become popular in alchemy and was reproduced in various texts.[20] Similarly, Michaël Maier (1568–1622), the German alchemist and Rosicrucian, employed the compasses (but not the square) in an alchemical metaphor. The etching appears in Maier's *Atlanta Fugiens* and shows a man holding an enormous compass up to a wall on which is drawn a circle; inside the circle is a triangle, another circle, and a square, enclosing the naked figures of a man and a woman. The writing that glosses the image behooves the reader to construct the geometry from the body of a man and a woman, which will, the reader is told, lead to the discovery of the philosopher's stone. The male and

ABOVE: The square and compasses is the best-known symbol of Freemasonry and is displayed in every Masonic Lodge. The letter "G" represents geometry as well as God, referred to as either the "Great Architect" or "Grand Geometrician."

body—the height of a ceiling, door, and window are in accord with the human body. In higher sense, geometry derived from the human body would seem to draw directly on the Virtruvian notion of the "squaring of the circle." (Dee, in his preface to Euclid's *Elements*, speaks of transforming a sphere into a cube, and vice versa.)

It is clear that geometry, as specifically regarded as revealing the relationship between man and God, entered Alchemy, where it was, unsurprisingly, symbolized by the square and compasses. The emblem did not become the exclusive property of alchemy but remained a common cultural image in Europe. It entered the rituals of stonemasonry, and later those of Freemasonry. During the seventeenth century, it also entered into the academic sciences that were equally, if not more, akin to Freemasonry than alchemy. The square and compasses can be seen on the front page of Johannes Kepler's *Rudolphine Tables* (1627). Here, the geometrician's tools are held, as with the alchemical Rebis, in the hands of a small figure. Unlike Rebis, the figure on the cover of Kepler's work is also shown with a draftsman's board, upon which is drawn some geometry, probably representing the course of the planets. Kepler was familiar with Dürer's mathematical works and seems to have borrowed from Dürer for his construction of polyhedrons or regular solids that were important for his astronomical theory. However, this

female figures are certainly drawn from, and probably represent, the alchemical Rebis. The notion of deriving geometry from the human body was not new and appears in Agrippa's *Three Books of Occult Philosophy*. It was a concept that is also known to the building trade, as all buildings are effectively built around the human display of the square and compasses is significant for another reason. Kepler was keen to publicly distance himself from magic and alchemy as well as from the very notion of pictorial symbolism.[21] He would probably not have allowed an overtly alchemical symbol to adorn his own scientific work, no matter how small the figure might have been.

Overall, the square and compasses appear so frequently in the sixteenth and seventeenth centuries that it would be impossible to note them all. They are found representing the arts that are based, or rely, on geometry, such as astronomy. Kepler's former employer Tycho Brahe (1546–1601) had been depicted with the square and compasses in a portrait printed on the front page of his *Astronomiae instaurate mechanica* (Hamburg, 1598). In 1703, it appears discreetly on the front page of Russia's first printed arithmetical textbook—Masons' lodges of the late seventeenth century, if not before, had already adopted the square and compasses, so this last example is unlikely to have affected the fraternity in any way. It is important to recognize that the square and

ABOVE: *Detail of the frontispiece to Johannes Kepler's* Rudolphine Tables *(1627). Note the figure (right) holding a square and compasses and standing behind a drawing board with geometry described on it.*

compasses remained a persistent symbol of geometry and related sciences right up to the point when the Masonic fraternity emerged from its cocoon in the early eighteenth century.

Chapter 3: Freemasonry and Rosicrucianism

Even before Freemasonry had appeared on the world stage, gossip about its existence had already begun with occasional newspaper reports implying that it was somehow alchemical or mystical.

Most frequently, it would seem, Freemasonry was being likened to the alchemically influenced philosophy of Rosicrucianism. By the second decade of the eighteenth century, the Craft had established itself across Britain, but the center of Freemasonry would be London. Here, the fraternity had really emerged and was performing rituals that were meant to teach its members history, mythology, and ethics. Although it constituted only a part of these rituals, a catechism, or set of prescribed "questions and answers," was repeated for new apprentices and older Masons as they proceeded through the Masonic degrees—by this method they learned all they could possibly want to know about the fraternity.

Early on, the catechisms may have constituted much of the bestowed initiatory process. Freemasonry continued to use them, but, as the society expanded philosophically and pictorially, they became a lesser part of the rituals. In 1723, an exposé of an alleged Masonic catechism was printed in the British newspaper *Post Boy*. This is interesting because the last few lines suggest that there are rituals or degrees well above the two or possibly three degrees that constituted British Freemasonry at that time:

Q. How many Orders of Masons are there?

A. Seven Orders.

Q. What is the highest Order that our present Masons can attain to?

A. Few exceed the Fourth Order.

A. What qualifies a Man for the Seventh Order?

A. These five Things. First, Conquest over Nature. Secondly, the Composition of the Grand Elixir. Thirdly, The Mastery of the great Work. Fourthly, The Chaining of the Golden Dragon. Fifthly, The enjoyment of the Silver Lady, &c.

The expressed qualifications for entry into these alleged orders are the mastery of certain alchemical practices: "conquest over nature" and the "great work" (or magnum opus, i.e., the whole of alchemy) are both familiar alchemical expressions. The golden or aquatic dragon and silver lady are also alchemical symbols.[1]

Although it would seem that this account hints at the existence of rituals or degrees of a higher caliber than Craft Masonry, it may simply be that the author

ABOVE: The ethical transformation of the Freemason is illustrated by the symbols of the Craft. "Fear God" is written beneath the compasses that symbolically "circumscribe" the passions of the Freemason, keeping him from succumbing to such immoral activities as are illustrated outside the circle.

considers Freemasonry as identical to alchemy and has reinterpreted it in light of the alchemical process as traditionally put forward by its practitioners and philosophers. While it is debatable that there existed, at that time, a type of Freemasonry composed of seven degrees, alchemical and Rosicrucian degrees eventu-

ally emerged within the fraternity, and the Rosicrucian banner became an important symbol in Freemasonry.

As a historical phenomenon, Rosicrucianism began with the publication of three pamphlets by the Lutheran pastor Johann Valentin Andreae (1586–1654) and his circle at Tübingen, Germany.

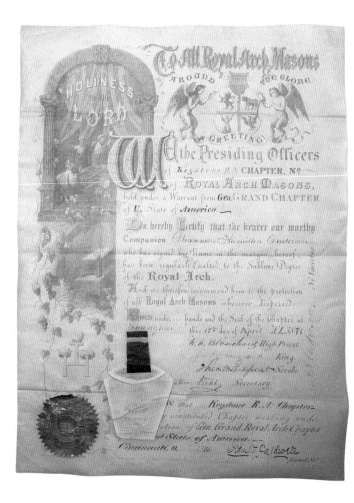

ABOVE: A certificate for the Masonic Royal Arch degree from 1871. A. E. Waite considered its origin to lie in a supposed "Rosicrucian" degree.

The first publication was that of the *Fama Fraternitas RC (Report of the R.C. Brotherhood)* in 1614 (though it appears that it had been circulating in manuscript form since around 1612), the second was the *Confessio Fraternitati RC (Confession of the R.C. Brotherhood)* in 1615, and the third was the *Chymische Hochzeit Christiani Rosencreutz 1459 (The Chemical Wedding of Christian Rosenkreutz, 1459)*, published in 1616, and of which

Andreae claimed in his autobiography to be the sole author.

The literal translation of the name Rosencreutz (or Rosenkreutz), and Rosicrucian, is "Rose Cross" or "Rosy Cross"—it is worth noting that Andreae's heraldic device was a St. Andrew's cross with four roses grouped around the center. Unlike his grandfather who had become a well-known Lutheran pastor and was affectionately nicknamed the "Würtenburg Luther," Andreae was almost unknown to his countrymen at that time. It is more likely, therefore, that the rose cross heralded in the manifestoes was understood by the Germans to be related to Martin Luther's infinitely more important heraldic device. Andreae must have been aware that the rose cross, and thus Rosicrucianism, would have been perceived in this way. A hundred years before the Rosicrucian manifestoes were issued, Luther had come to prominence in Germany by rejecting the authority, and what he felt to be the corruption, of the Roman Catholic Church. He translated the Bible into the vernacular and established the German, or Lutheran, Church. Well before the first Rosicrucian manifesto was issued, Luther was Germany's national and spiritual hero. The heraldic device he had created for himself was a black cross within a red heart, enclosed by a white rose.[2]

The Rosicrucian manifestoes heralded a spiritual and intellectual revolution, embodied by a secret brotherhood of Christian knights that were endowed with mysticism and represented a spiritual freedom that was afforded to Christians in Germany by Luther. Thus, in the narrative of the *Chemical Wedding*, we hear that the marriage was attended by an order known as the Knights of the Golden Stone, alluding with little subtlety to the philosopher's stone of alchemy. The order reflects the literature and myths of the knight that had sprung up in Europe in the late Middle Ages (the most popular of which were the stories of King Arthur and the knights of the Round Table, and those of Charlemagne). Also relevant in this regard were the honorary chivalrous, or nonmilitary, orders of knights, such as the Order of the Garter, which had been instituted by the various monarchies of Europe.

Although there are suggestions of a few Rosicrucian societies existing in Europe prior to the establishment of Freemasonry in the eighteenth century, Rosicrucianism largely remained an ideology until that point. It emerged as a society mainly through German Freemasonry, where it had become a semisecret inner society. As Freemasonry spread from Britain to Europe, the Craft provided the esoterically minded with a structure of rituals or degrees on which the Hermetic, the alchemical, and the knightly could be fashioned.

These various traditions occasionally manifested themselves as separate orders, but as this phenomenon advanced they were usually molded into a single order that housed a number of alchemical and knightly rituals. If Rosicrucianism had to wait for the emergence of Freemasonry to mold it into a practical, ritualistic society, Masonry in turn had almost certainly needed the Rosicrucian myth and spirit to further its own journey toward becoming a philosophical and mystic society. Freemasonry and Rosicrucianism had begun to be linked in the popular imagination, and to be men-

ABOVE: The eye on the flap is typical of Masonic regalia, though there seems little else to indicate whether this is a Masonic apron. Many other fraternities have emulated Freemasonry, and some have copied Masonic regalia, especially the apron.

tioned together in the seventeenth-century press. The first published references in which the two societies are mentioned together are, as might be expected, very brief. Rosicrucianism was probably known only to the most educated members of British society. Masonry was even more elusive, for, unlike the aforementioned society, it had never published any manifestoes for the public, nor trumpeted its philosophy. Even if the ethics and myths of Masonry went back hundreds of years, it was still finding its feet as an intellectual society.

ABOVE: *Detail of the Masonic Rose Croix apron showing the pelican or phoenix. To the right is a rose, symbolic of the Rose* *Sharon, and to the left is acacia, symbolizing the immortality of the soul. The Rose Croix degree appeared in Europe in th* *eighteenth century.*

One of the first mentions of speculative Masonry in the English language cites Rosicrucianism.[3] The work in question is *The Muses Threnodie*, a metrical account of Perth, Scotland, written by Henry Adamson in 1638. It appeared approximately three quarters of a century prior to the establishment of the premier grand lodge of England and well in advance of the Rosicrucianization of Masonry that occurred on the Continent in the eighteenth century. The relevant lines are:

> For we are Brethren of the Rosie Cross.
> We have the Mason Word and second sight.[4]

Similarly, in "A Divertisement," printed in *Poor Robin's Intelligence* in 1676, we also learn that

> the Modern Green-ribbon'd Caball, together
> with the Ancient Brotherhood of the Rosy
> Cross; the Hermetick Adepti and the com-
> pany of Accepted Masons intend all to dine
> together on the 31 of November.

In 1722, Eugenius Philalethes published *Long Livers*, a text on the alchemical universal medicine that was supposed to prolong life or bestow immortality.[5] Eugenius Philalethes (Noble Lover of Truth) was the pseudonym of Thomas Vaughan (1621–1666), a prolific English alchemist, whom Mackey calls "a celebrated Rosicrucian."[6] Indeed, in 1652, Vaughan had published a translation with his own preface of the Rosicrucian manifesto, the *Fama*. Considering the dates, it is clear that there were in fact two Philalethes, Vaughan being the first, and the second undoubtedly borrowing the name of the famous Rosicrucian to bolster his own claim to have found the correct ingredients of the universal medicine by living for 110 years.

Despite being an alchemical text, the younger Philalethes' work is dedicated to "the Grand Masters, Masters, Wardens, and Brethren of the Most Ancient and Most Honorable Fraternity of the Free Masons of Great Britain and Ireland," and thus suggests a concrete link between alchemy and Masonry. It is quite possible that Irish Masonic lodges did embrace other intellectual ideas, such as Kabbalah. Philalethes speaks in the magnificent tone that is common only in the history of alchemy and makes much of the image of the philosopher's stone, which he refers to variously as the "Celestial Cube" and the "Lapis Angularis" (Angular Stone). In his theatrical tone, he places the stone at the center of the mythopoeic alchemical world, replete with its familiar motifs, such as the Red King and his Queen, lions, and a dragon devouring its own tail. Yet all of this, Philalethes claims, is comprehensible to

> none but the Sons of Science and those who
> are illuminated with the sublimest mysteries
> and profoundest secrets of MASONRY.

Although addressed to Freemasons (as well as Sons of Science, i.e., alchemists), Philalethes' language is not Masonic, but is rather alchemical and Rosicrucian. Nevertheless, Mackey suggests that this second Philalethes was "a Freemason as well as a

ABOVE: *Masonic Craft certificate from the Grand Lodge of England, 1807.*

Rosicrucian," and that he was therefore "acquainted with both systems."[7] How correctly the term "system" can be applied to the Rosicrucian impulse at this point is open to conjecture, though it is not impossible that there were a few self-professed Rosicrucian societies with little or no connection between them. At various points, some of these societies may have influenced Freemasons, but we have evidence of this occurring only at a later date. Mackey's most interesting sugges-

tion is that Philalethes "alludes, in language that can not be mistaken, to a certain higher [Masonic] degree, or to a more exalted initiation, to the attainment of which the primitive degrees of Ancient Craft Masonry were preparatory"—this is a surprising statement from a normally cautious writer. Philalethes does address "my Brethren . . . of the higher class," though as Mackey also points out he does not use the term "degree." Masonry did indeed develop higher degrees or rites, many of which were certainly influenced by alchemy, although these did not begin to emerge for at least another ten years after the publication of Philalethes' text and even then were largely confined to France and Germany.

Despite his suggestion that Philalethes' text hints of a higher degree, Mackey is quick to highlight the contrast between Philalethes' fantastical, alchemical work and the *Constitutions of the Free-Masons*. The latter was, in a sense, the first official version of the mythology, ethics, and some of the practices of Freemasonry. It was written by James Anderson and published the year following Philalethes' *Long Livers*. Admittedly, despite its claim that Masonry was derived from the craftsmen at Solomon's Temple, being preserved by Noah and propagated by Euclid, the *Constitutions* seems very conservative and modest in comparison to Philalethes' text.[8] Nevertheless, after its publication, Anderson's *Constitutions* was openly criticized, if not attacked, by some Freemasons. The problem was not what the author had included in his history but what he had allegedly omitted. For the first time since the seventeenth

ABOVE: *Early-eighteenth-century hand-colored leather Rose Croix apron. To the right is a snake biting its own tail (a symbol of immortality), enclosing a chalice.*

century, the suggestion that Masonry was either connected to, if only by imitation, or derived from the society of the Rosicrucians was beginning to gain currency.

A poem entitled "The Knight," 1723, talks of the "Rosi-crucian Trade," and also of "A Charm for Masons," though the author is hostile to these societies and portrays them as superstitious. Similarly, in a spoof

ABOVE: This early and highly elaborate American Rose Croix apron is embroidered not only with the pelican, roses, and rosy cross, but also with the three crosses at Calvary, where Jesus was crucified.

advertisement printed in the *Daily Journal* on December 27, 1725, we find mention of the Rosicrucians and Freemasons (referred to as "kinsmen of the Hod and Trowel." A hod is a type of metal tray affixed to a pole and used for carrying bricks, and the trowel is one of the symbols, or symbolic tools, of

Freemasonry).[9] Printed in the same periodical on September 5, 1730, was the "Letter of A. Z."[10] Though much longer than the advertisement, it is a short history that vies with the history as published in the *Constitutions*. In regard to Freemasonry and Rosicrucianism, it states:

> It must be confessed, that there is a Society abroad, from whom the English Free-Masons . . . have copied a few Ceremonies, and take great Pains to persuade the World that they are derived from them, and are the same with them: These are called Rosicrucians, from their Prime Offices, (such as our Brethren call Grand Master, Wardens, &c.) being distinguished on their High Days with Red Crosses . . . On this Society have our Moderns . . . endeavour'd to ingraft themselves, tho' they know knothing of their most material Constitutions, and are acquainted only with some of their Signs of Probation and Entrance.[11]

Presumably the author of the letter meant to refer to the Mason's symbolic handgrips, or tokens, as they are generally called.

The author, however, is well informed as to the history and practices of Freemasonry and seems well aware of the *Constitutions*, Philalethes, *Long Livers*, and the former advertisement, with which it shares several points.[12] "The Letter of A. Z." also mentions the antiquarian and astrologer Elias Ashmole (1617–1692), his

ABOVE: *A masonic certificate of the Royal Arch Degree,1866. This degree concentrates on the rebuilding of the Temple and the discovery of a secret vault by three master builders.*

initiation into Masonry, and his history of the Order of the Garter, published in 1672. Like the first advertisement, "The Letter of A. Z." also speaks of Masonry adopting the patron days of the Rosicrucians, "being better inform'd by some kind Rosicrucian." Patron days are the traditional days given over to the celebration of saints; trade guilds, for example, each typically had a patron saint and celebrated their saint's specific day. The author of the letter mentions, correctly, the days of Saint John the Baptist and Saint John the Evangelist, both of whom are of symbolic importance to Freemasonry, especially in America where lodges are often said to be dedicated to Saint, or Saints, John. On the basis that neither saint had anything to do with architecture (proper to Masonry), the author of the letter asserts that Freemasonry appropriated these saints from the Rosicrucians, stating that the latter saint is the patron of that society. It is uncertain from what authority the author draws to make such explicit claims, although it would seem that he believed there was a society of Rosicrucians abroad, possibly in Germany. In Britain at the time, there probably were a few such societies, and it is possible that the author of the letter may have at least known of such a group and of some of their practices.

In 1643, the Austrian Rosicrucian Johann Permeier, who was connected to the monarchical circles of Sweden, had written to, among others, Denmark, Saxony, German State of Braunschweig, and Sweden, appealing for the establishment of a general council to consider the future of the Protestants. In his proposals of 1638, he included an initiation rite to be performed on the day of St. John the Baptist. Susanna Akerman connects Permeier to the story of a Rosicrucian masonic lodge at The Hague around 1637, though this date seems too early to warrant such a description. Permeier had settled at Emden in the Netherlands by 1630 and had started the Societas

Coronae Equestris Ordinis, which Ackerman thinks may have proved influential. If Freemasonry was distinct from stonemasonry at this point, it would seem unlikely that the separate, speculative type of Masonry had spread outside of the British Isles in any significant way. It is possible, however, that there was some Rosicrucian or other lodges on the Continent that practiced rituals and was dedicated in some sense to Saint John, and therefore similar to the later Masonic lodges. Interestingly, however, English lodges are generally dedicated to Solomon and Moses.

The most explicit and important criticism of Anderson's *Constitutions* came from the Briscoe Pamphlet (1724). To a great extent, the pamphlet is merely a reproduction of the history common to the Old Charges, but it also appears to identify the Rosicrucians and Freemasons as brothers of the same order. It states, unequivocally, that these orders are alike, that they are derived from the legendary father of alchemy, Hermes Trismegistus, and are therefore alchemical. In the preface to this rather odd piece of writing, the reader is treated to a peculiar story of a "Fellow at Vienna" and his overly inquisitive landlady. Suspicious that some of her pewter pots and dishes were missing, the landlady went searching around her lodger's room, half expecting to find them. Imagine her surprise when she found that her dishes had been turned to gold, due to her lodger's alchemical experiments—clearly this "Fellow" was an alchemist, Rosicrucian, or Freemason. One might wonder why an alchemist of such prowess had to steal pewter plates, but such was his bad luck that the landlady couldn't be bought off with the new dishes; the police were called, and he was sent to work in the mines of Germany.

The Briscoe Pamphlet makes much of the *Constitutions of the Free-Masons* and offers its reader constitutions that theoretically predate Anderson's by nearly two millennia. The author states that a copy of the "Original Constitutions" of the Freemasons had been found by Moses after making a search of the burial place of Adam and that

> the Original Constitutions of the Free-
> Masons, wherein the Grand-Secret is con-
> tain'd, and which might have remain'd so, as
> many Ages as it hath been hitherto kept, had
> it not been for an accidental Discovery which
> is too dangerous a Secret to broach: For as
> Rosy-Crucians and Adepts, Brothers of the
> same Fraternity, or Order, who derived them-
> selves from Hermes Trismegistus, which some
> call Moses. [13]

The *Constitutions*, in contrast, had excluded mention of the mythical Hermes Trismegistus, who is of course mentioned in some of the Old Charges. Much the worse for Anderson, the father of alchemy would become increasingly popular among the new philosophical Freemasons and would be spoken of in newer versions of the Old Charges, even in the eighteenth century. Thus, for example, the *First Foundation of the Craft of Masonry* (otherwise known as the *Dodd Pamphlet*, circa 1739) states that

ABOVE: *This certificate is from the United Grand Lodge of Ancient, Free and Accepted Masons of England (also known as the United Grand Lodge of England), 1845.*

> The great Hermes, sirnamed Trismegistus (or three times Great) being both King, Priest and Philosopher . . . He prov'd there was but one God, Creator of all Things. He divided the Day into twelve Hours. He is also thought to be first who divided the Zodiack, into twelve Signs. [14]

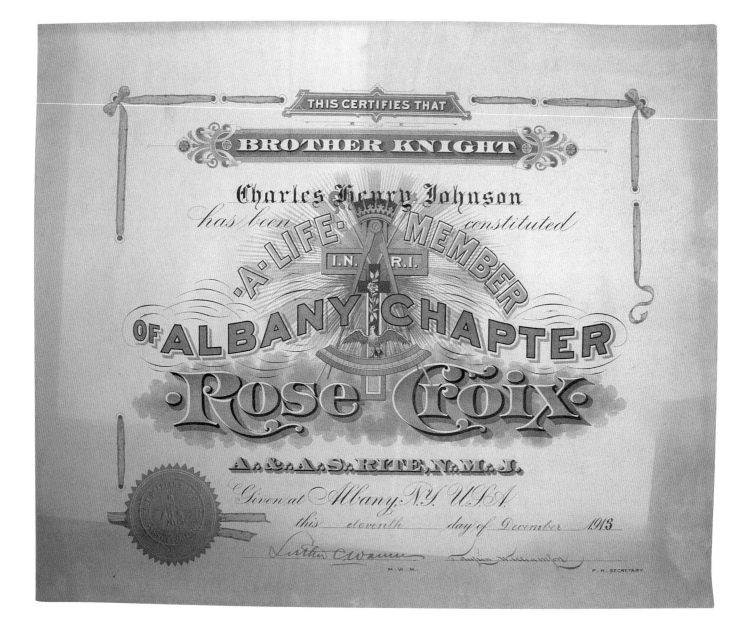

ABOVE: Rose Croix certificate, 1913. The Rose Croix degree is practiced by the so-called Ancient and Accepted Scottish Rite of Freemasonry. This society was established at the beginning of the nineteenth century, though its roots extend back into the previous century.

The pamphlet then goes on to discuss "Clerk Hermes":

> And then this worthy Clerk Hermes took to them these Lords' Sons, and taught them the Science of Geometry in Practice, for to work in Stone, all Manner of worthy Work, that belongeth to the Building of Churches, Temples, Towers, Castles, and all Manner of Buildings, and he gave them a Charge in this Manner. [15]

In chapter 1, we noted that there had been several Hermes, only one of whom was identified with the geometrician Euclid. It is most likely that in the *Dodd Pamphlet*, Hermes Trismegistus is not the same as Clerk Hermes, who again is probably identified with Euclid. The geometrician is referred to in the "History of the Free-Masons Miraculously Discover'd," in the Briscoe Pamphlet, as the scholar Eachlid or "Clerk Eachlid." Similar to the Old Charges, here Euclid is regarded as the teacher of the Seven Liberal Arts, and Hermes as the discoverer of the two stone pillars on which these arts were supposedly written.

Also included in the Briscoe Pamphlet is a section entitled "Observations and Critical Remarks on the New Constitutions of the Free-Masons," which casts Freemasonry in a glaringly alchemical light. The "New Constitutions" are Anderson's, and he is cited as the author. In this sense this commentary serves as an attempted correction to the official Masonic mythology. It is interesting to observe that the originators or heroes of Freemasonry are now alchemists.

> For in short, according to the Opinion of Sandivogius who copied after his Great Master Trismegistus, all Sorts of Sciences are contain'd in Masonry: Nay, Valentine in his Currus Triumphus, goes far as to say, an Artist cannot be properly call'd an Adept without he can build his Athanors, his Digestors, and his Reverberatory Furnaces with his own Hands, in which is required the skill of a Bricklayer, a Mason, a Smith, and an exquisite Geometrician. [16]

"Sandivogius" is the Polish alchemist Michael Sendivogius (1566–1636), and "Valentine" is that most famous German alchemist, Basilius Valentinus, or Basil Valentine. Athanors, digestors, and reverberatory furnaces are equipment proper to a medieval alchemical laboratory. Here, the author of the Briscoe Pamphlet clearly associates the arts or sciences of Masonry with alchemy, as he does Masons with alchemists. The text most explicitly states that the alchemist "Paracelsus . . . was as errant a Free-Mason as Adam," and that "Adam was the First Architect, copying after his grand Original the Maker of all Things." This perplexing statement, which surely infers that Adam and Eve where in some way Masons, is similar to the opening line of Anderson's *Constitutions*: "Adam, our first Parent, created after the Image of God, the great Architect of the Universe, must have had the Liberal Sciences, particularly Geometry, writ-

ABOVE: This twentieth-century decorative cross shows the Christian influence on the Rose Croix Degree. I.N.R.I. designates Jesus of Nazareth, King of the Jews.

So that as the Mechanical Arts gave Occasion to the learned to reduce the Elements of Geometry into Method, this noble Science [geometry] thus reduc'd, is the Foundation of all those Arts, (particularly of Masonry and Architecture). [17]

In the Briscoe Pamphlet, however, the sciences are considered as "contain'd in Masonry." In the *Constitutions*, Masonry is an essentially geometrical art, whereas in the Briscoe Pamphlet, the author contends that it contains other, nongeometrical arts—the most prominent of which now appears to be alchemy.

Masonry no longer primarily relates to the building trade, and it is not only speculative or philosophical but also esoteric or mystical—the teachers and exponents of Masonry are Paracelsus, Sandivogius, Valentine, and Hermes Trismegistus: the great names of alchemy. Here again, we encounter a competition in Freemasonry between championing a symbolic architecture on the one side and alchemy on the other.

Hermes, as noted earlier, is certainly mentioned in some of the Old Charges, although as "Clerk Hermes" he is probably to be identified with Euclid, who is included in Anderson's *Constitutions*. It may be, then, that Anderson wanted to present the Masonic fraternity as deriving from stonemasonry, to show the world a pure Masonic history unrelated to other philosophies, e.g., Hermeticism. Yet it was probably more likely that, like most other Freemasons, Anderson did not perceive there to be a connection between alchemy and Masonry and that most Masons probably

ten on his heart." Anderson continues, "No doubt Adam taught his Sons Geometry."

By "Liberal Sciences," Anderson means the traditional Seven Liberal Arts and Sciences: grammar, rhetoric, logic, arithmetic, geometry, astronomy, and music, which date from the Middle Ages and are still represented in the Masonic ritual today. What is interesting is that the arts, including Masonry, seem to be evaluated differently in the two texts. In the *Constitutions*, Anderson states, had only a very elementary knowledge regarding the science and philosophy of alchemy, if they had any knowledge at all. This does not mean that some men did not join Masonic lodges in the first few decades of the eighteenth century thinking it somehow Hermetic, wanting to learn the science of alchemy. Such men undoubtedly did join, but they were in the minority in British Freemasonry, even if they were occasionally among the most vocal.

Some Masons felt little need for restraint in criticizing Anderson's official mythology of Freemasonry and its development. This was somewhat unfair, since it is likely that Anderson had hurried the writing of the *Constitutions* and also had to take into account the wishes of his patrons—the premier Grand Lodge of England. Anderson both continued and broadened his studies of the Old Charges after the publication of the *Constitutions*, and in 1738 he published a new, second version that was different in some respects from the first. The Old Charges, which had provided the source material for Anderson, cover a vast area of knowledge: the Bible (from the creation of Adam to the building of Solomon's Temple), European history (especially of France, as well as late Anglo-Saxon and early Norman England), ancient Egyptian and Greek history, and some knowledge of the building practices and customs

from at least 1400. Clearly, given such a mass of assorted material, there would be every chance to overlook Hermes, especially if Anderson had thought Hermes to mean Euclid. Certainly Philalethes causes us to ponder whether there were some Rosicrucian societies or more mystical Masonic rites already appended to Masonry, if only few and far between and perhaps lasting only a very short time.

Some societies probably had formed in the first few decades of the eighteenth century, if not before, and simply claimed the title of "Freemasonry" for their own groups; this phenomenon became widespread on the European continent by the middle of the century. Another possibility is that some Masonic lodges may have been interested in alchemy or a number of other pursuits, including more orthodox science and philosophy. Certainly this later became the norm in Europe, but it might already have been the case in some English and Scottish lodges and, even more likely, in Ireland. Philalethes' dedication to the Masons of Ireland and England is certainly significant. Later in the book we shall come across some suggestion of unusual Masonic practices in Ireland at the beginning of the eighteenth century, perhaps connected to the so-called Royal Arch degree of Freemasonry that may have originated in that country.

Chapter 4: The Three Degrees

Initiation rituals into stonemasons' lodges are described in the later Old Charges, but during the seventeenth century, men with no aspirations to join the building trade began to be initiated.

Many of these men came from the opposite end of the social spectrum to that of the builder. They were often well placed in society, were educated, and some were leaders in intellectual fields. Despite the Old Charges' claim that princes, kings, and Biblical figures had all been masons, the first documented initiation of such a man is that of Sir Robert Moray (sometimes Murray), soldier and Secretary of State for Scotland. Moray was accepted into a Scottish masons' lodge in 1641 when his regiment—which presumably included members of the lodge—was stationed at Newcastle, in northern England. The second, though more famous, initiation was that of the antiquarian and founder of the Ashmolean Museum at Oxford, Elias Ashmole (1617–1692). He was initiated in 1646 in Warrington, England. Typical of the new type of mason, both were men of substantial education. It is perhaps not entirely coincidental that both were also instrumental in the establishment of the Royal Society, a British institution founded in 1660 in order to further the rational sciences as put forth by Francis Bacon—Moray was the first president of the society.

Ashmole and Moray also had a considerable interest in alchemy and Rosicrucianism, the latter of which had emerged earlier that century in Germany. A. E. Waite has suggested that Ashmole was already a Rosicrucian, or at least was associated with some practicing groups of like-minded persons at the time of his induction into Masonry.[1] Nevertheless, while Ashmole had recorded his Masonic initiation in his diary entry of October 16, 1664, it does not record any initiation into a Rosicrucian order. So, while Ashmole was undoubtedly connected to men that were interested in, if not devoted to, the Hermetic arts, if any sort of initiation took place into a Rosicrucian or Hermetic society it must have been very informal—there has been a tendency to overlook the importance of informal gatherings in contrast to structured, ritual-obsessed societies.

It is likely that Ashmole joined the Masonic group looking for, and perhaps even believing it to be in some sense, a Rosicrucian society, since there was a growing perception that Rosicrucianism and Freemasonry were linked. It is probable that, even if

The Most High, Puissant, and Noble Prince,
Charles Lenos, Duke of Richmond & Lenox,
Earl of March and Darnley, Baron of
Setterington, Methuin and Torbolton, Knt
of y most Honourable Order of y Bath.
GRAND MASTER. AL. 5725.
A D 1725.

A List of the REGULAR LODGES as CONSTITUTED 'till MARCH 25th 1725

St Pauls Church-yard	every other Monday from y 2 g of April inclusive
Knaves Acre	every other Wedn from y 28 of April inclusive
Brownlow Street Holborn	First Wednesday in every Month
Westminster	Third Fryday in every Month
Ivy lane	every other Thurs from y 20 of June inclusive
Newgate street	First Monday in every Month
Silver street	Second & Fourth Wednesday in every Month
in the Strand	First Fryday in every Month

Printed for & Sold by I. Pine Engraver over-against Little Brittain end in Aldersgate Street

ABOVE: *A list of Masonic lodges meeting at various London taverns, from 1725. The scene at the top left shows a master Mason holding the square and pointing to an architectural plan, presumably that of the Temple of Solomon.*

ABOVE: This Masonic apron shows a Craft lodge as well as various symbols of the master Mason, such as the anchor, the coffin, and the beehive. The working tools of the Royal Arch Mason can be seen bottom left.

the belief of a connection between the British Masons and the German Rosicrucians was incorrect, Englishmen who were interested in Hermeticism hoped to find a like-minded group of men in masons' lodges. Furthermore, while the seventeenth-century lodge was far less formal, and indeed far less symbolic, ritualistic, and perhaps even philosophical than the Freemasonic lodge of today, it did have the bare bones of ritual and a mythology that was substantial in its own terms and very much akin to the concerns of the sciences as they had been shaped at the end of the sixteenth century. Whatever the reason for Ashmole's joining Masonry, it is notable that six years later he would publish his compilation of alchemical texts, *Theatrum Chemicum Britannicum* (1652). Particularly pertinent is his comment that:

> After Hermes had once obtained the knowledge of this Stone, he gave the use of all other Stones, and therein only delighted: Moses, and Solomon, (together with Hermes were the only three, that) excelled in the Knowledge thereof, and who therewith wrought Wonders.

This is strikingly similar to the mythology of the Old Charges that Ashmole must have known and was almost certainly drawing on. Ashmole had participated in the lodge initiation ritual, which originally consisted in swearing an oath over a Bible but by the latter half of the sixteenth century also consisted of an opening prayer and probably the reading of the Old Charges to the initiate. This older mythology must have formed some part of the conversation among members of lodges of this period and later, especially as lodges were initiating intellectuals rather than potential builders. In the last quarter of the seventeenth and the first quarter of the eighteenth centuries, as men of intellect were increasingly being initiated into the lodge, reproduction of the Old Charges also increased.[2] This suggested that, by this time, the traditional legends of the builders interested the intellectuals more than it did those of the trade.

In his work *The Natural History of Staffordshire* (1686), Dr. Robert Plot gives a fairly detailed synopsis of the traditional mythology and speaks of the "scroll" or "parchment volume" of the Masons, these being the traditional form of the Old Charges. Though not a Freemason himself, Plot had been appointed keeper of Ashmole's museum and also knew Sir Christopher Wren, London's master builder and a member of the Royal Society. It is often alleged that Wren was the head, or grand master, of the Freemasons, though proof of this is lacking. With regard to the practices of Masons' lodges, Plot mentions that the new member is shown certain "secret signs," which we can be fairly certain were similar to the signs made by Freemasons today in their contemporary ritual or that they are at least their precursor. It is reasonable to assume that since Plot has recorded the mythology of the contemporary stonemasons' lodge, the mythology was not considered secret and may have been known to intellectuals before they were accepted into lodges. It would appear that these signs were originally employed by the initiated in order to prove their membership in the stonemasons' guild—no matter which specific lodge they had joined—though in Freemasonry such signs took on a greater intellectual significance, particularly as they increased in number along with the rituals themselves. Besides these guild signs, the so-called "Mason Word" was also given to initiates in Scottish stonemasons' lodges in the late seventeenth century, apparently for similar purposes. The Mason Word, along with a prayer, the myth of the Old Charges, and the signs, all entered into Symbolic Masonry, or Freemasonry proper. In this regard we may also note that, traditionally, newly initiated Masons in some parts of the European continent (particularly France) are given two pairs of gloves, with one pair to be passed on to the woman most esteemed by the junior Mason. A similar, if not identical piece of ritual is given by Plot, though the wording is rather strange:

> When any are admitted [into the society of
> Free Masonry], they call a meeting or lodge as
> they term it in some places which must consist
> of at least 5 or 6 of the Ancients of the Order,
> whom the Candidates present with gloves, and
> so likewise to their wives. [3]

In most lodges, all Masons wear white gloves and apron, these being derived from workman's clothing.

Ashmole remained connected to the lodge throughout much of his life. According to a note in his diary, dated March 10, 1682, he received a summons to attend a lodge to be held the following day at Masons' Hall in London, where he witnessed several men "admitted into the Fellowship of Free Masons." In his diary, Ashmole says of himself that "I was the Senior Fellow among them (it being 35 years since I was admitted)," thus suggesting a very limited hierarchy among the "Accepted Masons" (the intellectuals and gentry of the builders' lodges). There are several points worth considering in Ashmole's short diary entry. First, since Ashmole received, rather than sent,

the summons to attend the lodge, despite his being the "senior" member in that lodge (perhaps only on that day since more senior members may not have been able to attend), we might infer that the administrative and organizational tasks remained the privilege or duty of the stonemasons. Also, his seniority appears to be due to his time spent as a fellow ("brother" or "member") of the lodge, rather than due to a promotion to a particular title (such as Master mason) or office. Furthermore, the structure regarding the fee for admission into the lodge also seems to be rather loose, for we hear that, after the induction of the new members, the lodge dined together at the Half Moon Tavern in Cheapside, London, "at a noble Dinner prepared at the charge of the New-accepted Masons."[4] Presumably this fee would not to have posed too much of a problem for these new members, one of whom is listed by Ashmole as, "Sir William Wilson, knight."

Despite the fact that intellectuals were entering stonemasons' lodges in the seventeenth century, 1717 is universally heralded as the beginning of Freemasonry. While this may initially seem unjustifiable, it is not unreasonable. It is only at this point that we find the beginnings of a deliberate elaboration of the philosophy, ritual, and religiosity that had been embedded in the stonemasons' guild. This expanded philosophical side grew to become the whole, as an ethical, mystical, and social Freemasonry emerged out of and divorced itself from the building trade. The event that marked the beginning of this purely symbolic and intellectually driven Masonry, a "Speculative" Freemasonry, was the merging of four stonemasons' lodges to form the first grand body—the Grand Lodge of England (sometimes called the Grand Lodge of London). The social status of the men of these lodges varied greatly and, as was typical of societies of that time, the four lodges met in different taverns all around London (the Goose and Gridiron at St. Paul's Churchyard, the Crown near Drury Lane, the Apple Tree at Charles Street, and the Bunch of Grapes at Westminster). Three of the lodges were made up of men almost entirely from the building industry and as such represented the guild's past. The future was represented by the fourth lodge that met at the Bunch of Grapes at Westminster and was all but entirely composed of gentlemen and intellectuals. This lodge more or less equaled the other three put together. The four lodges met in February 1717 to discuss forming a grand body of Masons. On St. John the Baptist's Day (June 24) of the same year, Anthony Sayer, a man of fairly humble status, was elected to the position of grand master.

Those men who would prove to have the greatest intellectual influence in the newly formed grand lodge of Freemasons, as well as in the ongoing struggle to define and establish a "Speculative" Freemasonry, were undoubtedly the author of the *Constitutions*, James Anderson, and John Theophilius Desaguliers (1683–1744). Anderson was born in Aberdeen, Scotland, becoming a Presbyterian minister at the age of twenty-three in 1702. In 1709 he moved to London, taking appointments as a minister for various nonconformist churches. Also a man of the cloth, Desaguliers had been the son of a Protestant pastor, Jean

ABOVE: *From the earliest days of the Craft, communal dining has proved an important part of lodge activity. This creamer from the mid-nineteenth century, used at Masonic banquets, is decorated with the square and compasses.*

Desaguliers. Jean had lived and practiced his vocation in the then Catholic country of France where, under Louis XIV, those practicing the dominant religion had grown increasingly intolerant toward their fellow

ABOVE: *Anthony Sayer, the first grand master of the premier grand lodge of England, came from a humble background and even in later life earned a fairly humble living as a bookseller.*

Christians and, consequently, human rights regarding Protestants were eroded. While pastors like Jean Desaguliers were allowed to emigrate from France, they were not allowed to take their children, who by law were to remain to be raised Catholic. Despite this, Desaguliers and his wife left, smuggling their baby out of the country in a basket full of linen.[5]

Jean Desaguliers continued his vocation as a pastor to Britain's Protestant French refugees and died in 1699, while his son was still young. John Theophilius Desaguliers managed to go on to study theology at Oxford's Corpus Christi College and was later ordained into the Church of England, where he would earn several prominent positions. He also pursued his studies in the sciences, with which he had already had some success, and lectured in experimental philosophy, first at Oxford and later in London, where he concentrated on Sir Isaac Newton's discoveries.

It can hardly pass without mention that Desaguliers was elected a fellow of the Royal Society in July 1714, ultimately becoming its curator and demonstrator.[6] This was a position that afforded him a modest income and, more important, the patronage of Sir Isaac Newton, who was then the society's head. Fast gaining a reputation as a speaker on the Newtonian sciences, Desaguliers eventually delivered his lectures before members of the monarchy and thus became the second most important figure in the British scientific community, after Newton himself. Not long after the premier Grand Lodge was founded in London, Desaguliers entered the Masonic fraternity and by 1719 was elected its Grand Master. Influential and respected, he greatly affected Freemasonry, securing

ABOVE: *John Theophilius Desaguliers, grand master of the premier Grand Lodge of England, 1719, and friend of Sir Isaac Newton.*

Royal patronage of the Craft and winning members from Britain's most respected circles—especially, it would seem, from the Royal Society, a large number of whose members became Freemasons early on.

At this point, while the stonemasons of Britain had naturally subscribed to the prevailing religion of the country (formerly Catholic, and later Protestant Christianity), the grand lodge thoroughly disliked sec-

tarian religious dispute. It did not matter to its members what faith a man professed, and so the doors of Freemasonry were opened to those of different faiths. To quote from the first of the "Charges of a Free-Mason," published in Anderson's *Constitutions* (1723):

> But though in ancient Times Masons were
> charg'd in every Country to be of the Religion
> of that Country or Nation, whatever it was,
> yet 'tis now thought more expedient only to
> oblige them to that Religion in which all Men
> agree, leaving their particular Opinions to
> themselves; that is, to be good Men and true,
> or Men of Honour and Honesty.

Although they frequently conflicted in small details, the grand lodge set Anderson the task of compiling the Old Charges into a single, official history that would be the final word. In 1723, Anderson published *Constitutions of the Free-Masons* with the support of the governing body; the work has been published numerous times since. Desaguliers, who was then the deputy Grand Master, glossed it with a dedication to the grand master of Freemasons, the Duke of Wharton, and may also have

OPPOSITE: The frontispiece to Anderson's Constitutions, *1723. Euclid's 47th Proposition can be seen between the two central figures, the Duke of Wharton and the Duke of Montague, both Grand Masters of the premier grand lodge of England.*

played a supporting role as a cowriter of the main text.[7]

While the mythology of the *Constitutions* follows the same narrative as the Old Charges, they have been elaborated upon and details, undoubtedly historically questionable in many cases, have been added. More interesting is Anderson's treatment of the Temple of Solomon, which, in terms of the Old Charges, first appeared in the Cooke MS. The section on the Temple comprises an important, though certainly not lengthy, part of Anderson's text of 1723. Rather than drawing exclusively from the Old Charges, as we would expect of a Masonic historian, Anderson also derives his information on the Temple from the Bible. Needless to say, the Freemasons' Ritual would follow suit. Around this time, it is thought the simple ritual or rituals of the stonemasons' guilds were beginning to be refined, elaborated, and changed, emerging as something similar to the Masonic Ritual of today. It is almost certain that both Anderson and Desaguliers were instrumental in the philosophical development of the primitive foundation, in which the tools and procedures of building were elevated to the level of symbol and ceremony.

If the first few Grand Masters had helped to speed the growth of the Masonic fraternity, even before the *Constitutions* had been published, the grand lodge eventually elected a man who proved to be nothing but trouble. Philip, the Duke of Wharton (1698–1731) was not particularly well liked, but he was charming, convincing, and politically savvy, and also used to getting his own way. The Freemasons, while suspicious of the Duke, buckled under what was partly their own self-made pressure. The previous Grand

THE
NEW BOOK
OF
CONSTITUTIONS
OF THE
Antient and *Honourable* FRATERNITY
OF
FREE and ACCEPTED MASONS.

CONTAINING

Their *History, Charges, Regulations,* &c.

COLLECTED and DIGESTED

By Order of the GRAND LODGE from their old *Records,* faithful *Traditions* and *Lodge-Books,*

For the Ufe of the LODGES.

BY JAMES ANDERSON, D. D.

LONDON:

Printed for Brothers CÆSAR WARD and RICHARD CHANDLER, Bookfellers, at the *Ship* without *Temple-Bar* ; and fold at their Shops in *Coney-Street,* YORK, and at SCARBOROUGH-SPAW.

M DCC XXXVIII.

In the *Vulgar* Year of Mafonry 5738.

TO THE
Moft *High,* *Puiffant* and moft *Illuftrious* PRINCE
FRIDERICK LEWIS,
Prince *Royal* of GREAT-BRITAIN,
Prince and Stewart of SCOTLAND,
PRINCE of *WALES,*
Electoral Prince of Brunfwick-Luneburg,
Duke of *Cornwall, Rothfay,* and *Edinburgh,*
Marquis of the *Ifle of Ely,*
Earl of *Chefter* and *Flint, Eltham* and *Carrick,*
Vifcount *Launcefton,*
Lord of the *Ifles, Kyle* and *Cunningham,*
Baron of *Snaudon* and *Renfrew,*
Knight of the moft noble Order of the Garter,
Fellow of the *Royal* Society,
A *Mafter* MASON, and *Mafter* of a LODGE.

GREAT SIR,

ABOVE: The title page from the New Book of Constitutions, *by James Anderson, 1738. This was a reworking of the earlier* Constitutions.

Master had been the Duke of Montagu, and, if one believed the Old Charges, the fraternity had been patronized by kings, princes, and Biblical figures, even when it had been composed of humble builders.

In 1722, the Duke of Wharton became Grand Master of the grand lodge of England, and naturally appears alongside his predecessor on the frontispiece of the first edition of the *Constitutions.* Problems did not emerge until the Duke of Wharton had finished his yearlong term as the most exalted Freemason of London and the Earl of Dalkeith had been elected to take his place. Unsurprisingly, Wharton had no intentions of surrendering his latest title and influence, but the grand lodge rallied around the earl and Wharton was dismissed from the fraternity. Offended, the duke quickly joined, or possibly even established, what was certainly the first explicitly anti-Masonic society: The Ancient Order of Gormogons. Though revenge was very much on Wharton's mind, this was not the sole purpose of the society. The Order of Gormogons appears to have deliberately modeled itself on Freemasonry, while attempting to outmaneuver it at every turn. It, too, emphasized morality, sociability, and charity and had its own "secrets." Like Freemasonry, a potential candidate to the order was not evaluated according to his social status—although social status was always a bonus. The Gormogons' lodge appears to have been less formal than the Freemasons', and the fee for joining was lower than that of a Masonic lodge's. To add a bit of spice to the occasion, the charge was given in "rupees"—or at least the British monetary equivalent.

Despite its claim to hold within its fold men of education, especially concerning philosophy, engineering, and the like, a certain naïveté must have been common to members of the Wharton's new group, not least because of its radical claims. The society was said to have been brought to England by a Chinese Mandarin of some position in China, and its origin was claimed to predate even Adam, having been founded by Chin-Quaw-Ky-Po, the alleged first Emperor of China. Naturally, the Chinese philosopher Confucius also helped to mold the fraternity—even if British society as a whole had not actually read the words of Confucius, he was at least famous in some circles. Yet perhaps the most outrageous claim of the

ABOVE: This modern ceramic plate celebrates "brotherhood" as "the foundation of world peace." Freemasonry emphasizes respect for all religions and people, and requests that its members help those in need whether or not they are Freemasons.

Gormogons can be seen in an advertisement for the Ancient Order, which attempted to link it with the Roman Catholic Church:

> The Mandarin will shortly set out for Rome, having particular Commission to make a Present of this Ancient Order to his Holiness; and it is believ'd the whole Sacred College of Cardinals will commence GORMOGONS.

One can only wonder how the pope and the Sacred College might have reacted to the suggestion that this society was older than Adam, the first man created by

ABOVE: *On the right-hand side of the beehive on this Masonic apron is a book on which we see a skull and crossbones and some flames, such as we find on French floorcloths found in the third degree. To the right of the book is a perfect ashlar, or builder's stone, with a pyramidal peak, again more often found in French Masonry.*

God, and thus in contradiction to the teaching of Christianity.

While much, if not most, of the myths and proceedings of the Gormogons were absurd, the fact that the society linked itself to China, particularly to Confucius, may suggest some calculation on the part of the society. For Freemasonry, "East" is the symbol of the light of knowledge (because it is from the east that the sun rises) or the enlightened mind.[8] It was around this time that the Craft began to refer to its philosophy or doctrines as having been brought from the East, though this claim was also in line with the Old Charges that claimed to descend from the builders of the Temple of Solomon. Confucius emphasized ritual, morality, law, education, ethics, philosophy, and respect toward society and its hierarchy, especially to the emperor and ancestors. If there were ever a society in Britain that could be successfully compared to Confucian culture, it is the institution of Freemasonry, particularly the grand lodge as it was at that time. Like Confucianism, Masonry is not a religion, though it might look like one to the outsider. It perceives its function on the one hand to be the preservation of past tradition, and on the other the cultivation of the individual, especially through ritual.

Because of the Gormogons' anti-Masonic stance, any Freemason wishing to join the dizzying heights of Confucius, Chin-Qwaw-Ky-Po, and other supposed members of the society would naturally be required to renounce their membership in the Masonic order. To quote from a Gormogons' advertisement:

Nor will any Mason be received as a Member, till he has renounced his Novel Order, and been properly degraded.

The Gormogons remained a small group, and interest in them appears to have fizzled out quickly, and deservedly so, as their ruse was so utterly obvious.

ABOVE: French Craft certificate rendered in a classical style, 1835. Note the two pillars and the Temple of Solomon (center).

There can be no doubt that the acceptance of intellectuals into Masonry had a profound effect on its ritualistic practices and on accepted notions of hierarchy. At the beginning of the eighteenth century, there existed only one ritual or degree in England, and possibly two in Scotland. It is conceivable, however, that by the time the premier grand lodge had been established in 1717, two degrees were being practiced in at least some English builders' lodges, which may have then been altered and refined by the Freemasons of the early eighteenth century. Whatever the case, within about a decade of the formation of the grand lodge and the establishment of a solely speculative Freemasonry, there were three rituals or degrees—these constituted what is still referred to as the "Masonic Ritual," or "Craft Masonry." While the third degree concentrates more

ABOVE: A European Masonic past master's jewel, representing Euclid's 47th Proposition, suspended from a square.

fully on the life and death of Hiram Abiff (specifically on his position as master builder at Solomon's Temple, and his later murder by some of workers there), the first degree appears to be more in keeping with the ritual and trade practices of the stonemasons, though the latter has been made symbolic or philosophical. This degree puts forth symbols, such as the hammer and chisel for refining the rough stone, the drawing or tracing board, and other symbols that appear to refer to the drafting of the foundations for building work. Historically speaking, the second degree is the most difficult to evaluate. Even if the bare bones of this ritual were derived from the building trade, it is certain that it was developed by the grand lodge, and perhaps especially by Anderson. It elaborates upon the Seven Liberal Arts mentioned in the Old Charges, though it

also introduces a greater depth of Biblical symbolism than the preceding degree.

By the end of the seventeenth century, the lodges were practicing a ritual that was similar to, though still far simpler than, the Freemasons' Ritual of only slightly later. Although there is little evidence to suggest exactly when it occurred, it would seem that the motif of the construction of Solomon's Temple, particularly the account of the life and death of the semimythical Hiram Abiff, had expanded in importance in the first decade of the eighteenth century, becoming the Craft's central theme within a few years of the publication of the *Constitutions* in 1723. The role of Hiram Abiff had already become greatly expanded even by the time the book was published. Anderson gives some considerable space to Hiram in his text, pondering the meaning of the latter's name and the importance of his position, which he considers to be that of a master stonemason. Thus we read in a footnote that Hiram was "universally capable of all sorts of Masonry." Despite both the linking of Hiram Abiff with stoneworking and the redirection of the stonemasons' ritual by the grand lodge toward a more definite philosophical, mystical point, the pillars of Solomon's Temple are no longer made of brick and marble, as was claimed in the Old Charges. Instead, in the Masonic ritual, in accord with the Biblical description of the Temple, they are made of brass. In other words, while stonemasonry, and its rituals, trade practices, and tools had provided Masonry with a foundation for their ritual and symbols, these became a repository for intellectual concepts that resonated with the intellectuals of the lodges.

The symbolic number three—on which so much of Freemasonry is based—had begun to make its appearance in the Craft by the late seventeenth century, if not before. In the ritual catechisms, we learn that the lodge has three lights and three jewels. Though the symbolism has been subsequently developed, these terms have been retained in Freemasonry, which speaks of the three greater and lesser lights, and of the three precious jewels. However, while the three jewels of the seventeenth-century lodge were referred to by the now nearly incomprehensible terms—"Perpend Esler, a Square pavement and a broad oval"—today they are regarded as the tongue, ear, and heart.

The stonemasons' jewels are still found in Freemasonry, though in a slightly different form. The "esler" is today referred to in Freemasonry as an "ashlar," meaning either a rough stone or brick, while the

ABOVE: This statue depicts what is known to American Freemasons as the "Monument." It is composed of traditional third-degree symbols: the Weeping Virgin (representing the Temple) stands over a broken column (alluding to the death of Hiram Abiff), in her right hand a sprig of acacia (a promise of life after death), and in her left hand an urn. Behind her stands Time holding her hair.

broad oval is known as a "setting maul," which was a hammer once used by stonemasons. In the esoteric language of Freemasonry, an uninitiated man is said to symbolically be a rough ashlar, or rough stone, while the master Mason is symbolically a perfect ashlar, or a perfectly squared stone. This is because the Master Mason is supposed to have refined himself through the application of the moral lessons of Masonry, which are taught to him through the Craft Ritual. The symbolism of the stone is also expressive of Freemasonry's notion of equality. A Master Mason is regarded as one stone among many others that constitute the whole building (the community).

The nature of Masonic symbolism can be explored through the tongue, ear, and heart—the precious jewels of Freemasonry. Even a single symbol might represent various ideas, though these may, again, ultimately play off of each other and bring together various, otherwise disparate, elements of Freemasonry. Simplistically, the three precious jewels serve as a kind of symbolic shorthand for the process of learning the mysteries of Freemasonry. According to the ritual, the Freemason hears with the ear the lesson spoken with the tongue and keeps it in the heart, where all Masonic secrets are said to be stored. The three precious jewels can also be linked to the three principle officers of the lodge, or to the three lesser lights, the three rituals of Craft Masonry, and the like. It is more fruitful, however, to concentrate on one of the precious jewels: the tongue.

The tongue has attained special significance in Freemasonry, but, as with many other Masonic symbols, this significance may ultimately derive from its place in the ritual and symbolism of the stonemasons' guild. In Freemasonry, the Mason's tongue is often represented by a key, sometimes made of ivory, and suspended from a line of string. It is specifically represented as hanging (this being a visual pun), for the Mason's tongue must not "lie" (i.e., it speaks only the truth). A predisposition to truthfulness is regarded as a condition for initiation into a Masonic lodge and held essential to the Freemason. It is suggested by the importance of a new Mason taking an "obligation," in which he swears to uphold the principles of Freemasonry. With regard to the symbolism of the key in stonemasons' lodges, we read, for example, in the Edinburgh Register House MS:

Q: What is the key of your lodge?
A: A well hung tongue.

Q: Where lies the key?
A: In the bone box.

The bone box that contains the tongue is surely the skull, which became a symbol within Freemasonry. Again, it is clear to see how Freemasonry might have obtained the symbol of an ivory key as it works as an abbreviation of this question and answer. The symbol is given a richer context when the same text also speaks of the key being placed, rather gruesomely, "under the lap of my liver where all the secrets of my heart lie," as well as under a green turf and the setting maul.

It would seem that there are various ideas being presented here that may have some philosophical relationship. On the one hand, the key appears to represent both the requirement for secrecy and the ability to gain access to the lodge (probably by speaking the stonemason's passwords). On the other hand, in conjunction with the turf and setting maul, we also possibly find a reference to the myth of Hiram Abiff, the master builder. In the Freemasonic mythology, Abiff is sent by King Hiram of Tyre to direct the construction of Solomon's Temple. Before the building is completed, some of his workmen set upon and kill him in an attempt to extort from the master builder the "Word of Master Mason." With the death of Hiram Abiff, this word is, of course, lost—the myth of the murdered master builder is remarkably similar to the older French myth of Maître Jacques. In the Masonic mythology, Hiram Abiff is killed by a blow from a setting maul and buried in a shallow grave that is covered

ABOVE: *Freemasons stand around the floorcloth, forming the symbolic Temple. To the left the master of the lodge faces the candidate about to be made an apprentice of the lodge, who is kneeling on a stool, his right hand on the Bible. The orator holds a sword before the Sacred Book, protecting it.*

ABOVE: The top of this Masonic certificate shows a stormy scene in which a rock has been transformed into a Masonic altar. Above this is the All-Seeing Eye of God.

A similar enlargement of ideas can be found regarding many Masonic symbols. For example, in the first degree the letter "G" is said to represent geometry, while in the second degree it is explained as representing the Great Architect—in religious terminology, God. The earlier definition is not later invalidated, but is given a greater richness in representing both geometry and God. This expansion probably represents the historical process of Freemasonry. The first degree was probably largely derived from the ritual of the building trade, and again geometry was integral to the practice of Masonry early in the eighteenth century. Later we find the injection of religious symbolism, by Anderson for example, especially from the scriptures concerning Solomon's Temple. The meaning of any particular symbol in the Masonic ritual is dependent upon the context created by its narrative or myth. Thus, in keeping with the more Biblical language of the second Degree, and its description of the middle chamber and twin pillars of Solomon's Temple, the letter "G" becomes a symbol of the "Great Architect." Such a transformation in this and other symbols in the three rituals of Craft Masonry is not entirely due to Freemasonry's philosophical teaching, but is reflective of its development from its root in stonemasonry (illustrated in the first degree, where we find the hammer and chisel as symbols, and the "G" as representing 'geometry') to its philosophical development (reflected in the second and third degrees).

In the catechisms of the late seventeenth century, we read that the first lodge was held on the porch of Solomon's Temple, and this remains a fairly important part of the greater Masonic mythology. Then,

with turf; this is possibly what is being alluded to by the Edinburgh Register House MS and by other near contemporary builders' texts. Thus, the key represents secrecy (probably to keep the passwords, or "Word" secret), the ability to speak the "Word," and the master builder, Hiram Abiff, who is regarded as possessing the "Word," which was later lost.

ABOVE: A Freemason about to be raised to the level of master Mason approaches the lodge from the right and is confronted by the junior warden, holding a dagger before him, symbolizing the danger that ever threatens the man of integrity.

as now, the lodge was regarded as laid out from east to west, while the previously mentioned lights are described by the Edinburgh Register House MS, for example, as being placed in the northeast, southwest, and eastern passages (the placement of these lights is a little different today, as we shall see in the next chapter). According to the seventeenth-century stonemasons' catechisms, we hear that the apprentice

has been in the kitchen, while a fellowcraft (second degree of Masonry) has been in the "hall." "Kitchen" might refer to the physical lodge that was sometimes used by the stonemasons as a place to eat, drink, and relax between shifts, while it seems likely that the "hall" is the eastern "passage" and that this is symbolic of the body of Solomon's Temple. It is interesting to note that the lodge today is still divided

up into at least two rooms, namely the lodge room proper and an adjoining room, sometimes known as the "chamber of reflection," in which candidates are prepared and dressed or sit quietly and contemplate, prior to their participation in the Ritual.

Earlier in the eighteenth century, the lodge appears to have been marked off inside a larger room. It is not improbable that candidates were simply prepared outside this designated area, especially as lodges met in a hired room in a tavern. Perhaps as a consequence, in English-speaking countries, the anteroom is usually quite bare, while in French lodges, for example, the candidate is confronted by a more theatrical setting. Here he sits at a table on which is set a painting of a skull and crossbones; a cockerel; an hourglass; the three medieval alchemical symbols for the elements sulphur, salt, and mercury; and the acronym V.I.T.R.I.O.L., signifying *Visita Interiora Terrae Rectificando Invenies Occultum Lapidem* (Visit the Interior of the Earth and Obtain the Hidden Stone). Interestingly, a similar Chamber of Reflection entered the Knights Templar degree that emerged closer to the end of the eighteenth century in America, though it lacks the alchemical references in its furniture.

The most important and well-known Masonic symbol is the conjoined square and compasses that had entered the lodge by this time. In the oath of the apprentice, in the Edinburgh Register House MS (1696), are the words, "I am sworn by God and St. John by square and compass, and common judge to attend my masters service at the honorable lodge, from Monday in the morning till Saturday at night and to keep the Keys thereof."[9] The reference to the key to the lodge is really the tongue; to "keep the Keys" probably alludes to keeping the lodge's ritual and teachings secret. Whereas the stone-

ABOVE: *This Masonic jewel, worn at the lodge, shows the square and compasses at the bottom right. A figure representing the sun holds a mirror and level, a Masonic symbol of equality.*

OPPOSITE: *In this scene we see a Mason sitting at a desk, in a chamber of reflection, and awaiting the Degree of the Knights Templar.*

ABOVE: In this etching, the lodge has been laid out for the raising of a Freemason to the level of master Mason. Notably, as this is a third-degree ritual, there are three candles at three of the corners of the floorcloth.

masons had much earlier sworn an oath on a Bible, it would appear that the square and compasses have now been introduced. While they may not be identical to the earlier customs, the Freemasonic practices of today involve the square and compasses being placed on the

open pages of the Sacred Book, both at the swearing of an obligation to uphold the ethics expected of the Freemason and in the lodge generally. The square, compasses, and Sacred Book also constitute the "Three Great Lights" in Masonry and serve to symbolize those principles taken by a Freemason as his "guiding lights."

Other objects also began to enter the lodge, illustrating the philosophy and myths of Freemasonry while simultaneously drawing the Craft further from its roots in the building trade. Enough of this phenomenon was known for the Gormogons to mention it in their own self-publication, apparently deriding the Masonic lodge for it:

> This is to inform the Publick, that there will
> be no drawn Sword at the Door, nor Ladder
> in a Dark Room.

The sword has attained something of a special status in Freemasonry. At the time when the society first entered France, probably in the 1720s, the wearing of a sword had an aristocratic or noble connotation. Many French lodges, however, adopted the wearing of swords as a declaration that their brethren were equal, since, they contended, nobility was dependent on the substance of the person rather than on the circumstances of birth.[10] Likewise, in the "knightly" Masonic degrees, even of the English-speaking world, it is common to find members wearing swords, though these degrees did not appear until quite some time after the three degrees of Craft Masonry. In the reference by the Gormogons, the "sword at the door" refers to the practice of stationing a symbolic guardsman, known as a "tyler," at the door of the Craft lodge.

The "ladder in a dark room" is perhaps more enigmatic and enticing, and tells us a great deal more about the Masonic Ritual. Since most lodges at the time met in the hired rooms of local taverns, not all of them erected ladders or set up elaborate paraphernalia. There are numerous examples of lodges who did arrange their ritual settings in this way, however. The ladder, we might note, is a Masonic emblem linked to the Old Testament story of Jacob's Ladder (Gen. 28: 10–22) and is usually represented in the first ritual or degree. In the visual arts of the Masonic society, it is often represented as having only three rungs, as the Freemason is supposed to ascend ethically and spiritually through the virtues of Faith, Hope, and Charity. The ladder, then, also represents these virtues, which are spoken of in the New Testament (1 Cor. 13:13). With regard to the "dark room," during the rituals of the three degrees, there is a point in which the lights are extinguished in the lodge, before being relit with some bravado. This symbolizes the revelatory light of God and the light of knowledge of Freemasonry, whose symbols point the Freemason to God.

In a different sense, darkness is also a theme of the third degree, where we learn, for example, of the death and burial of Hiram Abiff. As we have suggested, the third degree is less directly related to the building trade or builders' rituals of the seventeenth century than the second or particularly first degree. Nevertheless, the greatly expanded role of Hiram Abiff in the Masonic mythology can at least be seen as implied in the stonemasons' rituals, though whether or not this was intended remains a matter for some debate.

We have already seen that the ritual catechisms of this era speak of a "green divot," or patch of grass,

ABOVE: A Freemason is laid on the floorcloth, representative of the grave of Hiram Abiff. The ritual illustrates the belief taught by various religions that the essence or soul of the person survives physical death.

which might be related to Hiram's grave. The burial place of Hiram Abiff was elaborated by Jeremy Cross (a prominent Masonic lecturer in early-nineteenth-century America), transformed into a complex structure composed of various symbols, and known generally as the "monument"—this compound symbol remains largely unknown outside the United States. The monument is an ingenious device that brings attention to those symbols that were left unconnected in the third-degree ritual and refer to the "Hiramic legend," as it is known—it includes an urn, the grave, a sprig of acacia, the hourglass, and a broken column. Elsewhere, we usually find the grave of Hiram Abiff represented by the traditional European-type casket, as well as a skull and crossbones. This emblem undoubtedly entered Masonry from the stonemasons' ritual, specifically from the "bone box" already mentioned. The sprig of acacia, or evergreen, represents the hope of life beyond the grave.

Chapter 5: Drafting the Foundations

As Freemasonry elaborated its symbolism and mythology, it began to develop its own genre of art, the so-called tracing board.

Today, the tracing board is a physical illustration or painting of the symbols for each particular ritual or degree, and is generally displayed as an accompaniment to lectures on the meanings of these symbols, and on the ritual and mythology of Freemasonry. Thus far, we have concentrated on written records pertaining to the development of Freemasonry and its rituals. In this chapter we shall examine Freemasonry's pictorial record.

In America, the tracing board has been largely confined to the earlier history of Freemasonry, while in the lodges of other English-speaking countries, as well as those of continental Europe, it enjoyed greater success and has consequently become one of the most important physical objects of the Masonic Ritual. In Britain for example, the lectures themselves are sometimes referred to as the tracing board. Nevertheless, even in America the tracing board is still considered one of the symbolic jewels of the lodge, and is spoken of as such during the Masonic ritual there, as well as in other countries.

Importantly, while the tracing board became an objet d'art, it would not be fully realized as such until later in the eighteenth century, having then developed through various distinct phases, the earliest of which tell us a great deal about both early intellectual and architectural, or building, influences on the Craft that are not otherwise recorded. In contemporary Freemasonry, the tracing board is generally seen as representing, and being derived from, the architect's or draftsman's drawing board. However, the tracing board is really an amalgamation of both the architect's plan and the builders' draft, the latter of which was traced directly upon the physical foundation of the building site. Although, as we shall see, the Masonic board owes something to both diagrams, in its earlier ritualistic use it derives more from the builders', while in regard to its philosophical and mystical aspects, it is more indebted to architecture.

Because of its long period of development within Freemasonry, the tracing board has otherwise been known as the forming board, mosaic pavement or mosaic palace, square pavement, and lodge board. We will refer to some of these terms a little later, especially as we examine the symbols of Freemasonry. The most important alternative to the term, however, is "trestle

ABOVE: This American tracing board is modeled on a frontispiece for Batty Langley's The Builder's Jewel, published in Britain in 1746. The three columns and the objects hanging from them are nearly identical to those in Langley's book. However, symbols found throughout the first three degrees are added.

board," which seems to have been used frequently in the eighteenth century and earlier. The term is still commonly employed in American Masonry. A man who is to be initiated into the Craft at a future date is said, for example, to be "awaiting the trestle board," while a Mason who has not yet reached the degree of master Mason is referred to as being "on the trestle board." The distinguishable meanings of "trestle" and "tracing" in this context seem to derive from stonemasonry, specifically in regard to the physical apparatus, or the function of the board. Thus, "trestle" would seem to refer to the fact that the board was originally laid on trestles, while "tracing" refers to the fact that it was originally the board on which the draftsman drew or traced. "Tracing" also did not originally mean copying, but rather technical drawing, especially in straight lines. The records or "fabric rolls" of York Minster (circa AD 1399), which are nearly contemporary with the Regius MS, contain the earliest reference to "tracying bordes" of operative masons. "Tracing" or "tracery houses" are known to have existed in the fourteenth century at Exeter Cathedral and Windsor Castle, and in the fifteenth century at Westminster Abbey and York Minster, all in England. In the sixteenth century, it is recorded that trestles or tracery rods were purchased for the tracery house at Westminster Palace.

While these considerations suggest that the later masonic tracing board was derived from the architect's small-scale plan, it did not enter into the Craft exactly in this form. Indeed, it is somewhat incorrect to speak of a tracing "board" in regard to early Freemasonry, since the image was originally traced, or drafted, directly onto the lodge floor, thus constituting a small ritual in itself (which we will refer to as the "tracing ritual"). The practice of drawing an architectural plan was, we can be sure, inherited from the requirement of stonemasons or builders to draft the full-scale architectural "plan" directly onto the ground of the site where the commissioned building was to be built. In early Masonic terminology, the comparable plan is simply called the "lodge" or "lodge board." The significance of this is undeniable. The ritual of Freemasonry centers on the mythology of Solomon's Temple and its master builder, Hiram Abiff. Each of the three rituals involves a symbolic reconstruction of part of the Temple, i.e., the ground floor, middle chamber, or inner sanctum. The lodge is held to symbolize Solomon's Temple, or varying parts of it, and the tracing was necessarily then the plan for this Temple, and for the Masonic ritual itself. While the lodge, or rather, the Temple, is not drawn on the floor today (except in some few cases), it is still constructed anew with each ritual, though today it is the members of the lodge themselves that represent the architecture, or "symbolic Temple," by being stationed at certain significant points in the lodge room.

In its earliest form, the Masonic tracing, or draft, was entirely geometric, usually rectangular (called a "double-square" in Masonry), though early exposés often show this with a triangular section at its top with three steps drawn at the bottom. Included in one of few American Old Charges, the Carmick MS

ABOVE: *An eighteenth-century French tracing board. At the top is the rope with tassels at each end, or the tessellated border. The Blazing Star can be seen at the center, and the mosaic pavement at the bottom.*

ABOVE: Fellowcraft tracing board; oil on canvas, 2002. This tracing board shows the symbols of the second degree, notably the middle chamber of Solomon's Temple, the two pillars surmounted with the celestial and terrestrial globes, the pomegranate and lilies, and the five columns.

(circa 1727) is an illustration of a triangle with a series of even numbers on left side and odd numbers on the right, and within the figure are placed several Masonic symbols: a square and compasses, two candles in holders, a trowel, and a plumb line. Importantly, above it is written, "this figure represents the lodge." As such, this figure might represent one type of Masonic floor tracing with the various Masonic objects placed or drawn inside it.[1] It is possible also that the drafted geometry or plan varied either from lodge to lodge, or alternatively according to what degree was to be performed, and thus what part of the Temple was required to be represented. Indeed, today, the symbolic architectural details of the lodge still change according to whether the first, second, or third degree is to be conferred upon the candidate. While in the entered apprentice degree there are three pillars, in the fellowcraft degree there are only two pillars, but also included is a winding staircase of fifteen stairs.

Freemasonry had, of course, borrowed from the stonemasons by continuing to transform the builders' tools into symbols and developing that symbolic language. It would seem that Freemasons also sought to develop the actual trade practices of builders for their own ritualistic purposes, molding them to prevailing intellectual ideas, which, with the sometimes slow but certainly steady expansion of science and philosophy into the rational (the so-called "Age of Enlightenment" or "Age of Reason"), may not have otherwise found a home. Outside of Freemasonry, Kabbalistic studies had to some extent focused on the dimensions and architectural properties of the Temple of Solomon.

However, the Temple had more recently been investigated by a researcher who was undoubtedly philosophically more acceptable to the premier grand lodge of England—Sir Isaac Newton.

Newton spent much of the latter half of his life investigating the construction of the Temple of Solomon as it was described in chapters 40–48 of the Book of Ezekiel and procuring a coherent plan from this Biblical text, which he studied in three different languages. He in fact reproduced the Temple's floor plan as he believed it to have been. Although Newton was in so many ways the epitome of rationalism, for the scientist the floor plan of Solomon's Temple represented not simply the perfect architecture or geometry as ordained by God but also a mystical key by which future events could be calculated. Newton amalgamated the plan of Solomon's Temple with other Biblical testament and, undoubtedly, his own Puritan Christian ideas,[2] using the plan to allot various dates for specific key events. Yet, if the great scientist saw in the construction of Solomon's Temple a geometric plan onto which the Biblical could be affixed, so did Freemasonry. Indeed, in many respects Newton's Temple plan parallels the Masonic tracing. Newton was not alone in his fascination with the geometry of Solomon's Temple, and there were other academics who occupied themselves in a similar manner, for example, Rabi Jacob Jehudah Leon, who certainly did influence Freemasonry, though there is no concrete evidence that he had a direct influence so early on. It is tempting to think that the ritual drawing of the architectural plan of the lodge (the symbolic representation of Solomon's Temple) was influenced specifically by Newton's notion of the Temple. For John Theophilius Desaguliers—as both one-time Grand Master of Freemasons and Newton's disciple in the Royal Society—was certainly in a position to bring Newtonian ideas into the lodge and its rituals.

As we noted in the preceding chapter, Sir Robert Moray and Elias Ashmole were both early Freemasons and members of the Royal Society, a British institution established to further Francis Bacon's approach to the sciences. It seems quite possible that the mythological and architectural notions and practices of the lodges were later circulated among some members of the scientific body, though not necessarily reaching Newton, of course. Nevertheless, it is also striking that Newton, like Moray and Ashmole, also had an interest in alchemy and Rosicrucianism and is known to have owned several works on these subjects, for example, the Rosicrucian manifestos, the *Fama* and the *Confessio*. More important, perhaps, he also owned a copy of Ashmole's *Theatrum Chemicum Britannicum*, which we have had cause to quote, and in which King Solomon is mentioned. A certain caution is needed, of course, when discussing Newton and alchemy. He had certainly read alchemical literature and may have even experimented in it to some extent, as a part of his scientific investigations. Certainly Newton took alchemy seriously, though his own scientific discoveries were ultimately different from, if not contradictory to, classical alchemy.[3] Even so, if Newton ultimately rejected alchemy, he persisted with his mystically oriented studies of the Temple of Solomon.

Francis Bacon, whose ideas were the inspiration for the Royal Society, wrote one work that has been considered as having influenced Freemasonry, especially perhaps in regard to its conception of Solomon's Temple, though not specifically its plan. This was his *A New Atlantis*, published posthumously only a year after the author's death in 1627. Not entirely without justification, Frances Yates compares the work to the Rosicrucian manifestos, as she compares the English Baconian movement of learning or science to the Rosicrucianism of Germany.[4] *A New Atlantis* is a story of a ship and its crew that land off the shore of an island called Bensalem. The crew is eventually allowed to land, after some initial skepticism by the islanders as to the character, if not the religious persuasion, of the strangers. The sailors are admitted, however, when they disclose that they are Christians and swear "by the merits of the Savior" that neither are they pirates nor have they spilled any blood unlawfully. While the story itself is not especially important, one motif appears that is perhaps relevant. At the heart, or "eye," of the kingdom is a Society of Salomon's (i.e., Solomon's) House, which apparently knows a type of Christian Kabbalah—Christianity being the religion of the island's majority, though we are also told that some Jews live on the island. As it would appear that precious little has not been considered to be the origin of Freemasonry, we might remark in passing that Francis Bacon has been thought its inventor, though this theory has been largely rejected by Masonic scholars.[5] If *A New Atlantis* contributes anything to our study, it is simply that it illustrates that the Temple had been adopted

ABOVE: *Craft apron, early 1800s. On the flap of the apron is the Blazing Star, while directly underneath is the tessellated border. Other symbols are the Temple, pillars, sun and moon, and acacia.*

into Christian intellectualism, and this, of course, we see repeated in the studies of Newton and elsewhere. Some early Masonic lodges also gave the Temple plan a Christian coloring, though of a more historical or practical type, and moreover, to a lesser extent. Whereas Newton claimed that the Temple's symbolic geometry revealed, for example, the second coming of Christ (although this date has passed without event), the Freemasons seem to have early on allied the Temple to the church buildings that stonemasons had constructed, and still were constructing. The zenith of the stonemasons' work was the construction and erection of the great Gothic cathedrals during the Middle Ages. The Masonic tracing ritual, although appearing centuries later, appears to have modeled itself on at least some practicalities of building, for example, of establishing the positioning of steps and pillars, though these architectural elements were now, of course,

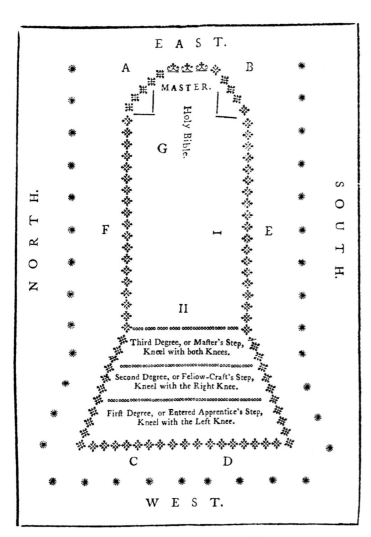

EAST.

A   B

MASTER.

Holy Bible.

G

NORTH.   SOUTH.

F   I   E

II

Third Degree, or Mafter's Step,
Kneel with both Knees.

Second Degree, or Fellow-Craft's Step,
Kneel with the Right Knee.

Firft Degree, or Entered Apprentice's Step,
Kneel with the Left Knee.

C   D

WEST.

EXPLANATION.

A Senior Deacon, with a black Rod.
B Pafs-Mafter, with the Sun and Compaffes, and a String of Cords.
C Senior Warden, with the Level, and a Column in his Hand.
D Junior Deacon, with a black Rod.
E Junior Warden, with a Column in his Hand.
F The Secretary, with the Crofs-Pens.
G H, I, Candles.
✳ Mafons ftanding round at the Ceremony.

N. B.

ABOVE: *A plan of the lodge from the exposé* Jachin
and Boaz. *It is very similar to the plan reproduced
in* Three Distinct Knocks.

treated as symbols. Yet, while we have plans of the drafted lodge from two exposés, or unofficial publications of the ritual, *Three Distinct Knocks* (1760) and *Jachin and Boaz* (1762), these illustrations do not show these details. Rather, it is the early ritual itself that speaks of the positioning of the pillars and other symbolic objects, as arranged necessarily around the plan. The ritual and tracing worked in harmony. In the apprentice catechisms of *Three Distinct Knocks*, it reads:[6]

Master: Why is your Lodge situated East and
    West?

Ans: Because all Churches or Chapels are, or
    ought to be so.

Mas: Why so Brother?

Ans: Because the Gospel was first preached in
    the East, and Extended itself to the
    West.

Mas: What supports your Lodge?

Ans: Three great Pillars.

Mas: What are their Names?

Ans: Wisdom, Strength and Beauty.

Mas: Who doth the Pillar of Wisdom
    represent?

Ans: The Master in the East.

Mas: Who doth the Pillar of Strength
    represent?

Ans: The Senior Warden in the West.

Mas: Who doth the Pillar of Beauty
    represent?

Ans: The Junior Warden in the South.

We can see from this passage how the Freemason participates in the architectural symbolism. Yet, while we read in this old exposé that the Pillar of Wisdom represents the Master, it would be more accurate to say that it is rather that the Master who represents the Pillar of Wisdom.

The notion of the "plan" obtains greater significance, though, when we consider it in light of the Biblical testament, as we must. The Christian influence can be seen in the above quotation, where the Gospel is being brought from the East to the West.[7] More importantly, it is from the Bible, primarily, that the Freemason derives his knowledge of Solomon's Temple and its construction. True, we find details of the Temple in the stonemasons' texts, but James Anderson, who returned the description of the Temple back to Biblical sources, reduced these in importance. The Bible played a significant part in the rituals of the stonemasons, particularly in regard to the taking of their oath. The Bible retained its importance in the ethics and teaching of Freemasonry, yet it also became an important symbol of the Craft, especially because of its descriptions of the architectural details and manner of construction of Solomon's Temple. However, the Bible is also often quoted in the Masonic Ritual. One of the most important sentences of the Bible, as far as the Freemason is concerned, would appear at first to have nothing to do with the Temple. The sentence is the opening line of St. John's Gospel: "In the beginning was the Word."[8] The so-called Word in Masonry has already been mentioned, that is the "Mason Word," which appears to have been used as a

ABOVE: *Master's chair, late 1800s. The master of the lodge is elected to ensure that lodge meetings are conducted responsibly and conscientiously.*

password among members of seventeenth-century builders' lodges, as well as the "Word" that was lost with the death of Hiram Abiff, according to Masonic myth. After the founding of the premier grand lodge in

ABOVE: Craft certificate, 1926. Steps form an interesting part of Masonic symbolism. In the second degree, for example, is the symbol of a flight of winding stairs of fifteen steps. Strangely, the Blazing Star has been placed on one of the sides of the altar.

London, the stonemasons' myth and practice was, to some extent, oriented by the Bible. It would seem, then, that this sentence from the New Testament was used to reinterpret the nature of the stonemasons' and Freemasons' Word. That is to say, the Master's Word, for example, might be regarded not so much as a password for obtaining higher wages in medieval stonemasonry or access to a Masonic lodge at the turn of the eighteenth century but rather as philosophically linked to the "Word of God."

The term that is translated as "Word" in the King James Bible,[9] and thus used in the English-language version of the Masonic ritual, is, in the original Greek, the broader and more complex term, *Logos*, which may with equal validity be translated as "reason," "thought," "proportion," "ratio," and most significantly in regard to Freemasonry perhaps, as "plan" or "design." (In Christian theology, and in St. John's Gospel, Christ himself is identified with the Logos or Word.) There can be no doubt that Freemasonry considered there to exist a philosophical or symbolic relationship between the Bible and the plan of the lodge. Indeed, Freemasonry still regards the tracing board as a symbol of the Sacred Book (i.e., the Bible[10]). In the Ritual the Sacred Book is sometimes called the "Trestle-board of the Grand Architect of the Universe" or is said to be the "real tracing board." This association is of significance for the tracing board, both in regard to its earlier, geometric stage when it was simply drawn on the floor and in its later, artistic form. In the earliest stage, as the tracing represented both the lodge and Solomon's Temple, it was regarded

ABOVE: This Masonic apron is embroidered with the badge of a past master (top left) as well the symbol of the mark master Mason degree (top right), which elaborates on the story of Hiram Abiff and introduces the idea of masons' marks.

as symbolically related to descriptions of the proportion, plan, and architectural details of Solomon's Temple, found, for example, in Ezekiel. In its later, artistic form, it appears essentially as a painting of various builders' tools, objects drawn from the stonemasons' lodges (such as the key), geometric shapes, and Biblical motifs, such as Jacob's Ladder, Noah's Ark, and the Temple of Solomon.

Among the symbols of Freemasonry there remain three geometric shapes that are undoubtedly

ABOVE: *This is similar to aprons worn by past masters today. In the center of the apron we see Euclid's 47th Proposition in a box suspended by the square.*

derived from the art of building. These are: 1) a somewhat enigmatic symbol made of a dot or point in a circle held between two vertical lines, 2) the pentagram, and 3) the Pythagorean Theorem, known to Freemasons as Euclid's 47th Proposition. The importance of this geometric theorem, supposedly discovered by the ancient Greek mathematician Pythagoras, is that it can be and indeed was used by builders to make a right angle. It is worth quoting

Vitruvius, from his *The Ten Books on Architecture*, on the construction of the theorem:

If we take three rules, one three feet, the second four feet, and the third five feet in length, and join these rules together with their tips touching each other so as to make a triangular figure, they will form a right angle. Now if a square be described on the length of each one of these rules, the square on the side of three feet in length will have an area of nine feet; of four feet, sixteen; of five, twenty-five. Thus an area in number of feet made up of the two squares on the side three and four in length is equaled to that of the one square described on the side of five.[11]

These geometric figures had previously been of enormous importance for architecture, and most significantly, they embodied what might be thought of as a philosophy of architecture, that is to say, aesthetic and intellectual ideas, and practical solutions to problems embodied in architectural practice, i.e., building. There can be little doubt that these ideas contributed enormously to the speculation of the early Freemasons, and that these symbols were employed in its tracing ritual of drafting the foundations of the lodge. It is specifically with these geometric symbols that we find the roots of much of the fully developed Masonic picture-symbolism and philosophy.

The symbol consisting of point, lines, and circle concerns us least of all. It's significance is probably derived from the fact that its constituent elements are the most basic elements of geometry (e.g., as defining a point, circle, and line), though it may refer to the Vitruvian notion of "squaring a circle." It is also worth pointing out, however, that among the students of Pythagoras, the point in a circle was said to have been called, among other things, the "Artificer."[12] The pentagram may represent the Golden Ratio (also known as

the Golden Section, Mean, or Proportion), which is embodied in the figure's construction. Supposedly based on, or at least related to, the proportions of the human figure, the Golden Ratio was held to embody the most aesthetically pleasing proportions, and figured prominently in architectural design up to, and

ABOVE: *Liverpool ware cup, early 1800s. The figure on the right-hand column holds a representation of Euclid's 47th Proposition.*

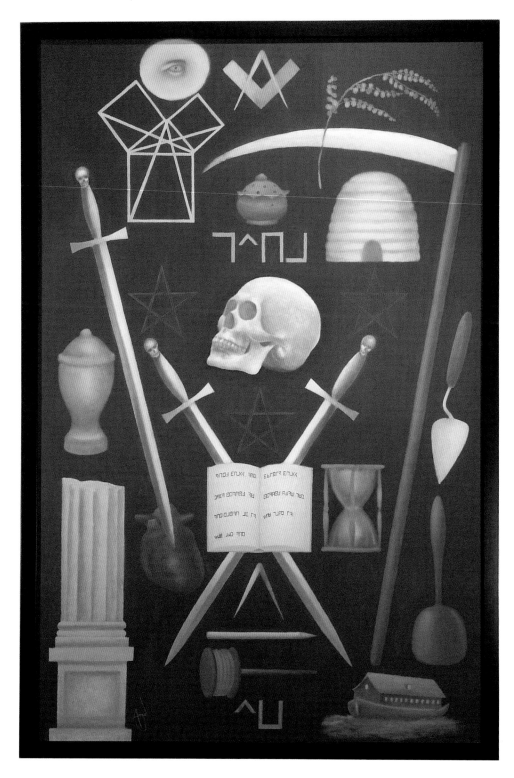

ABOVE: *This master Mason tracing board (oil on canvas, 2002) shows the symbols of the third degree. Note the beehive, Euclid's 47th Proposition (top left), and the pentagrams. Shortness of life is represented by the hourglass, while the Sacred Book is guarded from the profane by two swords. The possibility of triumphing over death is alluded to by Noah's Ark (bottom), the evergreen (top), and the All-Seeing Eye of God.*

even after, the emergence of Freemasonry. To quote Vitruvius on the human figure and its relationship to geometry, again from his *Ten Books on Architecture*:

> In the human body the central point is natu-
> rally the navel. For if a man be placed flat on
> his back, with his hands and feet extended,
> and a pair of compasses[13] centered at his
> navel, the fingers and toes of his two hands
> and feet will touch the circumference of the
> circle described therefrom. And just as the
> human body yields a circular outline, so too a
> square figure may be found from it.[14]

Not only the circle and square but also, of course, the pentagram could be produced by the model of the Vitruvian Man. In this regard, it is also notable that similar to the aforementioned Vitruvian theorem, as the candidate for initiation is brought into the lodge in the first degree ritual, the compasses is pressed to his chest.

Today, one of the more popular images of Freemasonry among non-Freemasons is that of the initiate with his pant leg rolled up. This undoubtedly looks comical to the outsider, who perhaps regards it as a fraternal prank, but its ritualistic significance is more complex than this. Over the course of the rituals of the three degrees, the Mason exposes both legs and feet, his arms, chest, and of course his head. It is very possible that this exposing of the extremities of the body is directly related to the construction of the pentagram, the Golden Ratio of architecture, especially as it

is viewed as related to the body of a man with his arms and legs outstretched in star-shape. It is noteworthy that the contemporary Mason's apron, while complex in its symbolism, is, loosely speaking, related to the pentagram in its shape, being rectangular with a triangular flap that is sometimes worn turned up. Also, it is symbolically associated with the covering, or skin, of the body.

However, it is the figure illustrating the Pythagorean Theorem, or Euclid's 47th Proposition, that undoubtedly proves the greatest potential for our understanding the early Masonic philosophy, symbolism, and Ritual, particularly that of drafting the lodge. Any stonemason of even the slightest skill would certainly have known the practical, architectural application of the 47th Proposition, by which the builder could make a right angle, or corner, which was necessarily the starting point of drafting the foundations of a building. In the earlier discussion of the medieval stonemason, it was mentioned that his methodology was based on geometry, not mathematics, and here we shall find an example. To practically utilize the 47th Proposition, the builder constructed what was sometimes called a "square" in the same manner as that quoted from *The Ten Books on Architecture*, though usually using a piece of rope or string divided into three sides and tied together at the ends, or sometimes three slats of wood. Although there were various methods, in essence the builders' square was held on the ground, its right angle marked out in chalk, and the first corner established. This method remained in use by builders until very recently and may still be used in a few cases in Britain. Within Freemasonry, it is certain that the stone-masons' square was conceptually and pictorially elaborated.

Although there are no records of how the plans of the Masonic lodge were drawn, there can be no doubt that the Freemason did make use of this method, as well as the builders' "square" (which should not be confused with the square of the square and compasses). We know for certain that they drew the lodge plans in chalk as the builders before them had done (though later cord and tacks were used), that their plans certainly included right angles in them, and that the geometry that lay behind the tool for constructing the right angle was to become one of the most promi-nent symbols in Freemasonry (the 47th Proposition of Euclid). Many Freemasons in the earliest years of the Craft were still stonemasons or builders by trade, and it is almost unthinkable that they would not have used their methods in such masonic construction. The meth-ods of drafting construction foundations probably constituted an essential part of the early masonic ritual that, with a steady progression into pictorial symbol-ism, ceased to be retained. The exposé *Jachin and Boaz* reads:

> While the Candidate is preparing, the Brethren in the Lodge are putting every Thing in Order for his Reception there; such as drawing the annexed Figure on the Floor at the upper Part of the Room: which is gener-ally done with Chalk, or Chalk and Charcoal intermixed; though some Lodges use Tape and little Nails to form it; which prevents any Mark or Sign on the Floor. It is drawn East West. The Master stands in the East, with the Square about his Neck, and the Bible open at the Gospel of St. John, and three lighted Tapers are placed in the Form of a Triangle in the Midst of the Drawing on the Floor.[15]

There are a couple of points of interest in the above quotation. The Master of the lodge wears a "square." While this was certainly the architects' set square, we cannot rule out that it was symbolically related to the use of the builders' square used in the drafting. Notably, today in America the Master of a Lodge still wears an architect's square, though in Britain, for example, the badge of a Past Master is the 47th Proposition. It is yet also significant that in *Jachin and Boaz* three tapers are placed in the middle of the draft, in the form of a triangle. We shall recall that the builders' (and even the architects') "square" is actually triangular in shape, as indeed is the lodge according to the Carmick MS. If their "squares" were made of string, builders often fixed them to poles that were stuck in the ground. Likewise, these tapers (candles) used in the Masonic ritual were also placed on similar supports. In English-speaking lodges, the tapers are placed around an altar on which rests the Sacred Book, while in French-speaking lodges they are often placed around a tracing board or floorcloth, again suggestive of an early recognition by Freemasons of the symbolic identity of the Sacred Book and tracing board. Considering that the tracing board and the Bible, in relation to the ritual, both represent the architectural plan, it is likely that these tapers symbolically represented the builders' square—the Masonic symbol known as the 47th Proposition.

In the eighteenth-century exposé *Masonry Dissected*, the lodge has three pieces of furniture, these being the mosaic pavement, Blazing Star, and indented tarsel. This last is otherwise known as the indented tessel, or tesselated border. Today, however, these three are known collectively as the ornaments of the lodge. In *Jachin and Boaz* we find a slight but essential movement toward the pictorial, for here the objects are rendered as the "Mosaic Palace," the "Throne beset with Stars," and the "Lace Tuft." This last change is particularly revealing. "Tessellated" means literally "squared" or "mosaic," but here it is referred to differently, apparently as some sort of fabric or thread. (Certainly we sometimes find "tessel" being confused with "tassel.") Interestingly, the Masonic representation of the tessellated border is not usually mosaic, but most often a cord, and certainly this seems to be the older image. Yet, it is likely that the tessellated border is related to the mosaic pavement, which is also sometimes known as the square pavement.

We learn from eighteenth-century tracts that the mosaic or square pavement was "for the Master Mason to draw his ground draughts on,"[16] that is to say, the master drafted on the ground, or floor. Notably, in *Masonry Dissected*, we are told specifically that the mosaic pavement is the ground floor of the lodge, and thus there can be no doubt that in this case

ABOVE: *Craft certificate, 1870. Drama has been added to the scene of the altar, the three tapers, Bible, and square and compasses by placing them on a rock surrounded by stormy weather.*

the master was drawing directly on the floor. It would thus appear from these texts that the square pavement is in fact but a name for the drafted plan of the lodge, which, as previously noted, was usually regarded as being a "double square" in shape. The tesselated border was almost certainly the rope tool, or "square," used by builders to establish the corner of their foundational draft. The term "tesselated border" (i.e.,

ABOVE: *This pouch is decorated with a scene reminiscent of early Masonic tracing boards. At the left and right are the rough and perfect ashlars, while in the center is a tracing board and the Bible.*

"squared" border), we can surmise, was derived from its relationship with the drafted Lodge, which, as we have noted, was frequently a double-square in shape.

We are left, then, with only the star in the center of the floor that, even today, remains a part of Freemasonry. From fairly early in the eighteenth century at least, the Ritual of Freemasonry included in its symbolism the sun and moon, as well as seven stars, all

of which were grouped together. However, given both the special status, and indeed the peculiar stationing, of this so-called Blazing Star, there can be little doubt that it refers to the pentagram and is therefore a representation of the Golden Ratio of architecture. If this were so, the tessellated border, square pavement, and star would seem to derive from and represent architectural theory and practice. Of course, this should hardly surprise us, considering that the ritual of Freemasonry was developed from the rituals of stonemasonry.

According to one account, at least, the master of the lodge drew on the square pavement. However, it is likely the square pavement, or lodge, was originally drawn by the so-called Tyler, whose function eventually became limited to that of an "outer guard," standing outside the lodge and introducing Freemasons at appropriate points. In stonemasonry, the tyler (or tiler) was the workman who literally laid the tiles, usually on the roof of the commissioned building, whereas we find him early on in Masonry laying the double square of the lodge's design. It is not difficult to see why the square pavement became the mosaic pavement of Freemasonry today, since a mosaic is composed of tiles. If the Tyler drafted the square pavement or lodge, it would seem likely then that that Master originally drew the pentagram and the symbol of point, circle, and parallel lines inside it. (Today, the latter symbol is still thought to be physically represented in every Masonic lodge, though this is rarely the case.) The drawing of symbols continued through most of the eighteenth century, and by the middle of the eighteenth century many, if not all, of the symbols of Freemasonry were being drawn on the floor of the lodge.

The square pavement, star, and border all became a part of the pictorial symbolism of Freemasonry and were soon being drawn on the floor or painted on cloth as small images among others, such as the trowel, chisel, and three pillars. Most inter-

ABOVE: *This apron shows a symbolic lodge at its center, with mosaic pavement, Blazing Star, and an altar around which are the three tapers. To the right is the 47th Proposition.*

estingly, as Freemasonry became more and more pictorial, it also began to manifest a greater depth of ethical and philosophical thought. The square or mosaic pavement became, and remains pictured today as, a black and white mosaic floor (and in the second degree is often pictured as diamond-shaped tiles) and thus became representative of fundamental opposites, such as good and bad fortune, that are certain to be encountered throughout life. The star became the Blazing Star and is representative in Freemasonry of the Divine presence. However, it is still often considered to be the center of the floor of the lodge, which is obviously an unusual place for a star, but a position that suggests how the figure was once drawn in the rit-

LEFT: The three rosettes intimate the master Mason, and a metal square suggests that this was owned by a master of a lodge.

ABOVE: A modern Blazing Star appears on the flap with a traditional one below. While the apron alludes to the mortal body, the pentagram was a symbol of health among the Pythagoreans.

ual. Lastly, we typically find the tessellated border pictured as a night-blue rope, often studded with stars, representing the heavens, the planets, and their paths. Here again we must wonder whether this is because of this border's earlier marriage to the star, or rather the star's original form of the architectural pentagram.

As Masonic imagery and philosophy became more elaborate, some lodges began to use metal templates so that they might more easily and accurately trace the shapes of the symbols on the floor. However, because such a tool was cumbersome and ultimately superfluous, it quickly fell out of favor. Other Masons began to paint the ritual symbols on small stone slabs, though these were often too small for use in the lodge. Most importantly though, some lodges soon began to place the actual, physical objects themselves (e.g., the ladder) inside the lodge draft. The lodge draft was a marked-off area designating the lodge proper, defined by a simple drawing of a "double square" or similar geometric shape. In a sense, this was the most natural development, as the rituals used by stonemasons' lodges at the end of the seventeenth century included the display of not only the Bible but, apparently, also the square and compasses. These three undoubtedly remained in the builders' rituals, being retained by those lodges that became Masonic during or soon after 1717. It is not impossible, of course, that a few other tools had entered the rituals even before this date, though it would seem that Freemasonic lodges eventually added numerous symbolic objects to their ritual, such as the sword and possibly also the heavy maul, ladder, and trowel, though these latter symbols are clearly derived from the building trade.

As early as 1733, another innovation was made when the symbols and objects of the lodge began to be painted on thick canvas or linen. Although these new painted "lodges" varied in size, their dimensions were restricted by the fact that they were either hung on a wall, laid on the floor or table, or perhaps stood on an easel. Typically the paintings were laid on the floor and were referred to as "floor cloths," though it became increasingly popular for the cloths to be stood upright, resembling something very close to the contemporary tracing board.

The new medium not only established a permanent and easily transported representation of the symbolic lodge but also had the added benefit that an artist could render the objects or symbols more naturalistically, creating something visually impressive. Eventually, of course, this compromised the necessity of drawing a new lodge on the floor each time. Perhaps partly because of this, the idea of such a permanent, painted lodge was not well received in all quarters, and in 1759 Saint Andrew's Lodge was ordered by the grand lodge of Scotland not to use the cloth they had been discovered owning—which had been discovered hanging immodestly in the window of a painter's shop. Despite this hostility, the floorcloth gained in popularity throughout the latter half of the eighteenth century

and seems to have been particularly favored by the largely upper-class Masons of France. In a set of engravings from the book *L'Ordre des Francs-Maçons Trahi* (circa 1745), we see different floorcloths with different symbols used for the appropriate degree, much like the tracing boards of today. (However, the use of the floorcloth was contrary to regulations.) For example, in the depiction of the initiation of an entered apprentice, the initiate is led to a cloth on which is painted the lodge, the two pillars (usually seen in the second degree), the five-pointed Blazing Star, and the indented tessel, along with the plum, level, and square. In other prints we find a master Mason's cloth, for example, on which is the image of a coffin (approximately the length of an adult male), a skull and cross bones, teardrops, and a sprig of acacia. Interestingly, the tapers are placed at three corners of the floorcloth, which again would seem to suggest that they were once placed at three corners of the lodge, the cloth representing the Symbolic Lodge, and the tapers, as we have suggested, derived from the three poles used to affix the builders' square.

Today in English-speaking countries, where the floorcloth has been retained, it has been confined to the third degree and features images similar to those mentioned above. As we have said, in English-speaking lodges, however, the three tapers are not placed around a floorcloth but are arranged around an altar, on which is placed the Sacred Book and the square and compasses. We have suggested that during the first half of the eighteenth century Freemasons considered the tracing or lodge board to be synonymous with the

Bible, both being the "plan." This has remained in Freemasonry's philosophical teachings, where the Sacred Book is said to be the "real tracing board." Today the three tapers symbolically light the entire lodge except the northeast corner, which is considered a place of darkness. This is particularly notable in view of the fact that, in the seventeenth century, one of the three lights was held to be in the northeast. It is difficult to say how this symbolic area of the lodge went from being a place of light to the place of darkness, except to say that both notions probably allude to it being the symbolic "first corner" of the lodge. In the first degree of Freemasonry, the entered apprentice is placed in the northeast corner, as he has not received the full "light" of Masonry. Again, in Masonic cornerstone laying ceremonies, the first stone is laid in the northeast corner (this ceremony will be examined further in the discussion of Freemasonry in America).

The members of the lodge are identified with its various parts, whether the corner, pillars, or even the perfect ashlars in the walls of the symbolic Temple. With the transformation of the tracing board from an object of geometry to an object of art, we naturally then find the once plain Masonic apron being painted, embroidered, and later printed with the symbolism of Freemasonry. Most strikingly, the painted and printed aprons are very often copies of tracing boards. This may suggest some intellectual connection between the lodge and the apron.

Naturally, with the expansion of Freemasonry into the world of pictorial symbolism, the tracing ritual all but disappeared.[17] Nevertheless, traces of it have been left behind, most obviously in Freemasonry's pictorial symbolism, which ultimately ended up as the repository of much of its geometric symbolism. The pentagram, as noted, was turned into an image of the Blazing Star, though this latter image, again, was later sometimes represented by a six-pointed star. The stonemasons of the late seventeenth century spoke of three jewels and three lights of the lodge. We have mentioned the three tapers (generally called the "lesser lights" of the lodge), with a probable root in geometry. These may have further transformed into the three pillars, referred to as Wisdom, Strength, and Beauty. Some Freemasons, however, have suggested that these latter pillars were derived from the three pillars of the Kabbalistic tree. We have noted the importance of Kabbalah for Laurence Dermott later in the eighteenth century, and it seems reasonable to suggest that, for those men who might be thought of as the philosophers of the Craft, Kabbalistic interpretations of Freemasonry were gaining currency. Certainly some Masons at the very least would have known of Bacon's *A New Atlantis*, and some might have made further studies of related materials. If so, it seems entirely possible that the three Masonic pillars were aligned to the pillars of the Kabbalistic Tree of Life. It seems unlikely, however, that Kabbalah was a major influence on the premier grand lodge of England in 1717, or later, and as such could not have affected the development of the symbolism of Freemasonry, nor its philosophy under this premier lodge. Kabbalah is not mentioned in Anderson's *Constitutions*, in effect the ground plan of Freemasonry, nor do we find it mentioned in the

LEFT: This entered apprentice tracing board (oil on canvas, 2002) shows the symbols of the First Degree, including the three pillars, the black and white tiles, and the ladder.

Masonic Ritual. Yet even so, it might be seen as one among many possible influences on the cultural development of Freemasonry (especially because it was mentioned by Dermott in his *Ahiman Rezon* and was likened to Freemasonry in the eighteenth century by Verus Commodus). It is this fact that renders the Craft neither geometric, alchemical, nor exclusively mystical or Kabbalistic, but rather something unique in itself.

Yet, while the inclination to reinterpret Freemasonry through Kabbalah, alchemy, etc., is problematic from a historical standpoint, such speculation and reevaluation might be seen as an integral part of the Craft. Eventually, such contemplation of Kabbalah, linked to Freemasonry's symbols, would affect the society both in the normally more conservative English-speaking lodges as well as in continental Europe.

Chapter 6: The Royal Art

By the middle of the eighteenth century a serious contender to the premier Grand Lodge of England had emerged.

It claimed to adhere more strictly to the old and authentic ritual tradition of Freemasonry, to possess some Masonic secrets and symbols that were otherwise unknown, and most controversial of all, to have a fourth degree, called the Holy Royal Arch. Such higher degrees had been appearing in and multiplying throughout the European continent for some time, but this was the first and probably the only major contender in Britain, and it would prove a major sticking point in relations between the grand lodges, like most lodges and Freemasons under them. It is likely that this new Masonry was influenced by the Masonic practices and rituals of the grand lodge in London. Not only were they similar in many respects, but having established itself as essentially "official" Freemasonry, other so-called Masonic bodies necessarily had to at least begin with the three degrees set down by the premier English grand lodge.

However, not all of the builders' lodges of England had come under the wing of the grand lodge at London, either in 1717 or later, and it is quite possible that some of the independent lodges had developed the stonemasons' rituals and practices differently, while retaining some old practices that the now popular Freemasonry had dropped. The Masonic rituals of England seemingly differed from the beginning, although common themes and motifs ultimately drew them together. The first references to the Royal Arch degree prior to the middle of the eighteenth century are slight and exist only in the records of the new grand lodge, which state that Laurence Dermott had taken the degree in 1746.[1] By the middle of the eighteenth century, this degree had been instituted in Scotland and probably northern England, and only slightly later had found its way to Philadelphia.

Though Dermott had taken this degree in Ireland, it was not official practice under the Irish grand lodge, which appears to have known nothing about it. Perhaps consequently—and despite it being populated early on largely by Irish Masons in London—some Masonic historians have sought to find its origin elsewhere. G. J. Findel, for example, thought that the rite had originated in France between 1738 and 1741 with one Chevalier de Ramsay.[2] It is unlikely, though, that the degree could really be accredited to Ramsay (who is discussed

ABOVE: This (probably French) Masonic apron shows the Temple in the middle, with the two pillars on either side. On the flap are symbols, such as the broken column, the beehive, and sprig of acacia. At the center of the flap is a serpent coiled around a globe, a traditional symbol of eternity.

later) or even to a single inventor. Nevertheless, there is also a strong similarity between the Royal Arch degree and the so-called Ecossais, or "Scots" degree, originating, ironically, on the European continent (more on this later). Waite claims that the Royal Arch was but a "revision of some Rosicrucian Grade,"³ and while this might ordinarily infer a Continental origin, it would appear that Waite was thinking of England.

Of course, the Irish might have found inspiration for the creation of a higher degree in Europe, but in this regard they could have done no worse than to look to England. For although it is generally overlooked, the premier grand lodge had itself introduced the idea of the higher degree, only its highest degree—tacked onto those of the stonemasons' guild—was the third. Though his life story in Freemasonry at least paralleled the life of Maître Jacques, Master Mason Hiram Abiff had been largely concocted by the first grand lodge of London. He had made only slight entry into the Old Charges, and even less into the rituals. The establishment of this new philosophical degree, and the death of Hiram Abiff found in it, was exactly the reason why pretenders to the Masonic throne could appear in such droves across Europe in the eighteenth century. Hiram Abiff died without telling anyone the secret. But perhaps Hiram had died simply without telling the Grand Lodge of England the secret, and perhaps the more adventurous Mason might find it. Europe's Freemasons were quite happy to point out where. Much to the chagrin of the premier grand lodge, the Royal Arch Mason likewise made no secret of having the secret. Interestingly, it has become a part of Masonic legend in the English-speaking world that the Royal Arch was once a part of the third degree.[1] It is not improbable that some elements of the Royal Arch—and by extension the newer type of

ABOVE: This Royal Arch jewel shows the Temple, the mosaic pavement, and the ark. Above is a ribbon that is sometimes found among the symbols of eighteenth-century Masonry. Beneath is the badge of a past master.

Masonry—were common to Masonic lodges even as the premier grand lodge formed in 1717, though it would seem unlikely that the entire Royal Arch degree existed and was simply cut away from that of the Master Mason then, or later.[3] Nevertheless, it has traditionally been thought of as the completion of the third degree and the crown or capstone of Freemasonry.

The most voracious advocate of the new grand lodge and the new type of Masonry was Laurence Dermott. Dermott was initiated into Freemasonry in Ireland around 1741, and by 1746 he was the Master of a lodge in Dublin. In the same year he also took the Royal Arch degree, which was then almost unknown, particularly in England. The conjunction of his reaching mastership of the lodge and joining the Royal Arch is perhaps significant, as traditionally only those Masons who had attained to the former position could join a Royal Arch chapter. However, in 1748 he left Ireland for England and joined the Craft under the Grand Lodge of England, or the "Moderns" as he would later call it, and all those practicing Freemasonry under its jurisdiction. Nevertheless, Dermott was far from the first person to refer to the Freemasons of the premier grand lodge as "Modern." It had, in fact, become more or less the stock insult.

Dermott would later leave the Moderns, apparently much dissatisfied. He joined up with another association of Freemasons, quite separate from the Moderns, who in large part were Irish. It is generally suggested that they existed on the periphery of recognized Masonry in England, incurring prejudice by the Moderns, though it is more likely that the separation was because of differences in their rituals. Dermott regarded the primarily Irish lodges in London as practicing a type of Freemasonry that remained unadulterated, authentic to its origin in stonemasonry, and thus "ancient." He styled a group of Freemasons who became known as the "Antients." The intellectuals of the premier grand lodge (such as Anderson) had refined the Craft, but they had also undoubtedly changed it in the process. However, contemporary Freemasons were not at fault for such adulterations made in Modern lodges, Dermott suggested, for they had been made earlier on, in the reign of King George I. The Moderns had merely inherited the problem. Previously, Sir Christopher Wren (whom Dermott, like others before him, considered the Grand Master of

ABOVE: *Ceramic mug, 1790. This English Masonic mug shows the arms of the Moderns. The figure closest to the shield is a master of a lodge, as he is wearing a square around his neck. Note the square and compasses resting on the Holy Bible.*

OPPOSITE: *The frontispiece to the second edition of Dermott's Ahiman Rezon, 1764. Above is the arms of the Antients, and below the arms of the so-called Moderns.*

The Arms of y^e most Ancient & Honorable Fraternity, of Free and Accepted Masons.

Holiness to the Lord.

The Arms of the Operative, or Stone Masons.

Freemasons) had allegedly neglected the lodges, and they of course fell into a state of decay. Despite this, some Masonic lodges had, Dermott suggested, continued in an "Antient" (ancient) fashion. Dermott's enthusiasm for this authentic Masonry was plain to see. Despite working twelve hour days in the employment of a "master painter," in 1752 he joined two Antient lodges. The same year he was elected Grand Secretary of the Antient grand lodge and remained in that prestigious position for more than three decades, when he was elected to be the Deputy Grand Master of the Ancient Grand Lodge. The earliest records of the Ancient Grand Lodge in England are from Dermott himself and date from his installation as Grand Secretary. Not surprisingly, the rules governing the Ancients appear to be derived from those of Ireland.

With Dermott's considerable scholarship, Antient Masonry went from strength to strength. Equality with the Moderns was secured with the installation of the Duke of Atholl as the Antients' Grand Master in 1771. Although Freemasons under the different jurisdictions sometimes fraternized together—occasionally in lodge meetings—the relationship between the two grand lodges was exceedingly strained. Dermott was often singled out for undeserved ridicule by some of the Moderns, and members of a lodge under one jurisdiction were not supposed to join, or even attend, any lodges under that of the other. That is to say, according to the rules of the grand lodges under discussion here, a Modern Mason could not attend an Antient lodge, nor vice versa—at least not until the next century. Although much of the hostility and snobbery issued forth from the premier grand lodge, in an address to the Antient Freemasons (and later published in the second edition of *Ahiman Rezon*)[6], Dermott would turn the tables. He claimed that the Modern Mason could not know all of the secrets of Antient Masonry—at least not without additional ceremony—though the Antient Mason knew all of the secrets of Modern Masonry.

Without having undergone the Antients' three degrees, the Mason could neither receive the Royal Arch, which according to Dermott was the "root, heart, and marrow of Masonry."[7] In fact, the Antients'

ABOVE LEFT: *A jewel bearing the heraldic device of the Grand Lodge of New York. It has clearly been modeled on the one adopted by the Antients, which appeared in London in the eighteenth century. The inscription at the bottom reads, Holiness to the Lord.*

ABOVE: This hand-painted apron is decorated with symbols of Craft Masonry, especially the third degree, except for the menorah, or candleholder, which is an emblem of Royal Arch Masonry.

ABOVE: *American Royal Arch certificate, 1801. This unique handmade document contrasts strongly with the French certificates of the same period. It is interesting to note that the artist has included a ladder in the bottom-left corner, since the ladder is not normally associated with the degree. According to the certificate, the Royal Arch degree was bestowed under the authority of a lodge at County Armagh, Ireland.*

version of the three degrees was different to that of the Moderns, though it stuck to the theme of Hiram Abiff and the building of the Temple. Nevertheless, as the eighteenth century progressed, some Modern Masons defected to the more complex Masonry of the Antients, and some rival lodges met together, working a mixed system.[8] Curiously, close to the middle of the eighteenth century, a group of actors in the York region of England received a charter from the Moderns' grand lodge to establish there a Masonic lodge, to be known as the Punch Bowl Lodge. This lodge communicated, and to some extent enjoyed unofficial joint membership, with a then revived Antient York grand lodge. From the Antients, the Punch Bowl Lodge received the Royal Arch degree, though again unofficially and so could not receive a charter necessary to legitimize its Royal Arch chapter.[9] Nonetheless, it seems to have proceeded to consider itself such an authority, sanctioning other Royal Arch chapters attached to Modern lodges. [10]

Similarly, and perhaps more strikingly, some high-ranking members of the premier grand lodge became Royal Arch Masons, even though the official policy of the grand lodge was that it had "nothing to do with the proceedings of the Society of Royal Arch Masons."[11] At this point the Antients were no longer equal with the Moderns but were rapidly becoming the more impressive of the two. Yet despite its successes in England, it was abroad that Antient Masonry would

ABOVE: "Frog Mug," late 1700s–early 1800s. This mug bears the arms of the Antients, with the inscription "Audi Vide Tace." Inside the mug is a sculpted frog, which would be revealed as the contents of the mug were drunk.

really shine. Incredibly, the once highly prestigious Modern Masonry was fast being reduced to a local, English phenomenon, while Antient Masonry was looking increasingly global, and increasingly powerful. By the end of the century there were Antient lodges as far away as India, though it would be in America that it would make its greatest impact. Even where Moderns' lodges had established themselves in these countries, as in England, they would begin to be replaced by those of their rivals.

There were undoubtedly a number of factors in the Antients' success. Though it had initially proved troublesome in England, both the political and social climate helped the Antients in America, even if the Moderns had arrived there first. The audacious claim to a higher degree, more secrets, and a greater antiquity apparently trumped the simple affluence and social prestige of its members in the game of Masonry. Yet, if the Antients' claim to be ancient was questionable, it was not an outright lie. On the one hand, they had apparently borrowed from the Ritual of the three degrees, established by the premier grand lodge. On the other hand, while the Antients had elaborated on the Masonic myth, they also insisted on keeping as close to the original form of Masonry as possible and criticized the innovations of the Moderns that neither accorded with stonemasons' tradition nor Biblical testament. Elaboration, for the Antients, did not mean innovation; it meant simply digging deeper at the ruins of the metaphoric Temple and, like archeologists, uncovering another, older layer, another foundation strewn with the broken pots and cracked jars of Masonic symbols not yet unearthed. Arguably, the Antients meant only to discover what was there already.

More complex and mystical than that of the Moderns, Antient Masonry was also arguably more intellectual. The Antient Masons had, after all, longer to reflect on Freemasonry than the premier grand lodge did before solidifying it in ritual. Though, as the three degrees had centered around the figure of Hiram Abiff, who had met his death already in the third degree, the Royal Arch degree could not so much complete the degrees, as is often suggested, but rather shifted the sights of the Freemason to a different and arguably more authentically Masonic horizon. Three time periods are found to be of symbolic importance for Freemasonry today. The first is the time of the construction of the Tabernacle (or the so-called First Lodge) in the wilderness of Sinai, after the exodus of the people of Israel from captivity in Egypt. The second period is that of the construction of Solomon's Temple (or Second Lodge) essential to the narrative of the third degree ritual. The third period is that of the rebuilding of the Temple under Zerubabel after its destruction, and it is this so-called Third Temple that is of importance for the Royal Arch chapter.

Under Dermott, the Antient grand lodge adopted a coat of arms composed of a lion, man, ox, and eagle. Dermott had apparently come across this in a collection of Rabi Jacob Jehudah Leon. The government of Holland had asked Leon to make a model of Solomon's Temple, which would serve as the basis for such a building to be constructed there. However, it appears that the cost was realized to be too high, though the model itself was exhibited fairly widely across Europe, for example at Paris, Vienna, and London during the reign of King Charles II. Leon also published an account of the Tabernacle and Temple, dedicating his work to the king. The lion, man (or angel), ox, and eagle had been the standards for four of the twelve tribes of Israel, and are mentioned in Ezekiel (1:10) as well as Revelations (4:7). They are also generally regarded as representing the four Platonic elements or building blocks of the universe: Fire, Water, Earth, and Air. In his work *Timaeus*, Plato conceives of these elemental qualities as codified in specific geometric shapes or "solids" (i.e., polyhedron) which, while infinitely small, are fitted together to create the universe and all it contains.

Later, the Royal Arch would elaborate on geometry, specifically the mystical geometry of Plato's *Timaeus*. Robert Freke Gould, past senior grand deacon of England and author of *The History of Freemasonry*, suggested that the title of the Royal Arch degree does not refer to a literal arch but means rather "chief,"[12] as in "architect" ("chief" or "premier" builder). Although we do find an arch among the symbolism of the Royal Arch as it stands today, this was not necessarily the case at its beginning, and considering the emphasis by the Antients and the Royal Arch on geometry, Gould's interpretation might prove the most valuable.

According to Plato, the universe was created by the "Master Craftsman" from the elemental solids of different regular geometric shapes *(polyhedrons)*. Thus, Spirit was given the geometry of the dodecahedron, Fire the pyramid, Water the icosahedron, Air the octahedron, and Earth the cube. These were then fitted together in various combinations, creating all different physical phenomena. The construction of the Platonic polyhedron is itself essential to the symbolism of the Royal Arch degree. Despite this, the degree is framed in a Biblical setting. The banners of the Twelve Tribes are present, representing the virtues of each, while the four main banners, already mentioned, are hung as

veils during the ritual, which the Freemason passes in his symbolic journey to the source of knowledge. It is not difficult to see why such advanced geometry entered the Royal Arch degree, yet given Freemasonry's grounding in stonemasonry and geometry, we should expect, rather than the Biblical, pictorial symbolism, that the geometry itself would prove the root of the degree. This is almost certainly the case.

To be sure, even by the medieval period the Platonic solids had become something to ponder in the Kabbalistic circles, and evidence of Christian Kabbalah can perhaps be found in the history of the Royal Arch degree. Dermott also seems to have connected a spiritual Freemasonry to Kabbalah (at least he had dreamed this while embarking on his authorship of *Ahiman Rezon*). In fact, he not only suggests that the Freemasons in Jerusalem and Tyre—who he asserted had gone to build the Temple—were the greatest Kabbalists, but also included in his *Ahiman Rezon* a prayer, supposedly said in Jewish lodges, which states explicitly, "number us not among those that know not thy Statutes, nor the divine Mysteries of the secret Cabala."[13] He includes a prayer for Christian lodges, we may note, in which there is no mention of Kabbalah, the prayer being of a very traditional Christian type. Nevertheless, by the seventeenth century, Platonism had made significant inroads into conservative academic circles, sometimes utterly hostile to the mysticism of Kabbalists, alchemists, and neo-Platonists, and this route back to the Antients, and their Freemasonry, should not be ruled out too hastily, especially as they also emphasized the study of geometry.

In the early seventeenth century, the Platonic solids had found themselves a matter of importance in the opposing worldviews of the English Rosicrucian-devotee Robert Fludd and the German astronomer and mathematician Johannes Kepler. Fascinatingly—in part because there has long been the notion of a connection between Rosicrucianism and Freemasonry—Fludd has been regarded by some Freemasons as the possible inventor of Freemasonry. This does not fit well with the fact that stonemasons possessed some sort of ritual, a very definite mythology, and undoubtedly some philosophical or esoteric understanding of architecture, geometry, and proportion long before the birth of Fludd, much of which was very definitely adopted by Freemasonry. On the other hand, while Kepler has not been seriously looked at by Masonic historians, it is far more likely that Kepler's theories did contribute significantly to Antient Freemasonry, possibly regarding the Antients' reference to the Platonic building blocks and certainly regarding another Antient Masonic symbol, the beehive. Complicating the matter, though, this symbol was stolen by Fludd, though not directly.

By the time the Antient lodges had appeared in England, a large section of the Royal Society were Freemasons, and certainly members of that scientific body would have been intimate with the works of Kepler. Fludd also had a more reasonable side to him, and in his time was also well known to the cultural establishment. He had graduated from Oxford University and, having studied medicine, went on to be one of the physicians at the court of James I. There were also at least one or two members of the Royal Society who still had an interest in alchemy, and they would probably have known of Fludd. Newton, of course, was one of them. However, while it is difficult to say when such influences might have entered Freemasonry, it seems unlikely that it would have been so late. Indeed, the importance for Fludd, in the theory that links him to the Masonic fraternity, is the possibility that he had helped to turned some lodges of stonemasons in the early seventeenth century into mystical or philosophical societies or lodges. Of course, the same could be said for Kepler.

In Kepler's *A New Year's Gift, or the Six-Cornered Snowflake* (on the front page of which he refers to himself as Mathematician to his Imperial Majesty), we begin to see how close he had come to what would later appear as Freemasonry. He inquires into the geometric qualities of the pomegranate seed, lily, beehive, and rose—as well as, of course, the snowflake. However, perceiving these objects of nature rather as geometric, Kepler implies that they are not natural per se, but instead must have been "designed." Necessarily, they must have been designed by God, specifically through geometry. In line with early Christian theology, Kepler viewed God as the Architect. Of course, he could look back to Plato and to the Bible to find confirmation of this idea, as had the theologian before him. He was not presenting a new idea but was using new methods of research and new observation (such as the paths of the planets) to reveal the truth of a notion that had existed for millennia. We can see that Kepler's unusual choice of the pomegranate and the lily was probably derived from the Bible's description of Solomon's Temple (1 Kings 7: 15–7: 22):

> For he [Hiram Abiff] cast two pillars of brass, of eighteen cubits high apiece: and a line of twelve cubits did compass either of them about. And he made two chapiters of molten brass, to set upon the tops of the pillars: the height of the one chapiter was five cubits, and the height of the other chapiter was five cubits: And nets of checker work, and wreaths of chain work, for the chapiters which were upon the top of the pillars; seven for the one chapiter, and seven for the other chapiter. And he made the pillars, and two rows round about upon the one network, to cover the chapiters that were upon the top, with pomegranates: and so did he for the other chapiter. And the chapiters that were upon the top of the pillars were of lily work in the porch, four cubits. And the chapiters upon the two pillars had pomegranates also above, over against the belly which was by the network: and the pomegranates were two hundred in rows round about the other chapiter. And he set up the pillars in the porch of the temple: and he set up the right pillar, and called the name thereof Jachin: and he set up the left pillar, and the name thereof Boaz. And upon the top of the pillars was lily work: so was the work of the pillars finished.

ABOVE: At the bottom of this Craft apron is a gavel, a sprig of acacia, and a trowel. In the center is the Temple of Solomon with two pillars surmounted by pomegranates. The Blazing Star is on the flap.

As the two pillars of Solomon's Temple appear in the second, or fellowcraft, degree of Freemasonry, so necessarily do the lilies, pomegranates, and "network" that adorn them. After the beginning of the eighteenth century, the two pillars of the Old Charges were modeled on those described in the Bible. The main difference to them being that, like those of the stonemasons' mythology, these were still considered to have been receptacles of written knowledge. In this case, however, the archives were said to be contained within the shafts of the pillars, which were portrayed in early eighteenth-century Masonic myth as being of hollow brass.

ABOVE: *This unusual past master's jewel shows a mosaic pavement, the two pillars, and an arch.*

ABOVE: *A past master's jewel composed of the compasses and sun. The Antients required that a Mason be made a master of a lodge before taking the Royal Arch degree. American Masons are still made symbolic or "virtual past masters" before they are allowed to take the Royal Arch.*

Nevertheless, that Kepler had transformed the pomegranate and lily into a serious matter for those contemplating geometry and intellectual mysticism surely affected the understanding of the more edu-

cated Freemasons, who were discussing such subjects in the lodge itself. Indeed, given that geometry played a greater part in Freemasonry at that time, it is reasonable to suggest that some lodges at least might have discussed the pillars in such terms. As we have seen, the plan of the lodge itself was geometric, and the pillars themselves formed a part of a fellowcraft lodge, at least.

More important at this junction, however, is the philosophical connection between the five Platonic solids and the hexagonal cells of the beehive, or even the hexagon generally, which Kepler seems to have favored greatly. It is important because it may lead us to realize why the Antient Masons had come up with their new interpretation of Freemasonry and why they had adopted the beehive as a Masonic emblem. Kepler was eager to ascribe to the construction of the cosmos, and the order of the planets, a Divine origin in which God is the designer of the Cosmic Geometry. There were five elements, he argued, because there were six planets (the seventh had not yet been discovered), and the elements fit between the planets as a kind of atomic tiling, the solids fitting neatly together through space. Similarly, Kepler speaks of pomegranate seeds being packed, or rather compressed, and in this way, the organic, or natural shape is made into a geometric one. Simply put, in this theory, the small berry-like pomegranate seed is pressed on all sides by the other seeds, and they by others, and so on and so on, until it is flattened from different angles, pressing it into a shape of many different flat sides, i.e., a polyhedron.

Of course, there are several different ways in which to pack spherical objects, for example in rows, with each sphere placed side by side and one above the other, which will of course compress the roughly spherical shapes into exact cubes. However, Kepler regarded the pomegranate seed as having been packed in a hexagonal arrangement, thus connecting it to the honeycomb (which is similarly packed), and again to the lily, whose geometry he also regards as such because it has six petals.

In Kepler's *Six-Cornered Snowflake*, he discusses at length the implication of the geometric shape of the honeycomb and the reason why bees build in such geometry.[14] Of all the reasons Kepler gives, the one that resonates perhaps most with Masonic ideology is that, composed of hexagons, each bee necessarily shares in the work of the other, with one bee building one side of the wall and the neighboring bee the other. The bee is a communal builder, and the beehive is, by implication, a community of builders.

In many respects the beehive is the most provocative of Masonic symbols. It is specifically a symbol of work, and, like Kepler's definition, a community of workers. Although it is not specifically stated by Freemasonry as to what type of work is meant, we need only to return to Kepler's assertion that bees are builders or, to use another term, Masons. True, these are not stonemasons, but in the eighteenth century the term Geometric Mason was also used by the Craft to mean a Freemason. Nevertheless, despite being connected to mathematics by one of the earliest Masonic exposés of Ireland, the definition of the symbol by Freemasonry proper excludes any mention of the fact that the beehive, like the floor of the early Freemasonic lodge, is geometric. Nor does it appear that it was taught as such much earlier. In one American tract of 1827, by William Morgan, we read only that:

It [the beehive] teaches us that, as we came into the world rational and intelligent beings, so we should ever be industrious ones, never sitting down contented while our fellow-creatures around us are in want, when it is our power to relieve them without inconvenience to ourselves.[15]

Pleasant though the sentiment is, as a definition of the Masonic symbol it is entirely unsatisfactory. According to Kepler, God taught the bee to build. The Creator had also, we must recall, taught the geometry of the Tabernacle (the so-called First Lodge), and it was this that also proved the design of Solomon's Temple. Similarly, God had also given the structural design for Noah's Ark, and this is partly why it is sometimes asserted that Noah was a Mason. We must wonder why, then, Freemasonry does not seek to explain or even mention the structural qualities of the beehive, but instead couches it only in moral or ethical considerations, especially as Kepler had made it so significant within the world of the sciences. It is entirely impossible that the early Freemasons had not noticed that the beehive was an object of natural geometry. Indeed, as we have seen, some lodges brought actual objects to the lodge to be displayed during the ritual or lectures, and it is known that this included the beehive in at least some Antient lodges. It would also seem entirely impossible that the Antients were unaware of the fact that the beehive had become a major theory and problem of geometry in the seventeenth century, and especially so in the early eighteenth century when practicing builders and architects appear to have played a greater role in the lodge generally. This was a period that particularly Dermott looked back on with admiration.

In the second edition of his *Ahiman Rezon*, he would complain that the Modern lodges had "thought [it] expedient to abolish the old custom of studying geometry."[16] Dermott's accusation is potentially signifi-cant for any real understanding of Freemasonry's history and development in Britain. Dermott would not have attacked the Moderns for dropping the study of geometry if the Antients were likewise guilty, nor if it had not formed an integral part of Freemasonry (i.e., the philosophical aspects of the lodge, whether that of the stonemasons or Freemasons proper). Furthermore, it was the continual practice of these "old customs" that gave the Antients their name, and reputation—if only among themselves. If geometry had been, and was still being, taught in the lodge—and this would seem to be the case—it is certain that many lodges would have known of Kepler's beehive, and it could very easily have entered at least some lodges as a part of any geometry lesson, delivered, for example, at lodge meetings, or after rituals. Given Dermott's insistence of the antiquity of the Antients, it is tempting to think that they had not so much adopted the beehive as the Moderns had dropped it, along with the study of geometry, though there is no evidence for that.

We have already shown that the basis of much of the pictorial symbolism of Freemasonry appears to have been derived from geometry. It is likely that as Freemasonry became more and more philosophical or speculative, and geometry consequently of less and less importance in practicalities, that it was still used to enlarge upon Masonry's symbolism and practices. Thus, the 47th Proposition, for example, might have been explained regarding its function in drawing the lodge. It is highly likely that the Golden Ratio was discussed in regard to its symbolic or geometric representation, the pentagram. Where it had not died out through lack of interest, a regular discussion of geometry might well have complemented the rituals, possibly following directly from them. Indeed, this is still the case in Freemasonry today, though Freemasons do not perhaps think of it in such terms. The American third-degree lecture still teaches the 47th Proposition, as it does the beehive. Similarly the symbol of point, circle, and parallel lines is spoken of in the first degree lecture, while the Platonic solids are explained in the Royal Arch lecture, partly concerning their physical construction.

While it is likely that polyhedrons were originally communicated in some—probably Irish—lodges, for example, these shapes, like the 47th Proposition, the pentagram, and symbol of point, circle, and lines, were probably related to myth and philosophy. This conversion of geometry to symbols of philosophy could have taken place as easily in the conversations of lodges in the early seventeenth century as in the revising of rituals in the early eighteenth century. Plato's myth of a Master Craftsman deity could be related to the Biblical story of God designing the Tabernacle and ordaining the building of Solomon's Temple, as, of course, could the Platonic elements be related to the four major standards of the tribes of Israel. However, if a Mason were to look for something outside of the Craft in the century that it was developing, which seemed to hint at the identification of the Temple and the Platonic myths, it would surely be Kepler's *Six-Cornered Snowflake*.

Dermott perhaps gives us a clue to how in-depth the lessons on, or discussions of, geometry might once have been. In the 1778 edition of *Ahiman Rezon*,

Dermott parodies the Moderns and their love of banqueting:

> Some of the young brethren made it appear,
> that a good knife and fork in the hands of a
> dexterous brother (over proper materials)
> would give greater satisfaction, and add more
> to the rotundity of the lodge, than the best
> scale and compass in Europe . . .

And furthermore added that

> . . . polygons, ellipsis, and irregular figures of
> all sorts might be drawn and represented upon
> Bread, Beef, Mutton, Fowls, Pies &c. as
> demonstratively as upon slates or sheets of
> paper.[17]

It is possible that Dermott infers that the Moderns had done away with the geometry lesson, replacing it with dining, which generally succeeds the conferral of any ritual, for example.

We may ask then, why is it that we do not find any explanation of the Pythagorean Theorem; the symbols of point, circle, lines, pentagrams; Euclid's 47th Proposition; or the beehive in the Masonic lectures and rituals in terms of geometry, but only in terms of what they represent ethically, morally, and spiritually? No matter how important geometry had been, Masonry was becoming more and more concerned with philosophy, myths, and pictorial symbols, of course. It is interesting to note, however, that in the

ABOVE: *This Royal Arch apron includes various symbols from the third degree. Likewise, the key in a circle of letters appears to derive from the mark master degree and is related to the mythological Mason's mark of Hiram Abiff. "Holiness to the Lord" is an important phrase in Royal Arch Masonry.*

Royal Arch, the geometry of the Platonic solids is still spoken of in the lecture and is of some significance for the Royal Arch Mason. As we have also remarked, by the end of the seventeenth century we find the square and compasses used by builders not only as tools but also as symbols in their ritual. It is not unlikely then that the geometry essential to the art of building was similarly taught half concerning its practical application and half its metaphor for the builder, and that the former trade aspect was dropped by the Moderns fairly shortly after they had established the Craft as philosophical and Biblical in leaning. It may also be that the Freemason of the seventeenth century (such as Ashmole), and the Antient Freemason up until a certain time, was expected to have an understanding of geometry, and that as such it was not formally taught, but rather there was simply, as Dermott says, some discussion of it.

Although, as a Masonic emblem, the beehive is largely associated with Antient Masonry in England, it does appear as an important symbol in one, apparently Irish, tract of 1724, addressed to the "society of Female Free-Masons" and entitled *A Letter from the Grand Mistress*. The text is exceedingly odd, and while it does betray much of the myth of the Old Charges, for example, it also reveals many practices and mythological elements not otherwise a part of Freemasonry. The author suggests that some or other secret word employed by Freemasons was derived from "a Silly Pun upon the Word Bee," though this is unlikely to have been the case. Most significantly, though, the *Letter* says that

A Bee has in all Ages and Nations been the Grand Hieroglyphic of Masonry, because it excels all other living Creatures in the Contrivance [i.e., manner of constructing] and Commodiousness [its physical construction] of its Habitation or Comb; as among many other Authors Doctor McGregor now Professor of Mathematics in Cambridge (as our Guardian informs us) has Learnedly demonstrated.

It is very interesting to note that the importance of the beehive derives in large part from its geometry, as taught by a professor of mathematics, who would certainly have been conversant with Kepler's works. Indeed, we can hardly doubt that one of the "other authors" who had considered the bee's habitat from an apparently mathematical or geometric perspective was Kepler, even if the author of the critique was unfamiliar with the works of the astronomer and mathematician. It seems likely that, given this background, the beehive had indeed entered Freemasonry because of its importance in geometry. Important also in the critique, the physical construction of the beehive is more definitely linked to the Masonic lodge, not improbably as this was originally drawn out as a geometric shape (e.g., a double square). The tract also appears to identify the Mason with the bee itself:

What Modern Masons call a Lodge was . . . by Antiquity call'd a HIVE of Free-Masons, and for the same Reasons when a Dissention happens in a Lodge the going off and forming another Lodge is call'd SWARMING.

ABOVE: The Rosy Cross engraving of Fludd/Frisius. In the center is the rose of the Rosicrucians (its stem represented as a cross). Bees hover around the rose, while beehives can be seen on the right-hand side.

Such terminology does not appear to have been widely used. Yet, even if we do not hear specifically of "swarming" elsewhere in Masonry, later descriptions of the beehive symbol makes use of parallel language, as we have seen from Morgan's exposé.

Despite what we must surely regard in our own time as a rather mystical interpretation of the universe, Kepler, as we mentioned earlier, was keen to distance himself from the world of the irrational and the occult, attacking the Rosicrucian sympathizer Robert Fludd of England, for example. Admittedly, Fludd had struck the first blow, writing an apologia accusing Kepler of dealing superficially with mathematics, although this was clearly not the case, as, for Kepler, his own mathematical and astronomical theories revealed nothing less than the Divine Nature, God—the supreme Architect. Not surprisingly, Kepler responded at length[18] to Fludd's accusations, to which Fludd again replied (although this time soliciting no response).

Despite this, the ideas of both Kepler and Fludd drew on the theories of Plato and the Pythagoreans. Thus, Kepler is able to prove Plato's thesis of a geometrical reality to the world, though this is to a large extent revised. There are, however, some rather more concrete connections in the philosophies of Fludd and Kepler. Both would employ the rose and beehive in their work. We have mentioned these in relation to Kepler's intellectual inquiries as expounded in his *Six-Cornered Snowflake*. With Fludd, these appear in the form of an allegorical etching. This etching would first appear eighteen years after Kepler's work, in Joachim Frisius's defense of Robert Fludd, *Summum Bonum* (1629). Frisius, however, appears to be none other than Fludd himself. As the Masonic scholar A. E. Waite pointed out, the style is the Englishman's, and it is known that it was he who sent it to the publisher—with instructions to print the defense separately from his own work, which Fludd had sent along with it. The publisher apparently forgot his instructions and printed the defense with Fludd's *Sophiae cum Moria Certamen*.[19] The etching next appeared in Fludd's *Clavis* of 1633.

The Frisius/Fludd engraving shows a bee hovering near a rose, its stem and branches somewhat cross-shaped (a most obvious allusion to the rose cross). To the right of the rose appears a row of four beehives, and to the left some elementary fencing between which we see a spider's web. Above the rose is the motto, *dat rosa mel apibus* ("the rose gives the bee honey"). The etching however, is an adaptation of one by the German Rosicrucian Daniel Cramer. A year after the publication of *The Chemical Wedding of Christian Rosenkreutz*, Cramer released a series of forty, somewhat naïve but nevertheless charming, etchings under the title of the *True Society of Jesus and the Rosy Cross*. In Cramer's etching, honeybees swarm around a Christian cross, which supports a spider's web in one of its top right angles. There is a small door in the cross, which thus alludes to the cross as a kind of spiritual beehive, and Cramer glosses his etching with a literary description of the sweetness of the cross. There is little hint of the alchemical, the neo-Platonic, or the fantastical, and as such it is closer to the original spirit of

Rosicrucianism, rather than to the later revisions and embellishments discussed in the next chapter.

It is easy to see why Kepler was upset with Fludd, and why the two learned gentlemen could so easily rub each other the wrong way. They tackled geometry—and such philosophy as could be drawn from it—from two conflicting positions. For Kepler had shown in his *Six-Cornered Snowflake* that, having a base of five petals, the rose embodied the geometry of the pentagram. As with the stonemasons, and probably early Freemasons, the pentagram was regarded as special by Kepler, because it embodied the Golden Ratio. Needless to say, that the rose embodied arguably architecture's most important mathematical design reaffirms Kepler's notion that God is the "Architect" of creation and that, in effect, the created world is architectural at root. Unfortunately, Fludd would reduce the rose to an ultimately nonsensical seven-petal rose, robbing it of its architectural significance. Similarly, Fludd had removed the hexagonal beehive from its place of prominence by the introduction of the imaginary, and predictably, seven-threaded spider's web.[20] It is curious, then, that Fludd has so often been considered a possible strong influence on the development, if not the inventor, of Freemasonry, which at its foundation is architectural.

Waite, particularly, was impressed by Fludd, and devoted considerable space to the aforementioned learned Englishman. His argument for connecting Fludd to Freemasonry, however, was published as an article for the *Transactions of the Manchester Association for Masonic Research* in the first quarter of the twentieth century.[21] It was also presented in a lecture[22] to the grand lodge of New York in 1918 by Ossian H. Lang, the then Grand Historian. According to Lang, the four lodges that had formed themselves into the first grand lodge of Freemasons in 1717 had earlier been a society within the so-called Masons' Company. This inner society has been given the name of the Acception by Waite, as intellectuals who joined lodges in the seventeenth century were called not Free Masons but rather Accepted Masons, as they were accepted into the trade guild even though they did not themselves practice the trade of building.

The records of the Masons' Company go back to 1620 and are almost contemporary then with the first announcements of the Rosicrucians in Germany. These early records are also contemporary with Fludd, though no one denies that the reason for this is that previous records were destroyed in the great fire of London. Although supposedly held within the Company, these four lodges, and others besides perhaps, are alleged not to have had any interest in the practicalities or trade of building, for which the Masons' Company certainly existed, but rather to have been a collection of purely philosophical, or rather occult, lodges or societies. Waite suggests that the lodge attended by Ashmole in the late seventeenth century was again a lodge held under the Masons' Company, the importance here being, of course, Ashmole's considerable interest in Hermeticism, or alchemy, and Rosicrucianism (we shall recall that Ashmole had earlier published a collection of British alchemical texts). The suggestion is that one might work backward in

ABOVE: *The working tools (bottom left) of the Royal Arch Mason appear on this apron, while in the apron's center is the Temple with symbolic veils, as pertains to the Royal Arch degree. The beehive, trowel, and hourglass are all from Craft Masonry.*

RIGHT: *This printed Royal Arch apron from the mid-nineteenth century is decorated with many of the symbols of its ritual. Aaron's rod is to the left, and the crow, pickax, and shovel are on the right.*

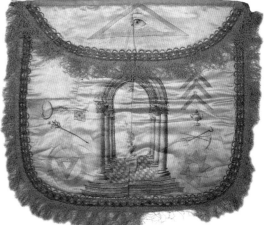

time, from Ashmole to the likeminded Fludd, placing the latter also in the Acception.

Needless to say, for Waite, it is here in the lodges of the Acception that the origin of a purely mystical Freemasonry is to be sought. Waite does not think it necessary to show that Fludd had started the society, but states that

> But if anything brought him within it, he would have changed it. However, it arose . . . the Acception was not impossibly a group of Hermetic students, of which there were many at the period, that Fludd drew them together or took his place among them, and that after this manner, and the manner of the Rosy Cross [i.e., Rosicrucians], they began to speak of spiritual building in a Hall of Masons, of a Hermetic Art in stone, and that in this way they contributed something to a figurative art of building.[23]

We shall recall that Ashmole had spoken of the Stone of Solomon, Moses, and Hermes, while Fludd's language is more Biblical. Perplexingly, it is Fludd's symbolism that Waite seems to feel passed into Freemasonry, though significantly he feels that the Acception may have stood in relation to other masons' lodges as the Royal Arch degree stands in relation to the three degrees of Craft Masonry, that is, as a more explicitly mystical, higher, or inner fraternity.

The initial problem of this theory—namely, that we do not find evidence of Fludd's philosophy in rela-tion to Ashmole's lodge or the premier grand lodge of England—is overcome when Waite infers that the Acception might prove the origin of the Royal Arch. Necessarily then, Waite attempts to distinguish the supposed mysticism of the Acception from those of other lodges, suggesting that rather than invoking the Old Charges, they spoke of "a House Mystic built up of living stones," and of "Christ . . . the corner-stone of the spiritual building." Furthermore, referring to the stone as Aben, Waite relates this term to the Hebrew words for father *(ab)* and son *(ben)*, and again to the Holy Trinity, Father, Son, and Holy Ghost, the last of the three being apparently implied. Some of the symbolism that Fludd appropriated from the Bible (e.g., the cornerstone) did enter the Royal Arch and some of the higher degrees; however, the latter at least appeared later in the eighteenth century, and it is unlikely that Fludd's works proved much of an influence. Moreover, the the Masonic fraternity had undoubtedly drawn such references as the cornerstone directly from the Bible, as it had regarding the Temple of Solomon.

Luckily for the bedraggled Fludd theory, there is some slight circumstantial evidence. Although Fludd was a resident in Beardstead, Kent, he also had a house in close proximity to the so-called Masons' Company, located on Coleman Street, London. Furthermore, as Waite has pointed out, it is only a relatively short period after Fludd's death that we begin to hear of the introduction of intellectuals with an interest in Hermeticism into the society. While this may not strike us as especially convincing, the Fludd theory still has some minor advantage over other such theories promoted as fact over the last few centuries. For, while Fludd certainly did not change stonemasonry into Freemasonry, he may have accidentally contributed something to the change in perspective. Even if he robbed the rose and beehive of their architectural association, he also, at least, presented a building-type symbolism drawn from the Bible. However, even if we accept such an idea, he must be seen as a minor figure in the development of a symbolic architectural language, such as was later developed by the Moderns and Antients.

Essential to Fludd's attractiveness for Waite and other Masonic historians, however, is that he is potentially proof for a wider theory that Freemasonry was born out of Rosicrucianism. Waite believes that Fludd's involvement in this mystical science or philosophy may have begun either with a reply to his apology or defense of Rosicrucianism, with "emissaries" visiting England to initiate him, or, otherwise, by his own interpretation of their doctrines. The latter is doubtlessly the more probable, for while many intellectuals published appeals for initiation into the Brotherhood of the Rosy Cross, apparently none received any response, and as such, Rosicrucianism appears to have initially developed as a personal or solo pursuit in which the devotee struggled with and generally promoted his notion of Rosicrucian ethics, morality, mysticism, and symbolism. However, Fludd, as Waite also points out, was traveling in Europe during what he suggests was the period of intellectual contemplation and refinement that finally produced

ABOVE: An old Masonic jewel with coffin, skull and crossbones, and beehive.

ABOVE: *This Royal Arch apron is decorated not only with Royal Arch symbols, such as the pickax, shovel, and Ark, but also with many symbols from the degree of master Mason, such as the anchor, hourglass, and the coffin. We also see a Calvary cross inside a star, traditionally associated with the Masonic Order of the Temple, or Masonic Knights Templar.*

Rosicrucianism. The timeframe for this period Waite gives as 1598 to 1604, important, he suggests, because during this period a society by the name of Militia Crucifera Evangeluca held their Congresses at Luneberg, and it is here that Fludd may have met Johan Valentin Andreae, still yet a teenager but destined nonetheless to be one of the influential members of the primary Rosicrucian group.

While we have spoken of Kepler's rose in regard to a semireligious architectural theory, it might also have some significance for Rosicrucianism. Kepler appears to have been much more genuinely connected to the Rosicrucians than Fludd; certainly he had some loose connection with the original Rosicrucian group, for want of a better term. He knew Andreae, the author of the *Chemical Wedding*—if not Rosicrucianism—and would appear to have been involved with his more conservative Christian unions[24] established some time after the publication of the Rosicrucian manifestos. The *Six-Cornered Snowflake* was written three years before publication of the first of the Rosicrucian manifestos. It is not impossible that Kepler's interpretation of the rose fed into the Rosicrucian group's understanding of their symbol. We have shown that alchemy adopted geometry as a new philosophical language and again have inferred that this geometry-based alchemy can be equated with Rosicrucianism.

While the high-profile and highly mystical Freemason Albert Pike considered that the square and compasses, as well as some other Masonic symbols such as the sun and moon and the triangle, were likely adopted directly from Rosicrucianism, Lang has gone further in his assessment of Masonic iconography. Dividing the Masonic symbols into three groups: symbols exclusive to Rosicrucianism, symbols used by both the stonemasons and Rosicrucians, and symbols exclusive to Freemasonry. Lang's most interesting contribution is his suggestion that the stonemasons and Rosicrucians shared several symbols that later penetrated into early Freemasonry: the square and compasses, level, plumb line, trowel, beehive, hourglass, and cassia tree (known as acacia in Freemasonry). While he does not state exactly where we might find such symbols in Rosicrucianism, it is certain that in regard to the beehive Lang was thinking of Fludd, though he may also have known of its significance in the works of Kepler and Cramer. The combined square and compasses was both a symbol of alchemy and a highly popular symbol of geometry, which itself had always been regarded by the stonemasons as synonymous with their own trade. However, there can be no doubt that Freemasonry had adopted this symbol because it had been used in the stonemasons' rituals of the seventeenth century, at least, and moreover that it represented geometry, not alchemy.

Regarding the similarity of alchemical and Freemasonic symbolism, however, we may briefly look at a secret society of the sixteenth century. In 1577 an esoteric secret society, the Order of the Unzertrennlichen or Indissolubilisten, was established in Germany. To a large extent the order was populated by owners of mines and metalworks. Notably, it had five degrees, the last of which was concerned especially with alchemy, while their lodges were furnished with a Bible, skull, and hourglass, among other symbols. Most significantly, perhaps, one of these was the compasses. Likewise, despite a metallurgical bias of the society, this fraternity also spoke of God in terms of being the Architect. The use of the compasses and the reference to God as such seem only to imply, again, that alchemy had begun to adopt geometry as a part of its philosophical vocabulary.

McIntosh links the society to the original Rosicrucian group at Tubingen.[25] However, the question that concerns us is, Was this a group of alchemists that had later initiated those somehow involved in metalwork, or was this originally a metalworkers' lodge that had been transformed into a Hermetic order? Whatever the case, that esoteric philosophers linked themselves in groups to some extent dictated by profession clearly parallels Freemasonry not much more than half a century later. We might begin to think then that the esoteric philosopher had, by the end of the medieval period, sometimes joined vocational lodges that reflected the symbolism then current in alchemy and like mysticism. Trade lodges other than those of builders, of course, also had some sort of ritual and mythology but doubtlessly often desired prestige and wealthy patrons—how both parties might have benefited is clear. While unjustifiable from a historical standpoint, it is interesting to note that Waite suggested the Acception might have used the supposed history of the mythical hero of the Rosicrucian manifestos, Christian Rozenkreuts, in the same way the contemporary Masonic lodge uses the myth of Hiram Abiff, or the Hiramic legend, as it is called.

In *A Letter from the Grand Mistress*, it seems quite likely that, while the contents of the letter are not related to Freemasonry in every aspect, it does reveal the mythology of a once existing society. For we find in this text a highly elaborate myth and set of practices that would seem not likely the invention of a single person—though that is, of course, possible. Considering that the text speaks of a society of female Freemasons, it would seem possible that an already existing women's society merged with a Masonic lodge, possibly a decade or so before the tract was published. However, a more interesting possibility also opens up for us: that the reference to female Freemasons may be taken literally, that at least some women had been initiated into a Masonic lodge. Indeed, the transition from builders' unions to intellectual society, as occurred in the eighteenth century, may well have made room for women interested in such pursuits, especially in the absence of an authority on the matter. Familiar to the reader by now, the text refers to the practice of Kabbalah (which, it is suggested, was later called Rosecrution, i.e., Rosicrucian) by various famous persons and also explains the secret Words of the society, which—being the names of various Hebrew letters—are probably connected to some sort of Kabbalistic philosophy developed by this group or lodge. Thus, for example:

When one says Gimel, the other answers Nun;
then the first again joining both Letters
together repeats Three Times, Gimel-Nun,
Gimel-Nun, Gimel-Nun, by which they mean

ABOVE: *The All–Seeing Eye, hourglass, skull and crossbones, sun and moon, Noah's ark, and the beehive are all Masonic symbols. Although this apron looks Masonic, it is an apron once worn by a member of the fraternity known as the Oddfellows. The symbols derive from an Oddfellow's degree called "Rebekah," to which wives and daughters were also admitted.*

ABOVE: This apron is embroidered with various symbols of Craft Masonry (the coffin, trowel, Blazing Star, the letter "G" for "geometry" and "Great Architect"). However, the traditional color for the Craft is blue, and is as such sometimes referred to as a "blue lodge." Unusually, then, this apron is predominantly red, a color typically associated with the Royal Arch degree. Similarly, the Knight Templar Masonry is usually associated with the color black.

that they are united as one in Interests, Secrecy, and Affection.

Although Waite has far overstated the significance of Fludd for a developing Freemasonry, evidence of his being in any way involved with the Masons' Company or any stonemasons' lodge being nearly nonexistent, in a much broader sense his thesis is worth consideration. If Fludd did not join a masons' lodge, it is still quite possible that his ideas were carried into the lodges after his death by Ashmole and others. Intellectuals were being initiated into masons' lodges for nearly three quarters of a century prior to the forming of the premier grand lodge; they knew the mythology, had experienced the ritual or rituals of the lodges, and would appear to have discussed geometry there. Moreover, as we have suggested, it was certainly not a one-way street—the intellectuals of the lodge of course derived much matter to speculate upon from the lodges and vice versa. Freemasonry, or Speculative Masonry, almost certainly began not in the rituals themselves, but in speculation on the trade rituals.

It was those intellectuals of the premier grand lodge that sought to preserve the speculation of the previous century in their ritual, particularly in the third degree. Although, as we might imagine, all sorts of material must have been entertained in the conversations of those lodges composed of builders and intellectuals, certainly it is easy to think that Rosicrucianism, Kabbalah, Fludd, Kepler, Plato, Pythagoras, Hermes, and Biblical testament must have counted for a significant portion of their conversations, as must have the art of building, geometry, the Old Charges, King Solomon, and the like. It is not unreasonable to suggest that builders' lodges were influenced to different degrees regarding the esoteric, or intellectual, sciences. While the Royal Arch certainly grew in grandeur throughout the eighteenth century, it is possible that it originated in a stock of knowledge not common to those lodges that became a part of the Moderns, and even may have been limited to one, or perhaps a few, lodges in Ireland, for example. On the other had, as we have noted, it is very possible that the Antients had retained elements that the Moderns dropped as the latter became more Biblical and ethical in orientation. Masonic rituals were not standardized until the nineteenth century and even today are somewhat varied. The rituals of America (generally derived from the Antients) are lengthier and more elaborate than those of England, for example, and they may vary again from state to state—though the differences may be rather minor.

Chapter 7: The Golden Fleecing

Despite the writing of James Anderson's *Constitutions*, Laurence Dermott's *Ahiman Rezon*, and other unofficial texts, Masonic lodges were not scholarly societies, and Masonic scholarship would not primarily take the form of literary criticism or written histories.

Rather, the new and generally highly questionable theories of Freemasonry's origin and prehistory (prior to 1717) would be expounded in the medium of Freemasonry itself, that is, in symbols, secrets, and rituals, or, as they are generally termed, rites or orders. To be fair to the inventors of this second wave of Masonry, it can hardly be doubted that they took their cue from Anderson and his mythology or history—among other things at least—and apparently found in his work many valuable clues to a supposed real origin of Freemasonry. Yet, if Anderson had neglected Hermes—the father of alchemy who can be found in some of the Old Charges—he would find himself in the minority. Myth and history, fact and fiction had never been entirely separate in Freemasonry. As the fraternity spread across Europe, a flair for the dramatic would prove far more valuable than an ability to demonstrate historical exactness, and rites with such names as Kabbalistic Master or Egyptian Master began to appear, all of them supposedly Masonic. During this same period, the line between drama and ritual blurred considerably as the cultural influence of Freemasonry spread beyond the Masonic lodge.

Writers and composers adopted Freemasonry as a theme and incorporated elements of the ritual into their art. In Germany, for example, Masonic rituals and rites were sometimes reworked and at other times created by those such as Friedrich Ludwig Schroder, a leading theater director of his day, and Adolph Freiherr von Knigge, a popular novelist.[1] Even Mozart would draw on the rituals and fraternity of the Freemasons for some of his compositions.

While we have already considered the Craft and Royal Arch degrees, others would emerge, especially in the countries of France and Germany, adding to the repertoire of the Continental Freemason. Where there were once just a few degrees, these quasi-Masonic degrees poured in with such a force that they totaled over a thousand by the end of the eighteenth century. In this new wave of ritualism, some degrees were bestowed on Masons as the inventors of the rituals traveled from one lodge to another. Still others were compacted into different series of degrees, or rites, and were adopted by various lodges or grand lodges. These questionable adaptations of Freemasonry were not regarded as legitimate by the grand lodges of England,

ABOVE: In the foreground we see the gavel, trowel, chisel, and square and compasses, all of which the Mason symbolically applies to himself on his journey. At the end of the mosaic pavement is an altar on which is placed the square and compasses and the Sacred Book. This visually striking apron is from the middle of the nineteenth century.

nor for that matter by those of America, as they began to establish themselves. Nevertheless, these same Masonic bodies would eventually adopt some of the degrees that first appeared on the Continent.

BELOW: Ceramic container and lid, "lusterware," early 1900s. The painted medallions contain symbols from the third degree. A Calvary cross is atop three steps, probably representing the three degrees.

Although diverse, all of the new rites were meant both to illustrate and, to some extent, prove their inventors' hypothesis of Freemasonry's origin. Typically, they would promote Freemasonry as being exclusively Christian, though their authors were not concerned with the golden age of stonemasonry and its link to the Church. On the Continent, where Freemasonry was often the concern of the wealthy, the aristocracy, and the monarchy, it seemed difficult to believe, or stomach, that Masonry had arisen from the building and architectural trade or, for that matter, from England. Not surprisingly, there would soon be reason to believe that Masonry's origin could—despite its name and symbolism of square, compasses, trowel, and brick (or ashlar)—be traced to Europe's old knightly orders, and of those, most particularly, the inexhaustibly enigmatic Knights Templar. In addition, Masons and Masonry would begin to take the association of Rosicrucianism with its own society very seriously, and nowhere more so—or more naturally—than in Germany, the birthplace of the so-called Brotherhood of the Rosy Cross. Consequently, voluntary societies claiming to be both Masonic and chivalrous, or Masonic and Rosicrucian, became increasingly popular.

A fascination with all things knightly began with a speech delivered around 1737 by the then Grand Orator for the grand lodge of France, Andrew Michael Ramsay (1681–1743), better known as Chevalier de Ramsay. His thesis was perhaps rather fantastical, but as fantastical things often do, it fired the imagination. He stated, as if a matter of fact, that various princes

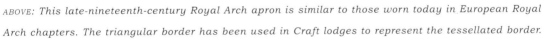

ABOVE: *This late-nineteenth-century Royal Arch apron is similar to those worn today in European Royal Arch chapters. The triangular border has been used in Craft lodges to represent the tessellated border.*

and kings returning from the Crusades in the Holy Lands had established lodges all over Europe, and being Scottish, Ramsay emphasized the importance he supposed Scotland to have had for the returning Crusaders. In 1282, James, Lord Steward of Scotland, he claimed, was Grand Master of a lodge at Kilwinning, and it was here that he had received Freemasons into the lodge (needless to say, over four hundred years before the establishment of the premier grand lodge of England).

Ramsay was born at Ayr, Scotland. His father (a baker by profession) ensured that his son would receive

ABOVE: Hand-painted silk Craft apron, early nineteenth century. The Monument is the central motif of this apron. Above the Monument is the emblem of a past master. To the right is a sword pointing at the heart, which might be interpreted as a symbol of courage.

a decent education. He studied first in his hometown and then went to the University of Edinburgh. Around 1709 Ramsay left Britain for the Continent. Then at the University of Leyden he met a Protestant minister, mystic, and founder of a Pietist circle, Pierre Poiret, who apparently educated him in his mystical philosophy. Nevertheless, Poiret encouraged Ramsay to visit the Roman Catholic Archbishop Fenelon. Within a year of this meeting, Ramsay converted to Catholicism. Having acted as a tutor in Britain, Ramsay soon found his skills in demand by the nobility and eventually found employment with Prince de Turenne. Steadily climbing the social ladder, Ramsay was made a Chevalier in a Catholic knightly order known as the Order of Lazarus. Around this time he also joined the Masonic fraternity, though it was the Order of Lazarus that connected Ramsay to the highest level of French society, introducing him to the Old Pretender, James III. Soon he had been given employment as teacher to Prince Charles Edward, or the Young Pretender, and Prince Henry.

Encouraging Ramsay's mystical pursuits, Archbishop Fenelon sent Ramsay to a mystic called Madame Guyon, to whom the former was connected. Guyon promoted a type of mysticism known as Quietism. Emotionally oriented, the doctrines of Quietism propounded such ideas as spiritual innocence. Though a Roman Catholic herself, Guyon nevertheless transcended the divide that ran though Christianity, attracting Protestants as well as Catholics in France, England, Holland and Italy[2] as well as other countries. Even so, Guyon's speculations were not tol-

erated by the Catholic church, and she was imprisoned for her supposedly heretical interpretation of the doctrine. There soon followed (in 1738, close to a year after Ramsey's speech) a papal bull[3] that ruled Freemasonry illegal.

The pope's edict against the Craft had no effect in Britain where the Roman Catholic Church had no legal power, but it nevertheless affected Italy, Spain, and Portugal,[4] where lodges had been established under the patronization of the premier grand lodge of England. Only two months after the pope had issued the bull, a court of inquiry was held at Lisbon, the records of which contain palpable suggestion of degrees or rites higher than that of the Master Mason, these being referred to as "Excellent Masons" and "Grand Masons."[5] While it is sometimes supposed that such new degrees were composed by Ramsay, it must be realized that he did not introduce the idea of higher degrees in his oration. Nor did he introduce any religious or ascetic ideals not already present in Freemasonry. What Ramsay did do was place Freemasonry in a different historical context, which is largely, as we have said, that of the Crusaders. Most interestingly, Heinrich Schneider considers that Ramsay had attempted to Catholicize Freemasonry, introducing an essentially medieval Christian, if not Roman Catholic asceticism, to the fraternity. Naturally, in other historical and philosophical settings the symbols, ethics, and rituals of Masonry appear differently, or rather different explanations can be given for each and all of them. For example, while Saint John, revered by Freemasonry, had been ascribed a

before it would be replaced by the order of the Knights Templar, which provided, albeit temporarily, a rather more convincing, though certainly no less a questionable, link between the Mason and the knight. The Knights Templar had begun in AD 1115 when Hugue de Payens recruited, or caballed together, the so-called poor knights in order to protect Christian pilgrims of Europe as they traveled to and from the Holy Land. Beginning modestly, the knightly order quickly received recognition and support. The Count of Champagne, founder of the Abbey of Clairveaux, was an early convert to the order, and King Baldwin gave the knights a wing in the royal palace of the Holy land itself, the mosque of al-Aqsa, supposedly built on the site of Solomon's Temple, which, as we have seen, was the site of the first stonemasons' lodge according to the Cooke MS and other, later, Old Charges. In 1127, de Payens met the influential Cistercian monk, Bernard of Clairvaux. Bernard reformed the Templars, gave them his rule (which would soon become the rule for all of the then emerging knightly orders), turning them into knight-monks. The Templars would center their lives on prayer and religious devotion, would remain celibate, and would even wear the habit of the Cistercian monk but slightly altered as the necessity of horse riding required.[7] But nevertheless, the Templars would remain knights.

While the Templars gathered force over the next century, spreading their order across western Europe and establishing a base at Jerusalem, other similar knightly and monastic orders would emerge, such as the Knights of St. John, the Knights of Malta, and the Teutonic Knights.[8] (The latter order required its knights to be of both German and noble blood, and settled what would become the German state of Prussia). Although these orders, and others like them, would continue for centuries to come until finally made obsolete as fighting bodies by developments in warfare or politics, the Templars were destroyed by Philip IV of France.[9] The French king was as greedy as he was treacherous. Having already plundered the Jews in France, he arrested the Templars on trumped-up charges and tortured them into confessing—though the only confessions extracted were to the most minor of the accusations leveled at them. Accused of irreligious and sacrilegious activities, their possessions were confiscated and the then head of the order, Jacque de Molay, and some of his fellow knight-monks were eventually burned at the stake. However, the death of de Molay is only the beginning of the myth that connects the Knights Templar to the society of Freemasonry—we shall examine this myth momentarily. The importance of the Templar myth in this new theory of Freemasonry's history was that the stonemasons and their lodges were viewed as the repository for the secrets of the Knights Templar.

At the time of Ramsay's oration, we should note, France was of enormous cultural importance to Europe. French had replaced Latin as the language of the elite and was the language of the Prussian, Russian, and other monarchies. Moreover, despite the cultural exchange of a more mainstream nature, British Craft Masonry (of three degrees) was rapidly spreading across national boundaries and making remarkable headway into Europe. To get to Germany, of course, it had to pass France. Germany, or rather those states that formed the Holy Roman Empire of Germany, was then naturally susceptible to the effects of Ramsay's oration. (Especially as it existed as a conglomerate of hundreds of States, the dominant three being the Rhineland, Austria, and Prussia, though these again were subdivided into provinces. The Rhineland was particularly divided, and, bordering France, it was also particularly prone to the influence of French culture.)

A part of the reason for the sudden explosion of neo-Masonic degrees was initially not simply the adaptation of Freemasonry's symbolism or ritual in accord with the new theories but also a further adaptation of these resultant degrees, and so on. A similar phenomenon can be seen in the Craft ritual itself, where, as we have shown, a symbol in the first degree (for example, the letter "G") will represent something quite different in a succeeding degree. In the case of the higher degrees we find in some cases a philosophy of one ritual being expanded and developed through a series of degrees or rituals compounded together into a so-called rite. Especially as the eighteenth century progressed, rites were compiled from degrees that had been practiced in various parts of France, which had no previous connection.

While some rites espoused alchemy or Kabbalah and developed these through a series of philosophical rituals, chivalrous rites also had to be reinterpreted, not only in terms of language but more importantly in terms of the nation's history and iconography, for example, as a degree or rite was taken from France to one of the German states, or vice versa. The adaptation of rites was probably partly necessitated as aristocrats of various countries gained important positions in some or other neo-Masonic knightly body, thus, for example, requiring a quintessential French rite for the French and, similarly, a German rite for the German aristocracy. However, while patriotism or nationalism played a minor part in some of the higher degrees, the ethos of the new Masonry remained as cosmopolitan as it had been in England, and thus it would seem probable that some heraldic imagery, for example, was adopted from other countries. Another possibility was that such symbols were appropriated merely as a part of the process of antiquing rites. However, these latter impulses do not significantly occur until the establishment of the so-called Ancient and Accepted Scottish Rite, discussed later in this chapter.

One of the earliest and most important embellishments of French and German Freemasonry was the so-called Scots Masonry or Scots degree, which emerged somewhere in or around the 1740s. Also of enormous importance was the Order of the Strict Observance (now defunct), which became increasingly powerful from about the middle of the eighteenth century, before its final, rapid decline. Most of the famous Freemasons of Germany (such as composer Wolfgang Amadeus Mozart [1756–1791] and playwright, poet, author, and scientist Johann Wolfgang von Goethe [1749–1832]) were initiated into the Strict Observance. Though apparently not its creator, the father and leading light of the Strict

ABOVE: This sword is similar to those used in the Masonic Order of the Temple, though the red handle and rosy cross on both the handle and sheath are only some of the features that distinguish this sword as one used specifically in the Rose Croix Degree.

Observance was for all intents and purposes Baron Von Hund. He had been initiated into a neo-Masonic body claiming to be the Order of the Temple (i.e., the Knights Templar) in France, by a so-called Knight of the Red Feather.

Connecting the Templars to the Strict Observance in a historical sense, von Hund proposed that, after the execution of de Molay, several Templar knights fled to Scotland where they continued the order. For whatever reason, however, these refugee knights had decided to disguise themselves as stonemasons on their journey, and as they reestablished the Templars in Scotland the knights adopted the symbols of architectural stonemasonry and the name of Freemasonry. If one accepts this idea, then the degrees of Freemasonry are really a treasure chest of Templar legends and symbols. In this regard, it has been alleged, for example, that Hiram Abiff, whom we hear of being murdered in the third degree, is really de Molay.[10] Problematically, the third degree was written hundreds of years after the demise of the Templars. There are several variations on the Templar theme, but with Scotland important for all of them—and Ramsay having already proposed it as the home of Freemasonry— it would become common for the high rites to be designated as Scots or Scottish. Thus, we find such degrees as the Scots or Scottish master and the Scotch knight of perfection, as well as such rites as the Scottish philosophic rite and the Ancient and Accepted Scottish Rite. Similarly, in the north of England there would appear various Masonic rites appended with the name "Harodim,"[11] "Heredom," or some variant thereof, Harodim allegedly being a moun-

ABOVE: Knight Kadosh apron, mid-1800s. There were several high degrees belonging to different and often competing Masonic systems of the eighteenth century, such as the so-called Scotch philosophical rite and the emperors of the East and West. This apron is an example of one from the Ancient and Accepted Scottish Rite, available to master Masons. The term Kadosh is supposed to be Hebrew, meaning "Holy."

tain near Kilwinning and near, therefore, James's Lodge. Even so, it is worth mentioning that though almost unheard of today, there were also a few Continental degrees purportedly of Irish origin—e.g., the so-called Irish Master, Powerful Irish Master, and Perfect Irish Master[12]—and that the Irish degrees may have faded into obscurity with the emergence of the allegedly Scottish degrees.[13]

On the European continent the Scotch Master degree was tacked onto the three degrees of Craft Masonry as a fourth degree. Then onto this was affixed the Strict Observance degrees. The fifth degree was

ABOVE: A parody of Count Cagliostro in a lodge in London, from 1786. Cagliostro (right) is in a Masonic apron decorated with the square and compasses. The table may be a spoof on the tracing board, as drinking glasses and a bottle of liquor lie on it, as do three candles, traditionally placed around the tracing board.

thus that of the novice in the Strict Observance order, while the sixth degree was that of the knight. However, those who were not of the nobility were given the title of Armiger.[14] Knightly and even Templar rituals appeared as one of the major trends of continental Freemasonry, especially in France. Robert Freke Gould has commented that the Templar degrees were created by the Scot's lodges (i.e., lodges that were responsible for conferring the Scot's degree), one of the earliest of which was the Kadosh degree that represented the vengeance of the Templars.[15] As an earlier king of France had been instrumental in the downfall of the

Templars, this was clearly a risky political theme; however, other such higher degrees appeared—no doubt in many cases mere copies of copies—and became known collectively as rites of vengeance. It was also, we might remark, a theme that utterly contradicts the principles of Freemasonry. Thus we read in the second charge of Anderson's *Constitutions* that, "A Mason is a peacable Subject to the Civil Powers, wherever he resides or works, and is never to be concern'd in Plots or Conspiracies." Indeed, Anderson remarks that "ancient Kings and Princes have been much dispos'd to encourage the Craftsmen, because of their peacableness and Loyalty." Undoubtedly Anderson was still reflecting on the Old Charges, where we read of stonemasonry being patronized by various kings and princes, such as Athelstan and Edwin, and of the more recent patronization of the Masonic fraternity by the Duke of Montague and the Duke of Wharton.

As mentioned, Rosicrucianism, Kabbalah, and Hermeticism would also take hold in the new Masonry, appearing also in various degrees. Yet, because Hermes Trismegistus, the father of alchemy, was supposed to have been an Egyptian, with the introduction of Hermeticism came also Egyptian myths and trappings to Masonic rites. (Hermes the Philosopher, or Hermes Trismegistus, we might recall, had been mentioned in some of the Old Charges.) The trend for Egyptian Hermetic Masonry would eventually appear on the German stage in the guise of Mozart's opera *The Magic Flute*, which in many ways reflects eighteenth-century Germany's neo-Freemasonry. It is still often referred to as his Masonic opera. Although less

ABOVE: *Royal Arch certificate, parchment, 1858. The lower left corner shows a secret vault in the Temple known to Royal Arch Masons.*

famous, the flamboyant and self-proclaimed Count Cagliostro,[10] for example, would continually attempt to establish his Egyptian Rite of Freemasonry, though he—like so many others—had originally been initiated into the Strict Observance. Similarly, there was the

ABOVE: *Hat; beaver fur, early 1800s. An earlier example of a ceremonial hat worn by the Masonic Knight Templar in America.*

Rite of African Architects formed probably in the mid-eighteenth century by C. F. Von Köppen (1734–circa 1798). They expounded, for example, the Egyptian mysteries as supposedly taught to Pythagoras by the priests of ancient Egypt and as was found similar between the teachings of Moses and those of the former priest. Notably, the first and second degrees of African Architects were the Apprentice of Egyptian secrets and initiation into Egyptian secrets, respectively. Yet the order had higher, or inner, knightly degrees that were supposedly more advanced in the royal science of alchemy,[17] though these degrees were called the esquire, soldier, and knight. Similarly, their lodge was

decorated with scenes of the Templars. It is this sort of marriage of alchemical and knightly rituals that typify much of the neo-Masonic rites of the latter half of the eighteenth century. Nevertheless, the order seems to have had a short life span and probably ceased to exist not long after the death of Von Köppen around 1798 and the issuing of an edict by the French king outlawing secret societies. Such edicts against secret societies would frequently haunt Freemasonry, though they sometimes included or excluded Freemasonry or certain Masonic lodges.

Elsewhere the Hermetic element would also appear alongside the knightly, sometimes invoking Greek mythology and adopting the image or name of the Golden Fleece, in what is certainly a reevaluation of Freemasonry's symbolism. Notably, in the Three Degrees of Craft Masonry, the apron is regarded as the

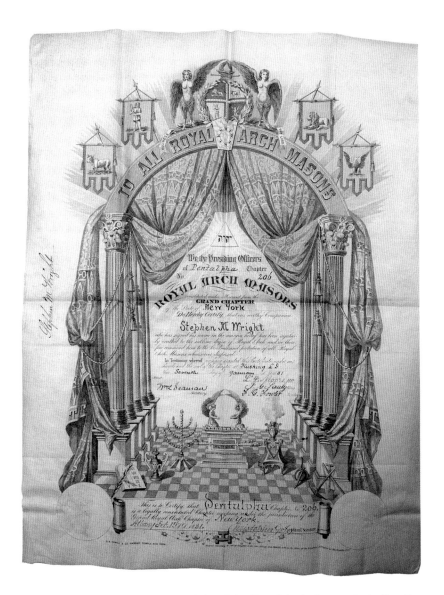

ABOVE: *A Royal Arch certificate, 1881, shows symbols of the Royal Arch degree, including the several veils hanging from the pillars at the sides, the ark of the covenant (lower center), and the four principle banners of the Royal Arch chapter above. In the lower right are the symbolic tools of a Royal Arch Mason.*

badge of the Freemason, and is held in higher esteem and considered to be of greater antiquity than the banner of the ancient Roman eagle, the Garter, or the Golden Fleece, the last two probably representing the chivalric orders of the same name. However, it is interesting to note that in the Irish publication *A Letter from the Grand Mistress* (1724), the Golden Fleece, Freemasonry, and even Kabbalah are linked together. Thus, "Jason a famous . . . Free-Mason used the Loadstone when he went in Quest of the Golden Fleece as it is called in Enigmatical Terms of Free-Masonry, or more properly Speaking of the Cabala, as Masonry was called in those Days." The mythical fleece had formerly made quite an impact on Europe's alchemists and Rosicrucians. The seventeenth-century alchemist Michael Maier employed the device in his book, *Antlanta Fugiens* (1617), and it appeared contemporaneously in Andreae's text, the *Chemical Wedding of Christian Rozenkreutz*, where it is of enormous importance, being presented to the hero of the story.[18] It is highly likely that this symbol was adopted by some neo-Masonic lodges precisely because it was perceived to be a symbol of alchemy and, possibly, Kabbalah.

Sometime around the 1760s, a lodge at Marseille called the Saint Jean d'Ecosse (Saint Jean the Scot) had two grades of interest, one being the knight of the Argonauts, and the other the knight of the golden fleece. Early in the nineteenth century, Europe would also see the awakening of the Rites of Memphis and Mizraim, each conferring over ninety degrees. Notably, in his first *Constitutions* Anderson placed the "Royal Art" of geometry or masonry in Egypt, had pointed out that one of the pyramids "is reckon'd First of the Seven Wonders of the World," and, most important in this regard, also stated that "Egypt is Mitzraim in Hebrew."[19] The Mizraim Rite had a degree known as the knight (or sometimes Sublime Prince) of the golden fleece. However, the rites of Memphis and Mizraim

merged in 1876, instituting the knight of the golden fleece as the tenth degree.[20] The emblem had yet already entered another new Masonic order—the Golden Rosicrucians that would encamp themselves most firmly in the German state of Prussia.

Freemasonry was established in Prussia, one of the three dominant states of the Holy Roman Empire of Germany, by Frederick the Great. It was an important step, not only for the development of the Craft in Europe but, as it would later transpire, in the additional symbols that it would lend to Freemasonry. While still crown prince of Prussia, Frederick was initiated into Freemasonry along with his close friend, Count Wartensleben, at a hotel in Brunswick on the night of August 14–15, 1738. The crown prince's father vehemently opposed Freemasonry, however, and the matter of the prince's initiation was kept secret from the king. When his father died in 1740, Frederick openly proclaimed his membership in the Masonic order and his service as Master of two Masonic lodges. Frederick ordered the building of a grand lodge in Berlin, initially called the Three Globes, but, in 1744, renamed Grand Royal Mother-Lodge of the Three Globes.[21] Prussia and Frederick the Great would become not only culturally important to, but also symbolic luminaries of, Freemasonry.

A turn from the chivalrous to Germany's native Rosicrucianism was facilitated when, in 1775, Johann Christoph Wöllner (1732–1800) was appointed Scots grand master of the Grand Lodge of the Three Globes, by Duke Frederick Augustus, in effect becoming the head of Scots Masonry in northern Germany.

Significantly, Wöllner was much enamored with alchemy and greatly affected by what Gould has called the "mystical mania of the day."[22] No mere spectator, he was already involved with the order of the Golden Rosicrucians.[23] His connection to this order was undoubtedly known to the prince, who would play a major role in the unfolding drama that would see the society in the ascendant.

The Golden Rosicrucians, we should realize, was yet another neo-Masonic order. However, the roots of this society can be found to exist before the introduction of Masonry to the Continent, or even the founding of the premier grand lodge in England. The first evidence of an order of this name appears in 1710, when Sincerus Renatus published a work that purported to be essentially a handbook of the order. It contained both the rules of the society and instructions in the art of laboratory alchemy,[24] which seems to have been widely practiced in Germany both inside and outside of this Rosicrucian society. To the world at large Sincerus Renatus appears to have been Sigmund or Samuel Richter, a pastor of Hartmannsdorf and a follower of the alchemists and mystics Paracelsus and Boehme. Richter claimed, however, to have been given the work by a master of the order rather than to have written the work himself. The claim is almost certainly credible, and as Christopher McIntosh suggests, Richter's adoption of the name Sincerus Renatus was probably not limited to his publishing of the text, though we

ABOVE: Round box with Masonic emblems, late 1800s. This box is decorated with the phoenix and the rosy cross from the Rose Croix degree surrounded by the emblem of a past master.

may assume that a pastor may have felt a need for caution in this venture. It is rather more probable that Richter was himself a member of the order of the Golden Rosicrucians, adopting this mystical nom de guerre when he was initiated or otherwise promoted to some position within the society, as frequently found with such mystical societies.

As might be expected from a history of a secret society, how or exactly when the order of the Golden Rosicrucians came to become a higher order of German Freemasonry is not entirely clear. Documents of the earlier, non-Masonic order bearing its name have been discovered throughout German-speaking countries and allow many possibilities, both in terms of place and date. However, McIntosh suggests that Hermann Fictuld,[25] an author of several works on alchemy, may well be a key in the transformation of the order. In his *Aureum Vellum*, published in 1749, Fictuld speaks of an order of Golden Rosicrucians and likewise gives them room in his subsequent writings. McIntosh suggests that Fictuld may have come into contact with some semblance of the order and either gave it a more coherent structure or established another group under that name. McIntosh suggests a date for its establishment as either 1747 (the year in which Fictuld wrote *Aureum Vellum*) or 1757, while Gould suggests 1756.[26] If Fictuld did reestablish the order, it is more likely that he came across only manuscript evidence and possibly that of Sincerus Renatus. However, it may also be that some groups, either derived from the earlier Golden Rosicrucians or identifying themselves as such, continued to exist throughout the first half of the century. Whatever the case, after the middle of the eighteenth century, the Order was ostensibly Masonic.

In July 1782, the Great Masonic Congress was held at Wilhelmsbad, Hesse Cassel, Germany, presided over by the Grand Master of the Strict Observance, Frederick, Duke of Brunswick. Importantly for the rise of the Rosicrucian order, the congress declared that Freemasonry was not derived from the Knights Templar and that there should no obligation for Masonic lodges to confer the high degrees of the Strict Observance.[27] On November 11, 1783, the grand lodge of the Three Globes declared independence by way of a circular, relinquishing its recognition of the by then tired Masonic Templar systems, though apparently observing both the Craft and Scots degrees. The Three Globes grand lodge was to become the center of the Golden Rosicrucians.

If a Freemason had received the Craft degrees as well as the Scots Master degree and was considered to be of the right caliber for further advancement, he would be invited to join the Rosicrucian order. At such an invitation he would report to a lodge of the Golden Rosicrucians wearing the ceremonial clothing of a Scots Master. Here he would be required to knock at the door of an outer room adjoining the main lodge room where the Golden Rosicrucians had formally gathered and where he would be tested on his knowledge of the Scots degree. He would also be required to wash his hands, as a symbolic act, before being welcomed to the lodge room. Once inside, passages from the Bible were read aloud, the Freemason removed the insignia of the Scots Master, and then he was accepted as a Rosicrucian. Next he was shown a floorcloth bearing the symbols the degree: the globe, the planets, candelabra symbolizing different aspects of wisdom, and a rough stone symbolizing the base or *prima materia* (primal material) of alchemy. These signs were explained to him, giving him then the most elementary teachings of the order. In conjunction with this intro-duction to the symbolism of Rosicrucianism and alchemy, the initiate was formally requested to study the art of alchemy for himself.

The order of the Golden Rosicrucians eventu-ally successfully established itself in Germany and spread to Russia, Poland, and elsewhere. Of greater significance for the order, however, was the initiation of Prince Frederick-William of Prussia.[28] Duke Frederick Augustus was particularly interested in the prince in this regard and instructed the prince's aid, Johann Rudolf von Bischoffswerder[29] (1741–1803), to recruit the prince. In 1779 Prince Frederick fell ill, and Bischoffswerder acted as his nurse. It was a position that proved ideal for enticing Frederick-William to the Golden Rosicrucians, not least of all because the order claimed to possess an elixir that could cure sicknesses and bestow longevity. (Attempts to manufacture such elixir had become one of the major preoccupations of medieval alchemy.) Naturally, this was given to the prince, who recovered only a short while later, though whether this was a direct result of the elixir must remain open to question.[30] In 1781, Prince Frederick-William was initiated into the order of the Golden Rosicrucians, assuming the fraternal name Ormesus Magnus.[31]

Although the Golden Rosicrucians appear to have originally bestowed only a single degree, it evolved into a rite of nine degrees, purporting to illu-minate its members in the mysteries of alchemy and Kabbalah. Aside from its elixir, the order also had a spirit-conjuring machine similar to one used by Count Cagliostro. Although this was no doubt more theatrical than practical, the Golden Rosicrucians appear to have earnestly viewed the rites and teachings of their order as a method by which the initiate might have ascended to the most sublime knowledge. It is notable that the degrees of the Golden Rosicrucians were aligned with the various planes or sephiros of the Kabbalistic tree of life. A member who had received only the initiatory degree was regarded as symbolically situated on the lowest plane of the Kabbalah.

Despite an attempt to develop an intellectual and spiritual system, the Golden Rosicrucians would follow the Strict Observance into extinction. In 1785, a ban on alchemy was issued in Austria-Hungary, leaving the order dormant there until the installation of Leopold II in 1790,[32] but only two years later Leopold died. With the death of Frederick-William II in 1797, the Golden Rosicrucians fell into rapid decline, losing its political presence with the dismissal of the Rosicrucians from court by Frederick's successor, King Frederick William III. On October 20, 1798, a royal edict was issued effec-tively banning all secret societies,[33] and while the three grand lodges of Berlin found themselves exempt, the three grand lodges of Prussia did not.

Chapter 8: The Higher Degrees Established

Around the middle of the eighteenth century, a degree whose emblem
was the rose and cross, named the Rose Croix, had begun to emerge
in the country of France.[1]

As Waite has observed, this title was already familiar to the more Hermetic-minded French, for when the Golden Rosicrucians were first heard of in that country, it was translated literally as l'Ordre des Rose Croix, or Rose Croix. Waite felt that the entirety of the Rose Croix degree is "reminiscent" of the Rosicrucian order[2] and points out its symbolism is congruent with, and almost certainly derived from, medieval alchemy. Despite superficial similarity of its symbolism to that order, the Rose Croix is a rather plain Rosicrucian degree if we may accept it as such, lacking all the frequently appearing bizarre elements of the Golden Rosicrucians, such as séances.

While simpler than the rite created by the Golden Rosicrucians, the Rose Croix degree would yet prove more enduring. Indeed, within a short space of time there would be several degrees with the title and sharing elements of the same theme and at least some of the same symbols. Nevertheless, different symbols and symbolic histories also crept into the various Rose Croix degrees. The Rite of Memphis, which we mentioned in the previous chapter, would include among its ninety-four degrees one entitled Maconnerie des

Chevaliers de Rose-Croix,[3] and, similarly, as the knight Rose Croix of Heredom, it became the forty-sixth degree of the Rite of Mizraim. Of greater consequence, the knight of the Rose Croix was one of twenty-five degrees of the chapter of Clermont and was also a part of the chapter of the Emperors of the East and West. Both of these rites form historical rungs on the ladder leading to the Ancient and Accepted Scottish Rite, in which the Rose Croix of Heredom is the eighteenth degree. The Ancient and Accepted Scottish Rite is one of a few rites acknowledged by Freemasonry today and is generally available to the Master Mason, though periods of waiting in which the Mason's suitability is assessed is not uncommon in France at least.

In the ritual of the Rose Croix of Heredom degree, as it is conferred by Scottish Rite Chapters today, the Mason is led through a black room and a red room, in which he finds various symbols and signs, such as a ladder, the skull and crossbones, the square and compasses, and the phoenix or pelican. Typical of the higher degrees, these symbols, derived from the three degrees of Craft Masonry, are reinterpreted through

ABOVE: *Although it is comparatively rare to come across this symbol in American Masonry, the All-Seeing Eye in the triangle is common to French Freemasonry, for example.*

the philosophy or ethos put forward in the higher degree. Notably, as in the first degree of Craft Masonry, here also the ladder represents spiritual ascent, as well as the virtues of faith, hope, and charity. However, traditionally, the Rose Croix degree was considered as a specifically Christian degree, available to those masons who professed Trinitarian Christianity, and so the ladder, along with the ritual's other symbols, reveal a specifically Christian coloring.

Thus, the ladder in the Rose Croix degree is also explicitly associated with Christ, as the way of ascent.

Again, the skull and crossbones, which we considered in relation to the Craft ritual, have again been reevaluated. In the seventeenth century it had become an important image of still-life painting, where Christian theology had become essential to understanding the symbolic message of the collections of painted objects. In this genre, and of this period, the skull had become a frequently occurring image representing mortality (a theme that is of great importance in Craft Masonry in particular) and was originally painted on the reverse of portraits in this context.[4] (It shall be

ABOVE: *Hand-painted Rose Croix apron, early 1800s. The Rose Croix is one of the most widespread of all the higher degrees. Versions of it have appeared in the European Rites of Memphis and Mizraim, and was once bestowed in Masonic Knight Templar encampments. In the Scottish Rite today, it is the eighteenth degree. The Mason who takes this degree is symbolically called a knight of the eagle and pelican, and also a prince of the order of the Rose Croix of Heredom.*

worth remarking that, similarly, a skull and crossbones symbol is sometimes embroidered on the reverse of aprons worn during the third degree.) Even before it had become an emblem of importance for still-life painting, however, the skull was sometimes included in paintings of the crucifixion, and it is in this same context, of course, that it is encountered in the Rose Croix degree.

The phoenix has traditionally been a symbol of Christ. However, as European alchemists adopted so much Christian imagery and symbolism, it also became a symbol of importance for this science and philosophy, representing the alchemical transformation of the lower into the higher, e.g., of base metals into gold. We may note that the journey through the black and red rooms of the Rose Croix degree loosely accords with alchemical symbolism, where we often find the colors of white, black, and red representing the process of transformation. However, the spiritual journey of the Rose Croix Mason also reflects the ritualistic and symbolic journey toward the East, spoken of in the Craft degrees. Lastly, the symbol of the Rose Croix, the rosy cross, was, as we have seen, a symbol of the Lutheran religion, as well as Rosicrucianism. However, in the Rose Croix of Heredom, the rose is again taken in the more traditional Christian meaning, of the rose of Sharon, again a symbol of Christ.[5]

Many of the higher degrees share much in common not only with the three Craft degrees but also with other higher degrees, and undoubtedly these must often have influenced each other, if only indirectly, with ideas

ABOVE: Reverse of the Rose Croix apron. The Rose Croix ritual involves two rooms, one black and one red. The color symbolism is repeated here.

and themes being circulated among lodges, both in secret rituals and open conversation. Remaining with the alchemical theme for the moment, we will look at the twenty-eighth degree of Scottish Rite Masonry, the Knight of the Sun. In this ritual the Mason is led through so-called philosophical and moral lodges, the symbols of the degree being explained in philosophical and moral terms. Notably, the ritual of the Knight of the Sun reveals symbols that are similar to the novice grade of the Golden Rosicrucians, though there is no direct link between the two bodies. In the Scottish Rite ritual the Mason is, for example, shown a globe representing the primal matter and the sum knowledge of alchemy, the seven planets representing the seven passions of man, and three candles representing youth, maturity, and old age.

LEFT: This ornate Rose Croix jewel shows the pelican or phoenix feeding its young with its blood, traditionally symbolic of Christ or the Word of God. Here the rosy cross has been transformed into a red, or rose-colored, cross of rubies, above which is the celestial crown. As with other Rose Croix jewels, the compasses rest on a semicircle reminiscent of the past master's jewel.

As in medieval European alchemy, for example, in this degree a dove represents the Holy Spirit. This Spirit, the Mason is informed, affects animal, mineral, and vegetable, while the sun nourishes the earth as God nourishes man. Vague and impracticable as it is, the Knight of the Sun touches upon the philosophy of metaphoric alchemy. Thus, though the Mason is introduced to the three alchemical elements: sulfur, salt, and mercury, though they remain mere symbols. Indeed, the Mason is not asked to practice alchemy, and the degree remains, as such, largely a dictionary in which the symbols of alchemy are defined.

Similarly, the teachings of an apprentice in the now defunct Egyptian Rite are elaborated upon in a now familiar alchemical, rather than Masonic, vocabulary. The essential point is surely that while a Freemason of the Egyptian Rite still encountered many Masonic symbols, they were not only largely interpreted as alchemical but moreover the process of refinement, or spiritual and ethical transformation, is also presented as alchemical in essence and at root. The sprig of acacia, which represents immortality of the soul in Craft Masonry symbolizes the Alchemist's

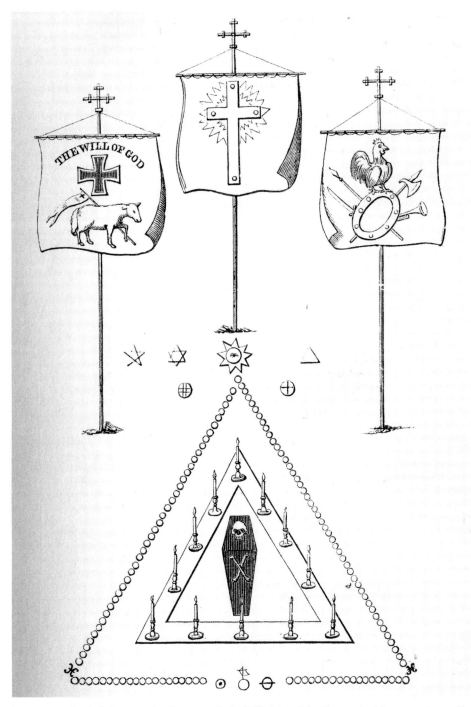

ABOVE: The banner on the left bears a lamb, a symbol of Christ, while the central banner shows the Calvary cross. Both of these symbols remain of importance in the Knight Templar degree. The triangle of candles is typical of the imagery of the Knight Templar degree.

LEFT: *Like the apron and collar worn during the Rose Croix ritual, the jewel itself is also reversible, having the pelican on the one side and the eagle, traditionally representative of Christ's oneness with God, on the other. The reverse of this jewel shows the compasses, semicircle, celestial crown, and eagle.*

primal matter in the Egyptian Rite. Again, the rough stone (or ashlar) that is regarded as the matter for chiseling a builder's stone or brick in Craft Masonry represents the alchemical mercurial substance in the Egyptian Rite and is regarded as being made cubic by the spiritual, alchemical process of purification. It would also appear that this is, again, associated with the Philosopher's Stone, regarded by medieval alchemists as liquid and solid, as well as symbolic or metaphoric. Notably, the apprentice is also told to transform the solid into liquid and then to turn that liquid into a solid. Such is very common in the instructions of alchemy. [6]

As with the Knight of the Sun degree, we also find a fondness for the number seven in the Egyptian and other rites. (It is interesting to reflect, though, on Fludd's use of the number seven, for example in his rose emblem.) Rather than seven planets (though they might be implied), the apprentice of the Egyptian Rite is told of the seven colors, for example. The significance of the colors is probably that they can be linked to the idea that at a certain point in the transformation of metals, the alchemist should see a rainbow of colors in the metal, sometimes symbolized as a peacock. This is not actually far-fetched, as white metals, such as tin and lead, do in fact produce some rather attractive colors when molten.

Despite being largely influenced by alchemical philosophy, a brief fantasy in the Egyptian ritual tells the apprentice that Solomon brought together twelve masters, twenty-four companions, and seventy-two apprentices. From the latter group, he is told, descended the Knights Templar, and from these knights supposedly arose the Freemasons. This myth seems entirely removed from the history of alchemy, and distinct even from Craft Masonry, yet it is in neo-Masonry that such myth and history merge, most often fusing chivalry and alchemy. We earlier noted this mixture in the society of the African Builders, and, we might recall, the first two degrees of that order also referenced Egypt. Even if no direct line can be drawn between these rites, there can be little doubt that among the many interpretations of Freemasonry, then, the alchemical was not only represented but was probably being passed from lodge to lodge, chapter to chapter, and group to group. These frequently appeared, disappeared, or were elaborated into, or consumed by, even more complex and elaborate rites, sometimes preposterous, and sometimes intelligent.

A. C. F. Jackson has suggested that the origin of the Rose Croix is to be sought in some degree associated with the Strict Observance influenced by Rosicrucianism. The Strict Observance had to some extent become influenced by alchemy, though nevertheless it would seem something of a departure from the Templar myth and ideals that were its raison d'être. Yet, some interpretations of the Strict Observance, in which the Templar or "vengeance" element had been diluted, were being given in France out of political, or sociopolitical, consideration in the eighteenth century. Yet, it is quite possible, of course, that the Rose Croix was developed by a French or even German Scots lodge or, for that matter, by any number of Hermetically inclined lodges, rites, or Masonic circles scattered across Germany and France.

In the late eighteenth and early nineteenth centuries in Britain and America, the Rose Croix of Heredom became closely associated with a neo-Masonic degree known as the order of the Temple[7] or, more popularly, the Knights Templar. August 28, 1769, is the earliest known date at which the order of the temple was conferred, the ceremony being recorded in the minutes of the first meeting of St. Andrew's Royal Arch lodge, held at Mason's Hall, Boston, Massachusetts.[8] Some ten years later, in 1779, there is evidence that the degree was being worked in Britain, but then only by the Antient lodges. The Moderns still only recognized the three degrees of Craft Masonry, much to the growing frustration of their brethren, who undoubtedly saw their counterparts spoiled by all kinds of glamorous Hermetic and knightly rites and honors. It has been asserted that the Antient's Athol lodges (named after their grand master, the Duke of Atholl) recognized both the Royal Arch and Knight Templar degrees.[9] It would appear that in Britain, Ireland, and America, the Knights Templar constituted an honorary fifth degree,[10] succeeding the Royal Arch degree, and also that this lat-

ABOVE: *This Masonic Knight Templar belt buckle is decorated with a triangle, twelve candles, a Bible, the symbol of a skull, and a jug (top). In a sense, the scene is a tracing board, representing the atmosphere of the Masonic order of the temple and the Christian teaching of life after death through salvation in Christ, central to this degree.*

ter degree was originally regarded as a prerequisite to admission to this chivalrous-type Masonic order, as it is today. In 1813, the Moderns and Antients finally put their differences aside and agreed to a marriage of the two Masonic grand lodges and their respective percep-

tions of Freemasonry. The Modern Grand Lodge must surely have felt the pressure to adopt some or other higher degree, not only because of the Antient Masons, but also because of the plethora of such degrees existing on the continent and sometimes finding their way to

England. With the compact of the Antient and Modern grand lodges and the subsequent establishment of the United Grand Lodge of England, the Duke of Sussex became the Grand Master. He had recently been installed as the Grand Master of the Moderns, while the Duke of Kent had been the Grand Master of the Antients. (The latter relinquished any claim on the title.) It is perhaps of interest that the Duke of Sussex was brought up in Germany, where Masonry was far more overtly mystical than in Britain. The duke had also developed a scholarly interest in Judaism and Kabbalah, had at least eleven Kabbalistic texts in his library, and, like Laurence Dermott, could read, write, and speak in Hebrew.[11]

A compact of the two competing grand lodges and Masonic systems was probably inevitable and, in truth, had been long overdue, though differences still remained to be ironed out and a contract worded very carefully. The main contention between the two parties was, of course, the Royal Arch degree, though the appearance of extra, supposedly higher degrees, such as the Knights Templar, couldn't have helped. The Moderns could not but hold to their view that three Craft degrees constituted Freemasonry proper, but the Royal Arch had to be accepted to get the agreement of the Antients and to make the compact in any way valuable for Masons under both of these jurisdictions. By all accounts many, if not most, Modern Freemasons wanted to participate in this degree especially, and some, as we have seen, already had. Some accommodating of the chivalrous degrees was also required.

ABOVE: *This masonic Knight Templar apron shows a Calvary cross in a triangle (one of the traditional symbols of the Degree) and the skull and crossbones, an enduring image of this type of apron.*

The second article of the Articles of Union, drafted by the Modern and Antient grand lodges, states:

It is declared and pronounced, that pure
Ancient masonry consists of three degrees,
and no more, viz. Those of Entered
Apprentice, the Fellow Craft, and the Master
Mason, including the Supreme Order of the
Holy Royal Arch. But this article is not
intended to prevent any Lodge or Chapter
from holding a meeting in any of the degrees
of the Orders of Chivalry, according to the
constitutions of the said Orders.[12]

ABOVE: *This plate from a Masonic Knight Templar banquet in 1901 shows the softer side of the Craft. As with the traditional arts generally, the imagery of Freemasonry has often used the female figure to represent one or other virtue. This plate appears to be purely decorative, however, and in this regard is unusual.*

The Royal Arch is thus no longer considered a degree in its own right, but is rather viewed as one of the three degrees. Perplexing though this may be, to put it more succinctly, the United Grand Lodge regarded the Royal Arch as the second part or completion of the third degree. Undoubtedly it is because of the specific wording of the second article of union that we find the origin of the myth that the Royal Arch was originally a part of the third degree. Indeed, it does not appear to have been viewed, or promoted, as such previous to this point, even if in some rare instances there may be similarities or crossovers in the degrees. The compact of the two grand lodges is remarkable, though, in that it did admit this one essentially higher degree as a part of Freemasonry proper, while other such degrees have always been treated with great caution by the English Freemason.

Regarding the aforementioned article of union, while we see that it was not meant to prevent Freemasons from taking the higher, chivalric degrees, the chivalrous order foremost in the British Masonic imagination at the time of the uniting of the two Grand Lodges was undoubtedly the Knights Templar. In a sense, the article may be read as a cautious endorsement of the higher degrees as conferred by the Antients.

It is possible that the Knights Templar degree in question was derived from those which had populated the Masonic lodges of Europe in the eighteenth century, such as the Kadosh, or those of the Strict Observance. The Freemasonry of France, especially, had become

RIGHT: This early-twentieth-century Masonic Knight Templar jewel is composed of a Calvary cross behind which are two crossed swords. Although it is a much misunderstood symbol, the skull and crossbones (center) has a long tradition in Christian art.

connected to the American in the protracted development of the Ancient and Accepted Scottish Rite (which would emerge first in the latter country), and, in a broader sense, the two countries had, of course, become closer with the American Revolution, and particularly with Benjamin Franklin acting as American diplomat in France—and where he would also exploit his Masonic connections in order to gain support for the U. S., as we shall see. However, the Knight Templar ritual is close enough to the Rose Croix in many respects to make us think that it might possibly have been influenced by this latter degree. As the Ancient and Accepted rite was not imported into England until the remarkably late date of 1845, English Masons had always received both the Rose Croix and the Knight Kadosh under the auspices of groups, or encampments of the neo-Masonic Knights Templar.[14] (These degrees, and others besides, we shall recall, floated around the neo-Masonic bodies and became established in various rites.)

After 1845, sole control of the Rose Croix and Kadosh degrees were solicited by the ruling bodies of the then newly established Ancient and Accepted Rite, as it is known in England, as these degrees were already established in this latter system, of course. Yet,

ABOVE: This is a typical example of an early-twentieth-century Rose Croix apron, with a rosy cross in red fabric, sequins, beads, and gold thread.

even so, a philosophical separation of the degrees had not been achieved. In England the Knight Templar degree was viewed as a prerequisite to being advanced to the Rose Croix. Similarly, on July 16 of the same year, the northern jurisdiction of the United States ruled that Masons petitioning for the degree of the

Rose Croix must first have attained the degree of the Knights Templar. These degrees have since attained a greater autonomy, especially in America, where the Knight Templar degree exists as part of the York Rite, which runs parallel to the Scottish Rite. Theoretically, as both in a sense meditate on the crucifixion and resurrection of Christ, and both use some of the same symbols such as the skull and crossbones and the Calvary cross, both rituals might be viewed as bestowing the same secrets. Of course, anyone who had read the New Testament would know these secrets, but that is not the point. The secret is, or rather was in the case of America, that various Masonic symbols pointed to Christian myth, history, and philosophy. It was always the reinterpretation of Masonic symbols that really proved the so-called secret.

Around 1800, several high-ranking Freemasons began assessing those rituals that would soon prove the backbone of the Scottish Rite's degree structure. However, it would appear that at least the honorary thirty-third degree ritual, as well as, possibly, one other, was only secured from France several years later. By 1801, this group had also begun discussing plans to establish a council of the Ancient and Accepted Scottish Rite, this occurring at Charlestown late in May of that year.[14] On October 22, 1804, the grand lodge of the Ancient and Accepted Scottish Rite was established in France, and on November 1 it released a circular announcing its establishment and offering, of course, superior rites to those available to Masons under the jurisdiction of the governing Masonic body known as the Grand Orient, as well as other grand lodges. The Grand Orient was troubled by the declaration and entered into a dialogue with the grand lodge of the Scottish Rite. In a remarkably short space of time, the two bodies had come to an agreement. On December 3 the two grand lodges joined, with the Scottish Rite holding itself superior. The Grand Orient already had its own Rose Croix

ABOVE: This Scottish Rite apron is worn in the thirty-second degree, called the Sublime Prince of the Royal Secret. The double-headed eagle appears twice on the flap. The symbol, as it appears on the right, with crown, sword, and steps, is related to the Knight Kadosh degree. Traditionally, the flag of the country in which the Scottish Rite body was located was shown on the apron s flap, along with the flag of Prussia.

chapter. Under the new arrangement the Grand Orient was allowed control of all degrees up to—but not including—the Rose Croix degree, while the Scottish Rite controlled this and all of the succeeding degrees.[15]

The Ancient and Accepted Scottish Rite initially claimed to derive its Masonic authority and historical legitimacy in part from two documents or constitutions that were held to have been granted to earlier rites adopted and developed into the Scottish Rite. The first of these documents was the *Constitutions of 1762*, compiled by the grand lodge of France, and the second the *Constitutions of 1786*, which, importantly, supposed the authority of Frederick the Great as the then supreme head and governor of those rituals authorized by the said constitution. According to Masonic legend, Frederick the Great had been granted authority of the Rite of Perfection by the young pretender in France. According to Masonic legend, Frederick was assumed to have revised the rite and its regulations in 1786, when he was close to death, enlarging the number of degrees in the rite from twenty-five to the thirty-three of the Ancient and Accepted Scottish Rite. This myth has been long dismissed by Masonic scholars, and it has been alleged, we may note, that one of the forgers of the constitution was Wollner, one time Golden Rosicrucian and aide to Frederick's successor.[16] Gould, on the other hand, felt that both of the constitutions could have been written in America. Regardless of their historical legitimacy, the lodge of Perfection in Philadelphia prepared an address for Frederick in 1785, and as early as 1770 the lodge of Perfection in Albany, New York, was directed to send their reports to Berlin.[17]

That the name of Frederick the Great, and of the state of Prussia over which he ruled, became attached to the rite is of interest as we consider the myths, symbols, and rituals of the Ancient and Accepted Scottish Rite. Although it had been one of the degrees in the older rite of the chapter of Clermont (which became a part of the Scottish Rite), a degree known as the Noachite, or Prussian knight, for example, became the twenty-first degree of the contemporary Scottish Rite. The ritual of the Prussian knight is concerned with what might be summed up as righteous judgment and mercy. Assemblies of this body are called grand chapters, while members of this body are known as Prussian-knight Masons. The traditional regalia of this degree is a black, triangular-shape apron decorated with an image of an angel and a naked arm holding a sword, as well as a triangular jewel suspended from the neck by a black ribbon and bearing the latter emblem together with an arrow. Also on the jewel is the inscription *Fiat Justitial Ruat Coelum* (Let justice be done, though heaven falls). This maxim has been ascribed to Julius Caesar's father-in-law, Lucius Calpurnius Piso Caesoninus, who died around 43 BC. However, this phrase was later adopted and slightly altered by Ferdinand I (1503–1564; Holy Roman Emperor 1558–1564), who used for his motto *Fiat justitia et pereat mundus* (Let justice be done though the world may perish).

It is stated in the allegory of the ritual that the Order of the Prussian Knights was formed at the time of the Crusades and established itself in Germany under the name of the Holy Vehme, taking the name

Prussian knights because it flourished in that German state. (We shall recall that the Crusades, as a theme important to neo-Masonry, began with Ramsay.) The Vehme was an order of judges that held particular sway in Germany during the medieval period. They appear to have had some type of ritual that remained secret to the noninitiated and to have tried cases in secret sessions if deemed unfit for evaluation before the general populace. The somewhat mythologized Prussian knights of the Masonic rite came to be called Noachites, the knight Mason is informed, because the order strove for the primeval judgment of Noah.[18] This Biblical figure is not especially important to Craft Masonry, though Noah's Ark is a symbol of the third degree[19] and Noah is mentioned briefly in Anderson's *Constitutions*.

Another emblem of significance regarding the German influence on neo-Masonry is the double-headed or Imperial eagle. The first we hear of it in a Masonic context is in a letter from Masons in Metz, Germany, to fellow Masons in Lyons,[20] France, in 1761, while one of the first Masonic images of the double-headed eagle is found on a tracing board painted for the knight of Kadosh degree, Albany, New York (circa 1767). The introduction of this symbol has led Jackson to conclude that Frederick the Great could not have been the head of the rite that was later transformed as the Ancient and Accepted Scottish Rite, stating that, as a heraldic device, the double-headed eagle belongs to the Hapsburgs, rather than the Prussian monarchy. This is undoubtedly true, though the Imperial eagle represented far more than the Hapsburgs.

ABOVE: The double-headed eagle was the heraldic device of the Holy Roman Empire of Germany and was also adopted into the imagery of alchemy prior to the eighteenth century. It appears to have been known to German Masonry, presumably for both reasons, and later became the symbol of the Ancient and Accepted Scottish Rite.

Late in the sixteenth century, the double-headed eagle had begun to enter the visual language of alchemy[21] and was certainly known to some continental Freemasons as such, especially those who frequented the various circles of the Golden Rosicrucians. Given the alchemical symbolism found in the Scottish Rite's Knight of the Sun degree as well as, possibly, the Rose Croix, the double-headed eagle's

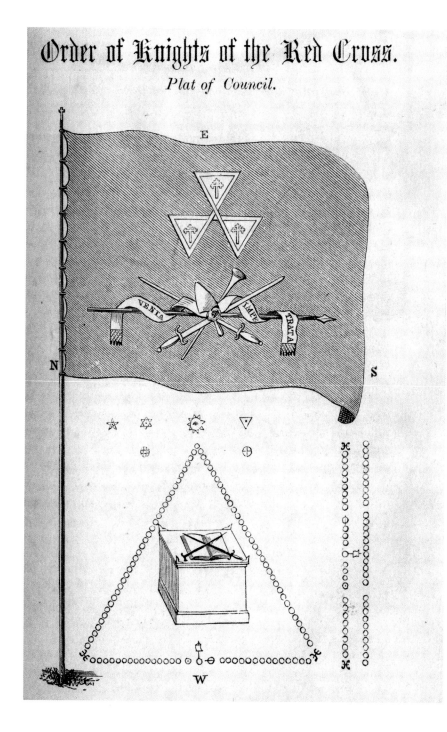

ABOVE: An illustration of the Masonic Order of the Red Cross, bestowed in Knight Templar encampments. In the center of the triangle is an altar and a Bible guarded by two swords.

appearance in this mystical philosophy is surely of significance. However, this symbolic figure had a much more worldly meaning. It was, in fact, the symbol of the Holy Roman Empire of Germany itself, and, thus, the then quintessential German symbol. This certainly does not suggest that Frederick the Great was actively involved in the rite, though it does suggest that those Masons who created the rites and degrees that were adopted by the Scottish Rite had deliberately chosen symbols that implicated Germany as significant. On the one hand it may be that some of the degrees were created in Germany, or that German Masons

added to French degrees as they were brought to their country. It is very probable that these degrees had continually circulated between the neighboring countries. In this regard it is valuable to take a brief look at the Holy Roman Empire of Germany and its political significance.

The Holy Roman Empire of Germany was established with the coronation of Charlemagne (Carolus Magnus or Charles the Great). As early as AD 771, Charlemagne had risen through the ranks to become king of the Germanic tribe known as the Franks (who would later establish the country of

ABOVE: *Lafayette bowl, ceramic. The Sacred Book is enclosed by the square and compasses, on either side of which is a beehive. This bowl was one used at a banquet in New York City, celebrating the Marquis de Lafayette's reception into the Masonic Order of the Knights Templar in 1824.*

France). On Christmas Day, AD 800, Charlemagne was crowned emperor by the pope at St. Peter's, thus establishing for the first time the often strained relationship between the offices of pope and emperor. Charlemagne's empire held within it different tribes and kings who, while theoretically subservient to the emperor, were—like emperor and pope—often antagonistic to one another. Nevertheless, as the founder of an empire that stretched across what is now France and Germany, Charlemagne became a national hero of both countries. Indeed, long before the eighteenth century, French stonemasons had also claimed the Emperor Charlemagne as one of the founders of their Craft.[22]

By the end of the eighteenth century, Napoléon Bonaparte began deliberately, and with typical audacity, promoting the notion of a similarity between he and Charlemagne. It is not known whether Napoléon was a Freemason. Evidence is lacking, but popular legend has rarely cared for facts, and myth suggests that Napoléon was made a Freemason on the island of Malta. Whether he was or was not a Freemason, Napoléon possessed a flair for the dramatic and married it to the type of symbolism and ritual that had earlier wooed half of France to Freemasonry as well as similar though lesser-known societies. Such bravado may not have been solely for the sake of self-aggrandizement, however—though Napoléon had no problem in that—but may have been executed with the intention of impressing the Freemasons of France. Indeed, even if many Freemasons had lost their heads in the French Revolution, many still retained powerful positions in society. Not only many of Napoléon's immediate circle of advisors but also members of his immediate family were Freemasons. Most interestingly, in Strasbourg and Milan lodges dedicated to Napoléon's wife, the Empress Josephine, had been established, and she became Grand Mistress of them.

In 1804, Napoléon would cajole the pope into crowning him emperor of the French, and for his coronation adorned himself with Charlemagne's spurs, sword, and sheath, along with a replica of Charlemagne's crown—the original remained out of reach in Germany. There must have been thousands of Freemasons across Europe with such titles as prince sovereign, sir knight, etc. Now, Napoléon unquestionably outranked them all. He was both emperor and the new Charlemagne. Soon after the coronation, the French newspaper *Moniteur* published its history of Charlemagne, translated into German, explaining also the apparent need to unify the Empire[23]—Napoléon meant to invade. In 1806, the emperor of the French would put an end to the Holy Roman Empire of Germany that his predecessor, Charlemagne, had established. Napoléon's armies defeated the Austrian forces, and Napoléon forced the abdication of the Holy Roman emperor. Dressed in the robes of his office, on August 6, the grand herald of the empire read the proclamation of Emperor Francis II of the Holy Roman Empire of Germany, renouncing his claim on the Imperial title and becoming Emperor Francis I of Austria.[24]

Although it was almost certainly made for the coronation of one of his successors, Emperor Otto the

Great (made emperor in AD 962[25]), the crown supposed to have been Charlemagne's was held at Nuremberg and ceremonially exhibited before the people every year around Easter in the Feast of the Imperial Insignia. Otto's crown must have been an impressive sight to the Germans: gold, surmounted by a tiara and Christian cross, set with two hoshen (a breastplate of twelve stones representing the Twelve Tribes of Israel worn by the high priest), and engraved with the figures of Christ and Kings Hezekiah, David, and Solomon. The Twelve Tribes of Israel may have been seen by Otto as synonymous with the kingdoms of the Holy Roman Empire that he, as emperor, held together. Emperor Otto wore not only the crown, but also the mantle and star-emblazoned tunic of the Biblical high priest, becoming his living symbol as he would the symbol of Christ the King.[26] It was the kind of symbolism that Freemasons loved. It had entered the Royal Arch degree, though undoubtedly drawn directly from Biblical accounts, and Dermott had even dreamed of this figure and had recorded it in his preface to the first edition of *Ahiman Rezon*.

It is important to note that when Charlemagne ascended to the emperor's throne he took an eagle (single-headed) as his symbol that in Christian iconography was the emblem of Saint John (we shall recall that some Masonic lodges were dedicated to Saint John, and Saint John the Evangelist and Saint John the Baptist are symbolically of importance to Freemasonry even today). When Otto became emperor, he adopted the double-headed or imperial eagle, making it also the symbol of the Holy Roman Empire of Germany as well as its subsequent emperors. It would also become the heraldic emblem of Nuremburg, the home to Otto's crown since it had been brought there in the fifteenth century by the Emperor Sigismund.

Chapter 9: Pledging Allegiance

In attempting to prove the superiority of Antient Masonry over the Moderns, Laurence Dermott highlighted the spread of Antient lodges across the globe.

The only country that he would cite as worthy of special praise, however, was America:

> [The] Freemasons of America . . . for their charitable disposition, prudent choice of members, and good conduct in general, deserve the unanimous thanks and applause of the Masonic world. [1]

In fact it would be in America that Antient Masonry would eventually settle. The 1813 compact of the competing English grand lodges of the Antients and Moderns had returned the ritual of three degrees to that of the far simpler Moderns' type. Both Masonic rituals followed the same themes (i.e., the construction of Solomon's Temple and the murder of Hiram Abiff), but the Antients used some symbols such as the bee-hive, almost unknown to the Moderns at that time, that remain in use in American Freemasonry. After the American Revolution (unthinkable fifty years earlier when the Antients were a small group on the periphery of acceptable Masonry), Modern Masons in America were expected to take the three degrees of Free-masonry again, though this time of the Ancient type, if they wanted to be recognized as legitimate Freemasons.

As we might expect, it is unclear exactly how Freemasonry came to the New World. It is possible that there were a few lodges in America, scattered here and there, even before 1717, though, as it is difficult to define what might constitute a Masonic lodge before this date in Britain, the problem is exacerbated in America. In 1634, Lord Alexander, Viscount Canada, was apparently inducted into a stonemasons' lodge in Edinburgh and soon after settled a colony near the St. Laurence River. John Skene, who had previously been inducted into a Masonic lodge at Aberdeen in Scotland, traveled to and settled in Burlington, New Jersey in 1682. Tradition also has it that in 1720 a Masonic lodge was founded at Boston, chartered by the premier grand lodge of England, though this governing body was then still very young, and only just beginning to enjoy a modicum of prestige or influence at home.

As in Britain, Masonic lodges in America were but one society among many. Members of various Christian sects left Europe to set up their own congre-

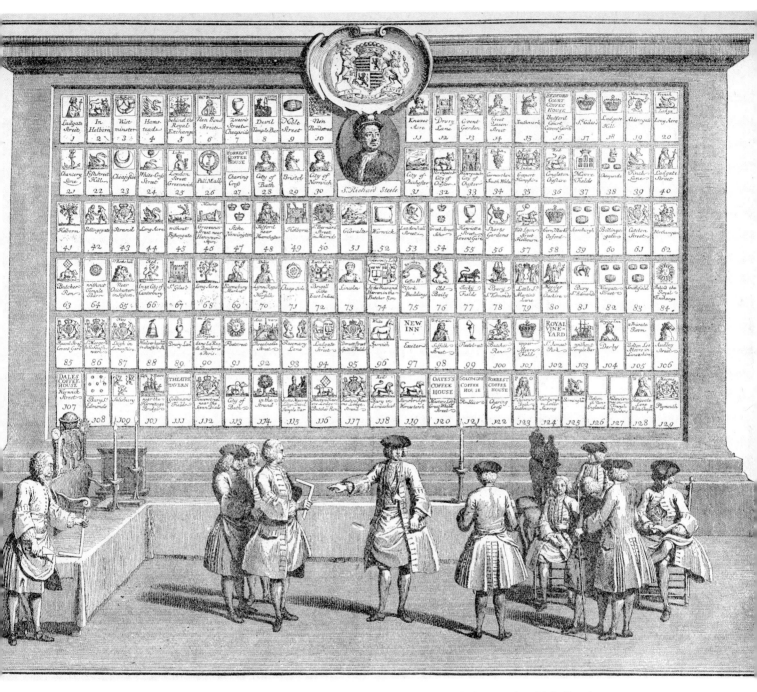

ABOVE: *A list of Masonic lodges from 1737. While most are from England, lodge number 72 is listed as located in "Bengal in the East-Indies," number 51 in "Gibraltar," number 124 in "Hamburg in Lower Saxony," and number 126 at "Boston in New England." Beneath the list are Freemasons at Lodge. To the left is the master's chair. The three tapers, or candles, are also displayed.*

gations without the fear of persecution, and some Rosicrucian sympathizers or even self-professed Rosicrucian groups also made a home in America. Likewise, as the colonists of America became increasingly troubled by the British crown revolutionary, pro–American independence political organizations such as the Sons of the Revolution would appear. The British charity the Saint George's Society was established in New York in 1770. As was typical of the time, these societies met in taverns, as did Masonic lodges, though in such an atmosphere the club's agenda must occasionally have been compromised. On one occasion in 1771, for example, no less than twenty-three toasts were given at a meeting of the Saint George's Society, the twenty-second being to "The Roast Beef of Old England."[2] Given the number of other clubs and societies, it is nothing short of astounding that Freemasonry would establish itself and, more significantly in American history, would itself play an important role in both the Revolution and the building of an independent America.

Although we cannot say with certainty when Freemasonry arrived on American soil, it is at least likely that it began to appear fairly shortly after the founding of the premier grand lodge of England, gaining a foothold as Freemasons emigrated from Britain to the colonies. The first few years of Freemasonry in the American colonies seems to have been plagued by administrative chaos, and lists of lodge were either not accurately kept or simply not kept at all, even by the premier grand lodge itself. Moreover, lodges were often simply constituted as required, or desired, and were presumably headed by one or more experienced Mason. These lodges sprung up here and there, sometimes lasted and sometimes simply fizzled out. This situation, although undoubtedly on a much smaller scale, was probably similar as Freemasonry entered the New World.

The story of American Freemasonry, as far as can be traced with any certainty, begins around 1730. On June 5 of that year, the first official act was passed by the premier grand lodge of England concerning the territories of America, making one Daniel Coxe (1673–1734) of New Jersey the Provincial Grand Master of the state of New Jersey as well as the neighboring states of New York and Pennsylvania. Early in 1731, Coxe apparently visited the grand lodge at London, where he was referred to in the expanded title, the Provincial Grand Master of North America. However, no records exist attesting to Coxe acting in this official capacity, and it is not known how his actual involvement in Masonry played out or even how many American lodges he chartered.

Already in 1730 there were several Masonic lodges in Philadelphia, Pennsylvania, and there were undoubtedly others scattered through the other colonies. Freemasonry not only established itself in Philadelphia to some effect, and early on, but in 1754, the Masons of the city erected the first Masonic hall in the country of America. Yet an ultimately far more important event would occur there even before that date, when the eminent Benjamin Franklin (1706–1790) was formerly introduced to the Masonic fraternity. Franklin's initiation into the Craft cannot be underestimated, concerning both the history of Freemasonry as well as that of Franklin himself. The moral lessons it espoused resonated deeply with Franklin and seems to have molded his outlook to a much greater extent than many other such notables who also joined the Craft—Franklin was, after all, a thinker, philosopher, and scientist and would prove himself a remarkable diplomat and politician. Moreover, Franklin, a man of redoubtable shrewdness, would turn his position in Freemasonry to the political advantage of America, winning much-needed support among the Freemasons of France for the American Revolution.

Franklin was probably aware of the existence of Freemasonry from his days in England and was maybe conscious of its ever-increasing prominence among, and importance to, the movers and shakers of Britain and Western Europe as a whole. In France, of course, Masonry was even more expressly aristocratic, and to a large degree Freemasonry in America would be quickly molded in this vein, though it would later adopt a much broader outlook. With social distinction less obvious in America than Britain and elsewhere, the colonial elites were eager to adopt Masonry and to use it as a marker of a man's status in the New World. Moreover, patronized by the minor aristocracy of Britain, Freemasonry elevated its American gentlemen members far above their peers, connecting them implicitly to the best of British society, which still, of course, drafted the laws for the colonists, much to their increasing displeasure. Though if the colonial Mason was an aristocrat of sorts, he was also an ethical elitist,

and that the moral and ethical code of Freemasonry resonated with him should not be underestimated.

In 1727, Franklin had formed a club called Junto, whose purpose and main characteristics seem to have strongly resembled the Masonic lodge—at least those whose members were more philosophically inclined.[3] Like Franklin, the men of the club had not reached the height of their careers nor presumably their self-education, of which the club was intended to form a significant part. Many of its members were, in fact, still apprentices, and for this reason it appears to have been originally styled "the leather apron club." The Junto met weekly, on a Friday evening, while excursions to the countryside were held once a month and a banquet was put on every winter. The stated aim of the Junto club was expressly to aid the "mutual improvement" of its members. Every member was held to produce at least one query on morals, politics, or natural philosophy, which was then to be discussed among its members, while they also took turns producing a paper on any subject—though undoubtedly loosely relating to the concerns of the club. The Junto grew, and, as it reached what was considered full capacity for a group of such a nature, other clubs were formed on the periphery.[4]

By 1730, lodges of Freemasons were becoming well known to Philadelphia, though their purposes and practices remained ill-defined by her non-Masonic residents. Gossip regarding the few lodges of the city had been circulating for some time, but on December 8, Franklin made the usually private society public by advertising that his newspaper would print an account of Freemasonry from London. Franklin was of course in a position that could have proved either very awkward or entirely beneficial to the society. Moreover, Franklin was of the right caliber for Freemasonry, as his establishing the Junto had shown, and he possessed a natural ability to persuade. Only a short while later, in 1731, he was accepted as a member of the Philadelphia fraternity's Saint John's lodge. On June 26, 1732, the *Pennsylvania Gazette* published notice that:

> Saturday last being St. John's day, a Grand Lodge of the ancient and honorable Society of FREE and ACCEPTED MASONS was held at the Sun Tavern in Water Street, when, after a handsome entertainment, the Worshipful W. Allen, Esq., was unanimously chosen Grand Master of this Province for the year ensuing, who was pleased to appoint Mr. William Pringle Deputy Master. Wardens chosen for the ensuing year were Thomas Boude and Benjamin Franklin.

Coxe, the Provincial Grand Master for North America, died two years later; Franklin's newspaper noted his passing but made no reference to his Masonic affiliation. By that time a resident of Boston named Henry Price had been given the position of Provincial Grand Master of New England in a ceremony in England, and, despite the distance that separated them, he and Franklin were certainly on familiar terms. The colonial lodges, of course, still adhered to the philosophy and regulations of the premier English grand lodge, the Antients having yet to emerge even in Britain. In 1734, Franklin published a facsimile edition of Anderson's *Constitutions*, and copies of these were sent to the brethren in Boston. In the same year, Franklin was presiding over the lodge, having been elected its Grand Master.[3] The *Philadelphia Gazette* published this account of his election to that Masonic office:

> Monday last a Grand Lodge of the Ancient and Honorable Society of Free and Accepted Masons in this Province, was held at the Tun Tavern in Water Street, when BENJAMIN FRANKLIN being elected Grand Master for the year ensuing, appointed Mr. John Crap to be his Deputy: and James Hamilton, Esq., and Thomas Hopkins, Gent., were chosen Wardens. After which a very elegant entertainment was provided, and the Proprietor, the Governor, and several other persons of distinctions, honored the Society with their presence.

However, all was not well in the burgeoning Freemasonry of Philadelphia. It was beginning to be afflicted by that peculiar Masonic curse—the establishment of self-appointed, or so-called irregular, rival lodges. Franklin refers to only one such lodge, which seems to have adhered to the very lowest standards. Worse still, the irregular lodge in question had even started to exploit gullible locals, charging beer as an initiation fee. Perhaps this should have been warning

ABOVE: Craft certificate from Saint John's lodge no. 2, North Carolina, 1793.

ABOVE: *Craft certificate, paper, from Boston, Massachusetts, 1850. The three panels include a pentagram, a figure resting with a lamb and lion, and Euclid's 47th Proposition.*

enough for the locals, but Franklin was rightly concerned by unfolding events and wrote to Price:

> I beg leave to . . . inform you, that some false and rebel Brethren, who are foreigners, being about to set up a distinct Lodge in opposition to the old and true Brethren here, pretending to make Masons for a bowl of punch, and the Craft is like to come into disesteem among us unless the true Brethren are countenanced and distinguished by some special authority as herein desired.[6]

That, according to Franklin, the members of this lodge were "foreign" is not without interest, for such a term almost certainly didn't refer to the English, and as such it might suggest the importation of a lodge of the more colorful European Freemasonry, with all of its exotic theories and oddities of ceremony. Indeed, it is possible that this lodge had enticed some of the Freemasons of Philadelphia to join them. In this regard it is interesting to see that Franklin ends the note with, "P.S.—If more of the Constitutions are wanted among you, please hint it to me." Surely this was the authority which set Franklin's and related lodges apart from the "false" and "rebel" brethren of which he speaks.

Despite such challenges, within a decade, Masonic lodges, coming under the jurisdiction of the grand lodges of Britain, had been established in Massachusetts, Georgia, South Carolina, New Hampshire, and New York.[7] Lodge membership was small, with only about twenty to fifty members per lodge,[8]

and Franklin's lodge was smaller than most. Early accounts of this lodge, at least since June 24, 1731, are contained in a small, handwritten book known as *Libr B*. The strange title is derived from an inscription on the cover, which reads "St. Johns Lodge Libr B" and above it, "Philadelphia City." It would appear that it was once called *Libr A*, but for whatever reason the letter "A" was effaced. At the date which records were first made in the ledger, the lodge had only fourteen members.

Franklin ascended rapidly in Freemasonry, and in February 1735 was elected to the position of Provincial Grand Master of Philadelphia (essentially the governor of the Masonic lodges for Philadelphia), and as late as 1760 he appeared at a meeting of the grand lodge of England, bearing the same title. An important shift took place in the makeup of American Freemasonry in 1758 when lodges under the jurisdiction of the Antients began to establish themselves in Pennsylvania. Within a few years they would surpass the older, Modern, lodges.

On July 1, 1776, the Continental Congress met to debate the matter of breaking with Britain, and though there was initially some wavering, the next day the motion passed with the unanimous approval of the thirteen colonies. On July 4, the Declaration of Independence was signed. Printers all over the country began producing and disseminating the declaration. The declaration was also read aloud in public. With war imminent, George Washington (1732–1799) moved his troops from Boston to New York, where the British army was expected to land. Here the declaration was read to Washington's army, whole regiments at a time. It inveighed against the British king, whom the Americans had come to consider a despot, and his government, though some elements in the British parliament—which had long maintained an uneasy relationship with the king—were to some extent sympathetic to the American cause. Democracy had been hard won in Britain also.

In the meantime the Sons of Liberty wrenched down a statue of George III at Bowling Green in New York City, later to be turned into bullets for the American army,[9] while Franklin was acting as a diplomat for America in France. No doubt this risqué political air added something to his already considerable charm, but as an inventor, printer, intellectual, Freemason, and, of course, foreigner, Franklin was an enigma by any standard, and he wasted no time in capitalizing on that fact. Declining to wear the fashions that obsessed the French, Franklin made sure that his clothes were that of the stoic, honest man, with just a hint of piety and religiousness. In France, the cult of reason, the Enlightenment, had taken hold of the intelligentsia on the one side and the popular imagination on the other. The Enlightenment expounded the ideals of brotherhood, justice, and equality, and held the importance of the church and secular government dependent on rational thought. Here, in this country of ideals, intellect, and glamour, Franklin became the Master of the prestigious Masonic lodge, the Nine Muses. More impressive yet, he officiated in this capacity at the induction of François Marie Arouet de Voltaire (1694–1778), philosopher, author,

and the brightest light of the Enlightenment. It was a coup for Freemasonry, and for Franklin.

Franklin wasted no time in pointing out how the ideals of the French opposed those of their tyrannical neighbor, Britain, though they were certainly at one with those of America. The French knew how awful the British could be. In 1761, British troops had swept across America, Canada, the West Indies, Africa, and India, forcing France to surrender her territories.[10] Such successes brought a heavy financial burden to Britain, and naturally, reparations were extracted from France, but they had saved the colonists of America from Gallic interference, or so Britain perceived, and with some creative taxation they too could be made to contribute. Soon parliament had levied the sugar tax on the American colonies as well as a number of other taxes directed at merchants. These taxes were highly unpopular and proved difficult to collect. The British then decided to impose the Stamp Act: all official documents would be stamped and taxed. To the British this seemed so much easier than collecting individual taxes on goods. But the colonists were not represented in parliament, and the Stamp Act only aggravated the hostility toward Britain that was being increasingly felt in America. In 1765, the new tax went into law but hardly into effect, as protests began to surface.

By this time, American Masonry was becoming increasingly divided into Modern and Antient camps, as more and more lodges of the latter type began appearing, some traveling from abroad, and some chartered by established lodges in the "old country."[11] In Boston one Antient lodge called Saint Andrew's, which met at the Green Dragon Inn, claimed to derive from Scotland but were snubbed by the premier Bostonian lodge of the Moderns' persuasion, which not only boasted a large membership but was also the grand lodge for the Moderns in the area. As a consequence Saint Andrew's lodge applied to the grand lodge of Scotland for a charter. This was granted, but Saint Andrew's next decided to become a grand lodge and received a charter to act in this capacity for other Antient lodges by the Scottish grand lodge only after they and several Antient lodges made up of military personnel had petitioned the Scottish Masonic authority. In one way or another colonial Masonic lodges began to take an active part in revolutionary politics, and while Franklin was busy in France, Saint Andrew's lodge in Boston had become equally well positioned in the fight against the British. Though this was not the only club to meet at the Green Dragon Inn, which had become a hotbed of revolutionary zeal.

In November 1773, a shipment of tea arrived at Boston Harbor, brought by the powerful, British-owned East India Company. Infuriated at Britain's increasing heavy-handed approach to colonies, Boston's residents met the ship and refused to allow the unloading of its sizeable cargo. Nevertheless, the ship refused to sail and remained docked. Events pivotal in the rise of the revolution would turn on the evening of December 16 at the Green Dragon Inn, not far from the harbor. What exactly their involvement may have been is unclear, but it seems highly likely that Saint Andrew's lodge was somehow mixed up in the ensuing drama. On that night, members of the lodge had gone to the tavern as arranged, but they did not go through the usual lodge proceedings. Supposedly, the lodge was distracted by a group of colonists disguised as Mohawks exiting the tavern (it is difficult to see how the lodge could have been so distracted—considering all Masonic meetings, as we have seen, took place behind closed doors). This group boarded the East India Company ship and threw 340 chests of tea into the water. Though some of these men were members of the Sons of Liberty, some were certainly Freemasons. Paul Revere is known to have been among the saboteurs, and his had been one of the names on the petition to allow Saint Andrew's to become a grand lodge. He later attained the position of Grand Master of Freemasons for Massachusetts. It seems reasonable to suggest that he was not the only Freemason who had involved himself in the scheme.

There had been Masonic lodges composed of members of the military ranks of various armies since the late 1750s, but with the outbreak of war, an increase of a British military presence also brought yet more lodges to America. Soldiers constantly traveled from one place to another and so could not join and hope to regularly attend a lodge permanently established at any town or city. As was the case in Britain, Antients' lodges were made up largely of artisans, merchants, and those just outside of the aristocratic circles, though this did not halt the appeal of the lodge, but quite the opposite. Membership had increased rapidly and was further swelled by those in the armed forces, both in Britain and America. The American Moderns and Antient lodges sided with the

ABOVE: *A Craft Masonic certificate issued under the jurisdiction of the grand lodge of New York, 1850.*

In the lower-right corner, a master of the lodge holds a scroll bearing the seal of the grand lodge.

revolutionary cause, even as the two camps remained split along Masonic and social lines.

Though the state of New York was given its first Provincial Grand Master by the Moderns of England, in 1739, this colony, too, was becoming increasingly dominated by those of the Antients. Within a short space of time after America's declaration to secede from Britain, Antient lodges formed a large part of the Continental army at Newburgh, New York. In 1752, at the age of twenty, George Washington had been initiated into Freemasonry at Fredericksburg, Virginia (though it has also been alleged that he was initiated into a British military lodge[12] during the war against the French and that he participated in lodge meetings then in a cave near Winchester, Virginia, known today as Washington's Masonic Cave[13]). It is worth noting, however, that while Franklin had joined a Modern lodge, Washington had joined the Antients, and these groups were not, of course, on speaking terms—Washington and Franklin may have been fighting for the same country, but could not have sat in the same lodge. During the Revolutionary War, Washington encouraged his soldiers to join lodges and liked his officers to be Freemasons. At Valley Forge, Washington approved a plan for the Temple of Virtue that not only became the meeting house of the whole camp but appears to have been used by the soldiers' Masonic lodges for their gatherings.[14] It is clear that, like Franklin, Washington also felt the fraternity's ideals suitable to a new America, uplifting for his men. In 1790, Washington wrote:

Being persuaded that a just application of the principles on which the Masonic fraternity is founded must be promotive of private virtue and public prosperity, I shall always be happy to advance the interests of the Society, and to be considered by them a deserving Brother.[15]

Leading Antient Masonry in New York was the Antient York Masons Lodge No. 169. It had followed a number of other military lodges up from Boston in an evacuation of British troops. In 1781, six Antient lodges stationed in New York City clubbed together, establishing an Antient grand lodge, held under the authority of no. 169.[16] In 1783, a peace treaty was signed between the British and the now independent nation of America. By this time the first, or Modern, grand lodge of New York had died. Initially excluded from the new Antient authority, Modern lodges were temporarily left to themselves. However, later the same year, the Antient grand lodge declared that these lodges might be brought under their wing, if they so wished. Now that the war had ended, of course, America, and all lodges and grand lodges on its soil, were utterly independent from Britain. The adoption of the old colonial Modern lodges by the dominant Antients not only made sense but also made for greater prestige. They were not only the old American lodges but, more important, they had proved so fervently pro-American and pro-independence in the face of the British. Given their age, patriotism, and the fact that the Moderns had frequently collected the more affluent members of society, among their ranks were a few

ABOVE: *A representation of George Washington as Freemason from the late 1800s. Washington thought highly of the Masonic institution, encouraging his soldiers to join lodges, and appeared in Masonic regalia for the cornerstone laying ceremony at the nation's capitol.*

men whose names had become near legendary, and that was surely a very large plus.

Though they had originally been issued a charter by George Harrison (made Provincial Grand Master for New York in 1753 by Lord Craysford), one of the most important Modern lodges in the Revolutionary War—New York's own Saint John's lodge—soon solicited for membership of the Antient grand lodge.[17] Another lodge of one-time importance was Union Lodge, no. 8. It had been headed at one point by Robert R Livingston, a well-known, well-liked, and certainly accomplished politician; he was a signatory of the Declaration of Independence and member of the Continental Congress, chancellor for the state of New York (1777–1801), and secretary of foreign affairs (1781–1783). He would soon be made Grand Master of the grand lodge of New York.

Of course some colonists had remained loyal to the British crown, and many of these emigrated to Canada after the war. Among them were a significant number of Freemasons who had fought with British troops. Notably, the first evidence of Freemasonry in Ontario is a certificate dating from 1780. It had been presented to Henry Nelles of New York, who had been initiated into a military lodge in the King's Own Regiment of Foot.[18]

When Franklin returned to Pennsylvania in 1785, the old Moderns were no more. The one-time Grand Master of a Pennsylvanian lodge, Master of the Nine Muses in Paris, and the man who had turned Modern Masonry to the benefit America and the rev-

ABOVE: *Early American dollar coin. On this early American dollar is the Eye of God, as well as thirteen stars representative of the thirteen original states. Around the edge is the inscription,* Nova Constellatio, *"A New Constellation."*

olutionary cause was not a member of American Masonry any more. American lodges were, for the most part, Antient, and any Modern Mason wanting to join an Antient lodge would have to go through the whole process again. Franklin apparently decided not to. At his funeral in 1790, the Antient Order of Free and Accepted Masons were one of the few groups that chose not to be represented. Washington, not Franklin, would become the symbol of American Masonry.

In the years that followed, Washington was elected the Grand Master of Freemasons in the state of Virginia, and the then grand lodge of Pennsylvania suggested that he be made the Grand Master for the

ABOVE: Corn, wine, and oil represent the wages of the stonemason and have traditionally been given to Freemasons on attaining the degree of master Mason. Some lodges still continue this practice.

whole of the United States of America. Neither of these suggestions came to fruition, however. In 1789, George Washington was unanimously elected to become the first president of the United States of America, the date for his inauguration set for April 30 of the same year. Present at the ceremony were General Jacob Morton and General Morgan Lewis, respectively the ceremonial marshal and escort for the president-elect—they too would become Masonic Grand Masters. Chancellor Livingston, Grand Master for New York, led the inauguration but in midceremony discovered that the Bible on which the oath was to be taken was missing. Being held on Wall Street, though, the inauguration was close to the meeting-house of Saint John's lodge, where a Bible was stored for use in their Masonic rituals. General Morton dashed to retrieve it, and the ceremony continued, with the first president taking his oath of office on the Saint John's lodge Bible (today generally referred to as the "Washington Bible"). This would not be Washington's last public ceremony.

On September 18, 1793, the cornerstone for the Capitol building in Washington, DC, was ceremonially laid by the grand lodge of Maryland, with the first president of the United States of America, George Washington, presiding in full Masonic regalia. Included in the *Columbian Mirror* and *Alexandria Gazette*, September 21, 1793, was a lengthy report, which stated:

> The plate was then delivered to the President, who, attended by the Grand master P. T. and three most Worshipful Masters, descended to the cavazion trench and deposed the plate, and laid it on the cornerstone of the Capitol of the United States of America, on which was deposited corn, wine, and oil, when the whole congregation joined in reverential prayers, which was succeeded by Masonic chanting honors, and a volley from the artillery. [19]

(Corn, wine, and oil, are held to represent "plenty" [i.e., abundance or good harvest], "joy," and "peace," respectively, and are symbolic of the wages of the stonemasons at Solomon's Temple. In Britain, sometimes a tracing board and a Bible is displayed at the construction site.

The prestige that Washington brought to the cornerstone ceremony cannot be overestimated. For the next hundred years this Masonic ceremony would be enacted before America's public, celebrating the beginning of construction of buildings large and small, while Masonic lodges became increasingly important to the cultural development of the country. The war had tempered American Freemasonry into a more pragmatic and rational institution than its European counterparts, and after the war it continued largely in this vein, extolling civic virtue and promoting the idea of community built on morality. If, in the first half of the eighteenth century, it had helped to reinforce social distinction, membership in the fraternity now helped members to blur the boundary separating the wealthy and the middle classes. Lodges in Boston also included

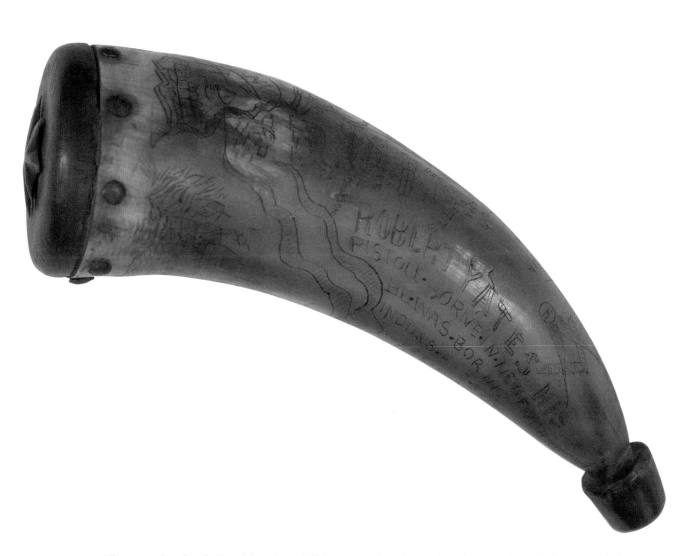

ABOVE: *Like many handcrafted and hand-embellished everyday objects from the post-Revolutionary period, this powder horn is inscribed with a Masonic emblem, in this case the square and compasses.*

men of African descent. While women were still unable to join Masonic lodges, they would also become increasingly accommodated by the fraternity, who would find ways to include them. Most significantly in this regard, Freemasons would either develop, or adopt from the European continent, rituals that were Masonic in principle but that drew on the history and biblical tradition concerning women, rather than men. These were then formed into various quasi-Masonic orders and were available to Freemasons and women (generally the wives and daughters of Freemasons).

Despite the initial moral and civic emphasis of American Freemasonry, it would slowly begin to align itself more fully with the European concept of the fraternity, which of course placed greater weight on its enigmatic qualities. Though it should not be forgotten that derived from Antient Masonry, the American rituals had more symbols than the Moderns in England and had originally been a more esoteric form of the fraternity. De Witt Clinton led the way in this resurgence when, in 1793,[20] he recalled to members of the fraternity the mythology that took Freemasonry back to the ancients. It had been the purpose of Freemasonry, he contended, to cultivate the arts and sciences—philosophy and geometry among those sciences being propagated among the intellectual elite of earlier times. With the war ended, the American Mason allowed himself the luxury of reflecting on the origins of the Masonic order and its mysteries and saw them among the so-called "Mystery Schools" of ancient Greece—in the secret society of the mathematician and mystic, Pythagoras, or in ancient Egypt, for example. Freemasonry may have been imported from Britain, but Britain, apparently, was but one stop on the greater journey that led the unadulterated and secret wisdom of the ancients to America.

Clinton had been initiated into the Dutch-speaking Holland lodge in New York City. It was a lodge that affected the city's cultural and artistic life more than most. It counted among its membership men involved in music, art, poetry, and theater, such as the "father of the American stage," William Dunlap,[21] while some of

ABOVE: This metal invitation was for the semicentennial celebrations of Morton Commandery of Knight Templar masons, held at the New York Academy of Music.

its members—including Clinton—helped in the establishment of various educational and cultural societies.[22] As in Europe, Masonry proved highly attractive to American visual and performing theater artists in particular. Steven C. Bullock has observed that Masonry allowed them to meet prospective patrons, while it gave the artist an air of being a part of America's cultural elite. Yet it was certainly more than this. Highly visual, theatrical, literary, and increasingly cosmopolitan, the lodge was in itself a sort of cultural center, a place of both ideas and natural creativity. It became standard in America (though not in Britain) that, at the culmination of the third degree, the lodge would perform a play about Hiram Abiff, his betrayal by his workmen, his murder, and the discovery and proper burial of his remains. Singing had long formed a large part of early Masonic gatherings—usually in conjunction with

ABOVE: *This handmade and hand-painted apron is from the late 1700s to early 1800s from early American Freemasonry. The three female figures represent Charity, Faith, and Hope. On the left, there appears to be a thistle, an emblem of Scotland, and as such it may be that the owner and/or maker of this apron was born in Scotland. Next to the thistle is a plum overlapping a rule. Another unusual feature of this apron is the single sandal or shoe to the left of Hope. The central arch strongly alludes to the Royal Arch.*

OPPOSITE: *The frontispiece to the fourth edition of Jeremy Cross's* Hieroglyphic Monitor, *1854, shows a knight arising to greet the day.*

highly ritualized forms of toasting—and Masonic songs were printed in the earliest Masonic books, such as Anderson's *Constitutions*. Organ-playing also became a part of lodge rituals. Last, and perhaps most important in regard to America, Freemasonry had a highly complex visual language. Indeed, Freemasonry had, as we have seen, developed its own genre of art, the tracing board.

Yet Masonry not only attracted professional artists and craftsmen, it turned men and sometimes women of lesser skills to the visual arts, though for purely personal enjoyment. Members of the Masonic community and women alike adopted Masonic imagery for their craftwork, carving the square and compasses emblem into a drinking horn or sewing it into a patchwork quilt. Most early-American Masonic aprons were hand-painted or hand-embroidered, sometimes made by Masons but more often by their wives or daughters. The most famous of this trend is certainly that of Mme. Lafayette (wife of General Lafayette), who embroidered a Masonic apron as a gift for George Washington. Such folk artists and artisans were certainly not being paid for their labors, and if non-artists were inspired to produce Masonic types of art, then we can only expect the same of the professional artists of the period.

Household items bearing Masonic imagery were not only manufactured in America but were even imported from abroad. For example, Staffordshire in Britain exported chinaware to America's shores decorated with Masonic symbols sometimes arranged to look like Europe's heraldry, largely, if not solely, used

by the aristocracy and monarchy. This transaction is particularly striking when we realize that Britain itself saw no such blossoming of Masonic decorated household objects, and the symbols of the fraternity were kept almost entirely inside the lodge. Indeed the grand lodges of Britain in particular showed a strong dislike of the pictorial tracing board as it began to appear. Unlike Britain, though, America was not only looking to build its communities, it was also looking to represent itself visually. With public displays by Freemasons such as Washington, first president of the United States, such an enthusiasm for Masonic symbolism was inevitable, because it sent the message that the morals and ideals of the newly independent America were synonymous with those of Freemasonry.

With a greater openness by the fraternity, and with a greater need for galvanizing the community, American Masonry began to cross thresholds that the British lodges would not. Even though it admitted men of other religions, American Freemasonry retained occasional references to the Christian religion in its Ritual until fairly late. Notably, one of the textbooks of American Masonry for 1869, the *General Ahiman Rezon* (traditionally American Masonic books are named after Laurence Dermott's Masonic textbook), reminds the reader that though lodges used to be dedicated to King Solomon, symbolically the first Grand Master of Freemasonry, "Masons professing Christianity" dedicated their lodges to Saint John the Baptist and Saint John the Evangelist.[23] Antient Masonry (the Father of American Masonry) had always nodded subtly to the Christian religion, acknowledging it in some of its rit-

uals also. As noted, Dermott had actually included prayers for Christian and Jewish lodges in his *Ahiman Rezon*. Again, while the Royal Arch was loosely Christian and the Knight Templar degree explicitly so, both of these degrees had of course been practiced, if not invented, by the Antients long before the Moderns adopted them.

Nevertheless, American Masonry was also cosmopolitan in its interest in, and appreciation of, religion. Indeed, there are extensive notes in the *General Ahiman Rezon* (1869) in which we find mentioned the Hindu deities Vishnu, Brahma, and Shiva; the sacred architecture of China, Japan, Greece, and Egypt; the ancient Egyptian god and goddess Osiris or Isis; and, perhaps most impressive of all, the Holy Book of the Persian, Zoroastrian religion, the Zend Avesta.[24] Unlike so much of the earlier European Masonry, however, these did not enter into the Masonic rituals themselves and remained largely study notes. At the time when European Masonry was really forging its exotic and questionable pseudo-Masonic degrees, the colonists of America were worrying far too much about taxes, practical independence from Britain, and human rights to have really been able to develop in this metaphysical direction, though some higher degrees did spring up in America (for example, the Knight Templar degree), we have seen. The trend toward the mystical ultimately became a more literary endeavor, though this itself fed back into the lodge in subtle ways. First of all, it must surely have affected the individual Mason's perception of Masonry. Secondly, while American lodges would admit men so long as they

ABOVE: *Masonic certificate, 1809, from Glenavy, County Antrim, Ireland. It shows that the recipient had attained the Royal Arch and Super Excellent Mason degrees, and was a knight in the Order of the Knights Templar.*

ABOVE: Mark master certificate. The Mark master degree elaborates on the Masonic mythology surrounding the construction of Solomon's Temple, specifically regarding masons' marks. In America, the mark master falls under the jurisdiction of the Royal Arch chapter.

adhered to those points on which the religions agreed, unlike British lodges, they began to advance requirements for initiation that hinted at deeper and more subtle mystical beliefs. New York, for example, requires that a candidate for initiation believes not only in God (of the candidate's religion)—this requirement is almost universal in Freemasonry—but also in the immortality of the soul. While this would hardly disenfranchise many religiously minded persons, it suggests, perhaps, that the potential initiate for American Masonry was supposed to have, in advance, some fairly mature religious concepts.

To some degree American Masonry has remained polarized, with some Masons regarding Freemasonry as essentially civic and community-based, and some others regarding it as mystical, or at least intellectual. While an oversimplification, it is true to a certain extent that this division is mirrored in the figures of Washington and Franklin, who tend to be regarded as model Freemasons by these two camps. Nevertheless, it is the Ancient and Accepted Scottish Rite—formed in the American south in 1802—that is most often championed as the epitome of mystical Masonry in America. Although the Royal Arch and Templar degrees existed elsewhere, in America they were compounded into the so-called "York Rite" that runs parallel to the Scottish Rite (the highest degrees of both are considered equal, despite their being a different number in each). Also in the York Rite is the "Cryptic Rite," the degrees of which (the Royal Master, Select Master, and Super Excellent Master) are considered as "optional." American Royal Arch chap-

ters also adopted other rituals: the Mark Master,[25] Virtual Past Master, and Most Excellent Master. In comparison to most of the higher degrees of the European continent, these are entirely conservative. It is worth taking a brief look at some of the degrees that we have so far not commented upon.

The Mark Master degree elaborates on the myth of Hiram Abiff and introduces the idea of masons' marks, though this ritual can in no way be considered as historically derived from the stonemasons. In America, the York Rite has been, and to a lesser extent still is, considered the "Christian Rite" of Masonry, though only some of the degrees really contain explicit references to Christianity, such as the Knight Templar degree. This degree has been traditionally bestowed on those Masons who professed a belief in specifically Trinitarian Christianity—a belief in the Father, Son, and Holy Ghost, or Spirit. Needless to say, this has led to numerous prominent Freemasons attacking the requirement, and the ritual, as un-Masonic, because Masonry does not discriminate according to a person's religion.

Regarding the Virtual Past Master, traditionally before receiving the Royal Arch, the Freemason would necessarily have served as the Master of a lodge. Advancing to this position, the Master-elect would be required to participate in a short, formal ritual where the "secrets of the chair" (i.e., the chair of the worshipful master) were given to him. As there was found to be a lack of qualified candidates among the Antients—and the Moderns where the Royal Arch was practiced—they adopted the practice of passing

RIGHT: This jewel is worn in the sixteenth Degree of the Scottish Rite, called the Prince of Jerusalem. The narrative of this Degree concerns the trials and tribulations of the builders who constructed the Second Temple. The hands of Justice hold the scales in equal balance, beneath which is a double-edged sword.

Master Masons through the ritual simply to enable them to receive the Royal Arch degree. This practice seems to have been at its height in the 1770s, though the governing bodies of British Freemasonry repeatedly took steps to stop it.[26] Nevertheless, this practice remains still a part of American Masonry today and has been established as the Virtual Past Master degree.

One report, or legend, of the degrees states that a neo-Masonic body called the Council of Princes of Jerusalem[27] was established in 1788 at Charlestown, and that one of its founders archived copies of the Royal and Select Master degrees that had been obtained from Prussia.[28] While it is likely that the degrees originated in Europe, the exact place of their authorship is unknown. Prussia had become a part of myth and symbolism of the Scottish Rite. The narrative of the Select Master degree once again concerns the master builder Hiram Abiff; however, it differs from the third degree in that this ritual states that Hiram Abiff buried treasure in a secret vault.

Other rites, of course, appeared in America, but where they were not able to attach themselves to the ever-enlarging Masonic family of rites and rituals, they simply died out. Nevertheless, they are historically noteworthy. In the first decades of the nineteenth century, for example, the French Rite was popular in New Orleans, compromising the position of both the York and the Scottish Rites.[29] This rite had been created by a French grand lodge called the "Grand Orient" in 1786 and was constructed from seven degrees: those of Craft Masonry, plus the Elect, Scotch Master, Knight of the East, and the Rose Croix. This would most certainly have upset the Scottish Rite Masons, as the Rose Croix degree was given by their body.

Although the Scottish Rite existed early on in America, it did not come to fruition until considerably later, when it was revised and elaborated by a prominent Freemason by the name of Albert Pike (1809–1891). Pike was born in Boston on December 29, 1809. His childhood surroundings were humble; his father was a shoemaker and farmer. It must have seemed that the child was not destined for much. Nevertheless, early in his life the young Albert Pike seems to have betrayed an innate yearning for greater knowledge and broader horizons, throwing himself into whatever learning was available to him in his meager circumstances and displaying a particular enthusiasm for poetry. By the age of fifteen he was teaching by day, saving money from his job to apply for the esteemed Harvard University, while engaged in his own curriculum of learning by night. Pike became not only a Freemason but also an adventurer, a thinker often ahead of his time, and most controversially, a general in the Confederate Army, emerging as one of America's most colorful and sometimes controversial Freemasons. There is still erected in the nation's

Capitol a statue of Pike in Masonic regalia, though his influence is confined to those who have elected over the years to take the Scottish Rite degrees, and this certainly does not include all Freemasons.

Like Benjamin Franklin, Pike was also involved in a type of society not dissimilar to the Masonic fraternity, joining the fraternity of the Oddfellows in 1849, just prior to his initiation into Freemasonry. A year later he entered a Masonic lodge in Little Rock, Arkansas, and within a year had been made a Master Mason. Freemasonry seems to have made an enormous impression on Pike, galvanizing his sometimes contradictory tendencies to philosophizing and adventuring. Pike pursued Freemasonry's myths, its mass of symbols, and its teachings, with such vigor as he had displayed in his youth toward learning generally. It was undoubtedly another adventure for him. Indeed, there is a sense of urgency about Pike's journey through the very many degrees of American Freemasonry. In 1850, Pike became a Royal Arch Mason, and in only a few years more had taken the Knight Templar degree. On March 20, 1853, he entered the Scottish Rite and had all degrees—from the 4th to the 32nd—bestowed on him at Charlestown, South Carolina.[30] The honorary 33rd degree was presented to him a year later in New Orleans. In 1859, Pike's rapid advance through Freemasonry was crowned when he was awarded the position of Sovereign Grand Commander for the Scottish Rite of the Southern Jurisdiction, in essence instituting him as the head of the rite for the southern states.

At the time many of the rituals were in a scant

condition, and most of these were not even enacted but were simply bestowed in name alone, as was largely the case with Pike's reception into the Scottish Rite degrees. The rite, with all its potential, its treasure trove of symbols, and its strange history, nonetheless impressed Pike. He resolved to rewrite them, to add his insights, and imbue the rite with his own understanding of myth and religion, to turn them into a footprint of a giant philosophy. He immersed, and perhaps even lost, himself in the project. He withdrew into his library in Little Rock. Removed from the world, Pike was at one point reported dead, and suitable eulogies printed in the newspapers, though naturally the adventurer and his friends simply took this as an excuse to note his reemergence and held a festival to celebrate his return to the world.[31]

Pike's work, however, would be temporarily interrupted by the turmoil that would soon overtake America. Since the Revolution, the gulf between the northern and southern states had increasingly widened. During the colonial period slavery had existed throughout America. It had even been proposed that the Declaration of Independence should blame Britain for all the evils of slavery, though this was dropped after some reflection showed the accusation to be highly questionable. Nevertheless, slavery died out in the North, and for some time after the Revolutionary War it seemed that it would simply fizzle out in the South as well. However, in 1793 Eli Whitney developed the mechanics that allowed textile mills to use short-staple cotton in their production.[32] The South could grow this in abundance, and a cheap labor force would keep the cost of production down, making the mills competitive in international trade. By 1860, cotton had become a massive industrial and economic force, accounting for 57 percent of all American export. Slavery had, once again, become a factor in the South's economy.

In 1860, however, presidential elections were held. The Republican Party nominated Abraham Lincoln, whose opinions regarding slavery were perhaps self-consciously restrained. The Democrats were split on the issue, and the southern and northern wings of the party nominated different candidates, costing them the election. Worried all along about the election, South Carolina's legislature remained in session awaiting the results. When news of Lincoln's victory reached the legislature, they voted to withdraw from the Union. Soon the states of Alabama, Georgia, Florida, Louisiana, Texas, and Mississippi followed, forming themselves into the Confederate States of America. In 1861, Senator John J. Crittenden of Kentucky drafted a compromise that might, at least, have brought the southern states back into the Union. Accordingly, slavery was to be banned in the North, but would be protected in the South, while states could enter, or rather reenter, the Union, in a semi–self governing capacity, answerable to its constituents, and more or less free to withdraw again if deemed politically expedient. There were other provocative issues in the relationship between the North and South, of course, but slavery proved the sticking point for Lincoln, who refused to sign the treaty. [33]

When the Civil War broke out not long after,

charters for lodges composed of military men of one or other regiment were granted by grand lodges, though with a definite unease. Generally speaking, grand lodges had always demanded to be the sole authority for their state. A lodge composed of soldiers, though, would be bound to cross state lines, and even if the states in question were on opposite sides of the political gulf, this seemed like a violation of the principle.[34] In the first year of the war, New York, for example, issued charters for eight traveling lodges, though near the close of the war under a new Grand Master it refused to charter any more. A large number of soldiers and officers were Freemasons and considered each other brothers, whether on the same or opposing political and military sides, and this certainly yielded a number of remarkable events that seem largely out of place in war. Masons felt they should help fellow Masons, but the lodge impressed upon its members their duty to help the community as a whole, and it was probably this that weighed most on the individual's conscience. Freemasons still thought of themselves as the builders of America, as well as the mortar that held it together as one. Even before the outbreak of hostilities, Freemasons wrote letters to grand lodges on the other side of the divide, imploring them to help avoid an outbreak of war, though they were not in a position to affect any political decision-making.

As the Union Army attacked Little Rock, the

RIGHT: Tobacco pipe, mid-1900s. This tobacco pipe is decorated with the square and compasses and the letter "G." These symbols are traditionally found together in American Freemasonry.

Grand Master of Iowa and commanding general Thomas H. Benton had Albert Pike's house and library guarded.[35] Similarly, close to the outbreak of hostilities, Jackson H. Chase, quartermaster of the Third Regiment of the New York Volunteers, came across an abandoned building used as a Masonic lodge as his regiment moved through Virginia. Masonic furniture, regalia, lodge records, and a charter were all found inside, and the rightful owner discovered to be one Tammany Lodge. The Volunteers' commander, Major-General Buttler—himself a Freemason—was informed, and Tammany Lodge's possessions were sent under a flag of truce to the grand lodge of Virginia for safekeeping until they could be returned to their rightful owners.[36] These are but two examples of many.

The Civil War ended in 1864 as the Confederate forces found themselves beleaguered, exhausted, and outmatched. Afterward, Pike resumed his rewriting of the Scottish Rite's rituals and in 1871 published his seminal work *Morals and Dogma*, intended as a guide for Scottish Rite Masons. Although this lengthy work dedicates a section to each of the degrees, one could gain very little information on the rituals themselves, as the text is deliberately much broader, discussing philosophy, religion, and symbols as might be related to the Scottish Rite. In this way, *Morals and Dogma* reflects the intellectual approach that American Masons have taken since early in the eighteenth century, and which is reflected in the extensive notes of the *General Ahiman Rezon* that we mentioned earlier, as well as works by British Masons such as William Preston.

Pike would not rest on his laurels and continued to devote himself untiringly to the Masonic fraternity. On October 4, 1877, he instituted the Provincial Grand Lodge of the Royal Order of Scotland and is referred to as "Sir and General Albert Pike" ("Sir" being the title bestowed on a member of the Royal order) in a warrant for the said grand lodge issued at Edinburgh. The Royal Order of Scotland, we might note, is a Masonic society, generally made available by invitation to Masons who have passed through at least thirty-two degrees of the Scottish Rite. Three years later Pike attained the highest position in a Masonic Rosicrucian society then known by the name of the Societas Rosicruciana Republicae Americae. His exalted title: Supreme Magus.

ABOVE: Pointing the Way, *Paul Orban, 1950s. In this painting Orban appears to play on the tension between the colonist and the native American, portraying Freemasonry as the ethical banner.*

Chapter 10: Last Rites

In 1866 two prominent British Freemasons, Robert Wentworth Little and Kenneth Mackenzie, founded the Societas Rosicruciana in Anglia (the "Rosicrucian Society in England"), availing it to only a few master Masons that they deemed suitable for initiation.

Mackenzie had previously been initiated into a Rosicrucian society in Austria and had apparently received a charter to establish a Rosicrucian society in England, while Little had come across writings of a German Rosicrucian order and translated them. In addition, it is possible that an older strain of British Rosicrucianism also fed into the society. Indeed, it is notable that the rituals translated by Little were not adopted wholesale; rather, the rituals for the British society were written somewhat gradually. Moreover, from the beginning of the Societas Rosicruciana, there were branches in both England and Scotland (the latter called the Societas Rosicruciana in Scotia), and it appears that, in the first few years after their formation, the rituals for both branches differed and were not then lifted from one central source. These were not the only differences between the two groups. While membership in the English society was limited to Freemasons, this does not appear to have been the case in Scotland,[1] though even in England the society was similarly viewed as distinct from and not otherwise being a part of Freemasonry.

Some groups or clubs claiming to be Rosicrucian were active in Britain during the nineteenth century. One such society, which had at its head a Doctor Falk,[2] was established in England in the first half of the century. As late as the 1860s, a group called the Manchester Rosicrucians was still in existence in that city, though it had become little more than a diner's club by that point. This group in turn claimed to be derived from, or a revival of, an older Rosicrucian group. One claim regarding the origin of the Societas Rosicruciana is that this older organization may have fed into what is sometimes thought of as the revived Societas Rosicruciana in Anglia[3] when it was founded by Little and Mackenzie. Nevertheless, it can hardly be doubted that another catalyst for the establishment of such a group was the introduction of the Ancient and Accepted Scottish Rite into Britain only a comparatively short time before, and indeed, there are at least some similarities between the two bodies, though the raison d'être of the Societas Rosicruciana has always been more literary than ritualistic. In its early years, however, members of one local group wore their

ABOVE: *Today in Britain and continental Europe, the apron of a master Mason is emblazoned with three rosettes. In America, however, a plain white apron is typically worn.*

ABOVE: A highly elaborate, hand-painted apron illustrating the story of three related degrees from the Scottish Rite of Freemasonry (these are the ninth, tenth, and eleventh degrees, called the Elect or Elu of the Nine, Elu of the Fifteen, and Elu of the Twelve, respectively).

Masonic Scottish Rite regalia to the society's meetings, though this was certainly frowned upon by other groups under the umbrella of the Societas Rosicruciana.

However, the differing elements of the rituals and proceedings merely serve to hint at the different opinions about the purpose of the Rosicrucian society. Curiously, Little had wanted to make the Societas Rosicruciana a branch of Freemasonry, specifically an honorary or "side-degree" to that of the Red Cross of Constantine[4] (this is an honorary Masonic body, existing also in America). Notably, the society's first periodical was frequently taken up with information on the aforementioned degree, written by Little. In 1872 the Societas Rosicruciana in Anglia and the governing body for the Red Cross of Constantine started putting out a joint periodical called *The Rosicrucian and Red Cross*, though this eventually ceased to be published. Despite this, the Rosicrucian society in question was meant to provide a forum for its intellectually active and philosophically inclined members, whose collective research would, it was hoped, dispel much of the nonsense that has always surrounded—and, indeed, still surrounds—such subjects. Not all of the early members were inspired by the notion of a literary Rosicrucian society, however, and it appears that few attempted to contribute any articles to the then semi-Rosicrucian periodical, and this, in fairness to Little, was at least part of the reason for the degree of concentration on Freemasonry. [5]

Masonic research lodges have since sprung up, and many continue to prosper. Unlike other lodges, these do not bestow any degrees and are generally open only to Master Masons, their aim being the exploration of the history of Freemasonry along scholarly lines. It must be admitted, however, that the "scholarship" of the Rosicrucian society was, and is, in many senses closer to personal theory or philosophy. William Wynn Westcott, who became the Supreme Magus of the English society toward the end of the nineteenth century, would complain that members of the society had rarely entered into historical research, even regarding the history of the Societas Rosicruciana itself. Yet members did adhere faithfully

ABOVE: *Christian symbolism is evident in this jewel of the Societas Rosicruciana, established by Freemasons in the nineteenth century.*

ABOVE: *New York Mason Society certificate, 1805. The New York Mason Society was not a part of Freemasonry, though this club adopted much Masonic symbolism. Note the arch, the stonemason s tools, and the two figures with their hands gripped. In various ways, Freemasonry has always been linked with other, similar societies.*

to the aims of the society, which is in part the study of the Kabbalah and intellectual and allegorical alchemy.[6]

The Rosicrucian Society spread to America (it was originally titled the Societas Rosicruciana Republicae Americae, though it is currently called the Masonic Societas Rosicruciana in Civitatiibus Foederatis, or the Rosicrucian Society in the United States), Canada, and elsewhere by the end of the nineteenth century. The Rosicrucian Society in York, England, initiated a group of Freemasons visiting from Pennsylvania, who later received a charter to establish their own branch from the Societas Rosicruciana in Scotia. This project came to fruition in 1879 with the establishment of the Pennsylvanian branch. A year later another branch in New York had been established.[7]

The Rosicrucian Society is in fact more widely known as a sort of stepping stone to the creation of yet another society, the Hermetic Order of the Golden Dawn. The Hermetic Order was created somewhere around 1887, in large part by William Wynn Westcott and S. L. MacGregor Mathers, another leading light in the Rosicrucian society. One legend has it that Westcott discovered the foundational documents of the Golden Dawn among a collection of books originally owned by one of the members of the Societas Rosicruciana in Anglia, another that these were uncovered by chance in a bookstore in London, and yet another that they were discovered in a Masonic library in London. This last legend, notably, is identical to one story regarding the origin of the Societas Rosicruciana, and it would seem that the histories of the two societies have become confused.

However the Golden Dawn came to acquire the "cipher manuscripts," as they are known, it was alleged that they contained the name and address of a Rosicrucian and resident of Nuremberg, Anna Sprengel, with whom the founding members supposedly corresponded, obtaining the necessary charter to establish the Hermetic Order.[8] Notably, the year following the creation of the Hermetic Order, a book of German Rosicrucian secret symbols was displayed to a branch of the Societas Rosicruciana. It had previously been in the possession of the Reverend A. F. A. Woodford, who is listed in their records of the meeting as belonging to the Golden Dawn, though, for unknown reasons, he had declined repeated invitations to join the Rosicrucian Society.[9]

The previous year Westcott and Mathers had met Dr. Anna Kingsford, a vocal feminist, author of papers on women's rights, and owner and editor of a women's magazine. With her encouragement, the Hermetic Order of the Golden Dawn began to accept women as members,[10] unlike the Masonic and Rosicrucian societies[11] that they otherwise belonged to. Members of the Golden Dawn were expected to study spiritual alchemy as well as Kabbalistic philosophy and the symbolism of Tarot cards, though the purpose of the society was not so much intellectual study as it was the practice of ritualistic mysticism. Eventually the Golden Dawn would embody an extraordinarily elaborate structure of almost countless rituals and degrees. The degree, or grade, structure of the Golden Dawn, which is more or less identical to that of the Golden Rosicrucians, became compartmentalized into distinct orders, the second being an obvious reference to Rosicrucianism: Ordo Rosae Rubeae et Aureae Crucis (Order of the Ruby Rose and Golden Cross).

The Golden Dawn attracted not only some important and forward-thinking women to the order but also a few prominent men who were not a part of the Masonic fraternity, not the least of which was the Irish poet W. B. Yeats, initiated in 1890. Yeats had met an actress by the name of Florence Farr when her brother-in-law had painted his portrait.[12] Farr was soon acting in the central role of *A Sicilian Idyll: A Pastoral Play in Two Scenes*, and Yeats busied himself in helping to arrange the scenes. As Mary K. Greer observes, Yeats had come across such theatrics in the Golden Dawn,[13] whose rituals verged on being plays, albeit ones laden with occult symbolism. Farr was beautiful and intelligent, she read poetry and had an interest in ancient civilization, and naturally Yeats lost little time in introducing her to the Golden Dawn.

Perhaps the most flamboyant and controversial character to be initiated into the Golden Dawn was the twentieth-century adventurer, mountaineer, poet, author, sometime dabbler in the fine arts, and practicing magician, Aleister Crowley. He was initiated into the Hermetic society in a hired Masonic hall in London in 1898, though he first came into contact with Mathers two years later. This contact led him to travel to Mexico City, where he was formerly introduced to the mysteries of Freemasonry, being awarded the thirty-third degree of the Scottish Rite. The Masonic body that he had joined, however, appears to have edged itself toward an unorthodox ritualized mysticism and was not considered legitimately Masonic by regular Masonic lodges, so Crowley was not acknowledged as a Freemason once back in Britain. The adventurer, for his part, was not overly impressed with his supposed Scottish Rite experience and considered himself to have learned little from it.[14] Crowley later went on to form a secret mystical society called the Argenteum Astrum (Silver Star), of which the British fine art painter Austin Spare was at one point a member.

Another prominent and esoterically inclined Freemason, John Yarker, also became involved with a literary or philosophical-type society espousing various mystical teachings, called the Theosophical Society, established in New York by Mme. Helena Blavatsky. Yarker sent Blavatsky two certificates giving her membership in two different orders. One of these was a co-Masonic order (i.e., one having a membership composed of men and women), and the other was Sat B'Hai, a Hindu society founded by members of an Anglo-Indian army regiment and brought to Britain around 1872. The Theosophical Society of New York adopted the secret signs of the Sat B'hai, though this practice did not last long, as the society disliked the idea of straying away from knowledge, or theory, into the dangerous world of practice. Yeats himself was thrown out of the Theosophical Society for participating in Hermeticism after he joined the Golden Dawn. However, many of the early members of the society were Freemasons, and at one point Blavatsky and members important to her society considered associating it with a Masonic body. One

ABOVE: Red leather Scottish Rite apron, hand-painted with sun and moon, later 1800s.

swami, Dayānand Sarasvati of Bombay, apparently promised the prominent Theosophist Colonel Olcott that he would write suitable rituals for the society's London and New York branches, though the society did not proceed with these plans.[15] Blavatsky appears not to have acted on her high-ranking, and highly questionable, neo-Masonic credentials and seems not to have really understood what the award entitled her to anyway. Nevertheless, after she had established her group, Blavatsky returned the favor to Yarker, awarding him honorary membership in the Theosophical Society.[16]

ABOVE: Although this less-than-subtle medal bears the square and compasses, it is not Masonic but belongs to another fraternity called the Junior Order of United American Mechanics.

BELOW: Shriner-figure whiskey bottle, early 1900s. The Shriners' Society is in effect a kind of spoof on Masonry and is well known for its parades in which Shriners drive around in miniature cars.

The writings of Mme. Blavatsky had perhaps their greatest effect in Germany, especially regarding the philosophies of that country's various secret occult societies. It is interesting to note that Crowley would eventually become the head of one such order, the Ordo Templi Orientis (Order of Oriental Templars), which had been modeled after numerous rites, such as Memphis and Mizraim and the Scottish Rite, though, as most Freemasons would point out, not with much legitimacy. Nevertheless, the order still bestows various rituals modeled on such Masonic degrees as the Rose Croix, though, because it is drawn from a wide range of myths, philosophies, and rituals, it is naturally far removed from the ritual as it is practiced in regular Freemasonry.

Over many centuries, Freemasonry has spread all across the globe and can be found as far afield as Australia, Japan, Egypt, and Jamaica. Australia is a relative newcomer to Freemasonry, seeing the first Masonic lodge established in Sydney in 1803. This, however, was dissolved by the governor of the city, who may also have had some of its members arrested. Nonetheless, seventeen years later a military regiment was stationed in Sydney, and had within its ranks a lodge dating back to 1752, when it had been chartered by the Irish grand lodge. They established what was essentially the first permanent Masonic lodge in Australia. Later lodges were also chartered by the Scottish and English grand lodges. Masonry in Australia is now independent of these mother countries, and grand lodges exist for its various provinces, including Tasmania, New South Wales, South Australia, and New Zealand.[17]

As in the United States, the first Masonic lodges in Canada appear to have been of the Modern type. The first lodge in Quebec ultimately derived its authority from a charter issued by Saint John's Lodge in Boston. Later, as America won its independence from Britain, emigration to Canada brought more lodges, most of which were, again, of the Moderns. By 1818, Canada had a Grand Royal Arch chapter. In 1855, forty-three lodges held a convention to unify the lodges of Canada, though problems surfaced when the council essentially established itself as a grand lodge. This upset various other Masonic lodges in the country, though the matter was eventually resolved.

The history of Freemasonry in any country makes for interesting reading, not least of all as it has often taken on local characteristics and has invariably found itself a part of the greater culture, reflected in its arts and crafts. Freemasonry was established in Madrid, Spain, at the beginning of the eighteenth century, though it was persecuted until the ascent of Joseph Bonaparte to the Spanish throne. Political upheaval in the twentieth century again saw Free-

masons attacked. A similar situation can be found in Russia. The Craft was subject to various bans over the eighteenth century and disappeared with the establishment of Communism in the twentieth century. Though, as Russian society has edged its way continually closer to democracy, Freemasonry has begun to reestablish itself in a small way.

With the spread of Masonry, the fraternity has developed somewhat differently from country to country. Perhaps one of the major differences between the Masonry of various countries is the addition of extra rites and clubs that have sometimes become appended to the Masonic structure. Though quite active in America, for example, the Order of the Eastern Star (open to male Freemasons and women) does not exist in Britain. Likewise one of the most well known fraternities in America is the Ancient Arabic Order of the Nobles of the Mystic Shrine, more commonly known as the "Shriners." What is generally not known about the club is that its membership is composed of Freemasons and is, in essence, another Masonic club. However, this society parodies the Masonic institution, albeit in a good-humored way.

There are several myths that surround the origin of the Shriners. Purportedly, the original rituals of the Shriners were translated from Arabic texts kept in the archives of the Order at Aleppo, Syria, and brought to the West by Rizak Allah Hassoon Effendee, a scholar of Arabic poetry and history.[18] Another popular myth suggests that the comedian William J. Florence was touring outside of America when he met Yusef Churia, a well-known scholar of East Asian culture.

ABOVE: Matchbook holder, early 1900s. This matchbook holder is embossed with a square and compasses, trowel, gavel, and level, among other Masonic symbols.

Florence supposedly impressed the scholar and was taken to the sultan who headed the Shrine, being inducted into the Order at Cairo. According to Florence, however, he was introduced to the Shrine in France, then headed by Yusef Churi Bey, and was given a copy of the Shriners' rituals. He departed for Algiers shortly afterward.[19]

It is certain, however, that in 1871 a group of Masons met in New York to discuss the establishment of the Shriner fraternity, which was accomplished a year later with Mecca Temple.[20] Only Freemasons who have become Knight Templar or thirty-second degree Scottish Rite Masons (i.e., have attained the highest degrees of either the York or Scottish Rites of Freemasonry in America) are allowed to join the Shrine, which also suggests that it might have originally been meant as some extra esoteric rite. However, even if this was the intention, the fraternity has become a sort of spoof on Masonry and, except for their emphasis on charity, there is nothing serious about the society at all, which is essentially anti-elite and exists otherwise only for fun. It is notable that one of its founders was a comedian.

The Shriners run numerous hospitals for children that are free of charge to the general public. The society is well known to the general public for its fund-raising activities, such as putting on circuses and parades in which they often drive miniature cars while wearing their trademark red fezzes. Similar to the Shriners is a lesser-known American social and charitable society called Mystic Order of Veiled Prophets of the Enchanted Realm, wisely referred to as

ABOVE: Shriner fez, mid-1900s. This fez bears the insignia of the Shriners along with that of the particular Shriner group or "Temple" that the member belonged to.

ABOVE: *A highly ornate pin worn by members of the Mystic Order of Veiled Prophets of the Enchanted Realm (the Grotto).*

cordant bodies are considered to be merely optional; they are not promoted by the grand lodges and are similarly not pursued by every Freemason. Again, not all of the societies and clubs we have mentioned exist in every country: the Shriners, for example, are largely an American and Canadian phenomenon and do not exist in Britain. We have already noted the existence of research societies or lodges that are situated at the opposite end of the Masonic spectrum. Such lodges exist all over the world and naturally attract Freemasons who are inclined to historical research and who are eager to be involved in dialogue regarding the history and development of Freemasonry. In addition to these lodges, there are also various groups of Masons that meet informally to discuss the history and symbolism of Freemasonry as well as similar, and related, phenomena. Though these formal and informal intellectual societies have gained little attention outside of the Masonic institution, they reflect the early history of Freemasonry as a cultural society, whose purpose is to aid the growth of its members intellectually as well as ethically or spiritually.

The Masonic fraternity often speaks of its "mysteries," and it is undoubtedly true that the Craft embodies many interesting intellectual and cultural elements and themes that have been lost elsewhere. The three degrees of Craft Masonry alone took centuries to evolve through the practices, rituals, and myths of stonemasonry and parallel the evolution of society at large. Yet, while we have encountered Hermes, King Solomon, and Euclid in some of the stonemasons' myths—and while these myths remain in

the Grotto, and this again is open to Freemasons, although attaining any degree beyond that of master Mason is not required. Not to be outdone by the Shrine, a black fez is standard regalia of the Grotto.

Freemasonry is a complex institution, composed of various clubs, societies, and rituals, although it must be stressed that in English-speaking countries at least, Freemasonry proper is considered to be only the three degrees (as well as, sometimes, the Royal Arch degree). In those countries, the higher degrees and various con-

LEFT: Unusually, this early Shriner ornament contains the double-headed eagle, symbol of the Scottish Rite.

many ways an enigma—we have noted the intellectualization of stonemasonry in the seventeenth and eighteenth centuries and the emergence of Craft masonry, or Freemasonry proper, at the beginning of the latter century. We have seen also the emergence of other, neo-Masonic rituals, which drew for example on alchemy and Kabbalah. Again, apart from this more obvious mysticism, it is highly likely that far subtler mystical concepts, expounded through the language of geometry and architecture that can be found in the early Christian notion of God as Architect, were deliberately adopted by the Masonic fraternity. Yet we have also witnessed this tradition in a broader context: in myths and studies of Solomon's Temple and in the studies of John Dee, Johannes Kepler, and Sir Isaac Newton, among others. It seems no exaggeration to say that Freemasonry embodies a mystical tradition that has been lost elsewhere.

Appendix: Women and Freemasonry

If Freemasonry is typically seen as a men's club, some other societies have only ever admitted women, such as the Princesses of the Crown and the Society of Sappho, both of which were established in the latter half of the eighteenth century, the former in Saxony and the latter apparently in Paris. An Order of the Happy Ones (Felicitaires) was established in the early 1740s in France, admitting men and women and strongly resembling Freemasonry, though its rituals and symbols were based on the narrative of a voyage from the Isle of Felicity. Remarkably, the ban on Freemasonry by the Roman Catholic Church itself helped to create one of the more famous Masonic-like societies, the peculiarly named Order of Mopses, which likewise admitted both sexes. The Order seems to have been created by a number of German Catholics who were caught between their desires to join Masonry and to comply with the wishes of the Church. Like Freemasonry, the Order had secret signs, passwords, and a ritual that is in many ways very similar to that of Masonry. Thus, for example, a square and circle were drawn on the floor and given symbolic meaning explained to the initiate during the ceremony. (The square represents the foundation of society, and the circle the actions of a Mopse.) Because the Order espoused love and faithfulness, they took their name from the German word for pug dog, *Mops*, which they regarded as symbolic of these attributes.

However, regarding Freemasonry, it appears that women began to be admitted into Masonic lodges in a systematic way in France somewhere in the 1740s, becoming what is now variously called co-Masonry or adoptive Masonry. However, rumors suggest that at least a few women were initiated into lodges here and there even before this. Though the details of the story might be questionable, it is clear that one Miss St. Leger was made a Freemason at the beginning of the eighteenth century. According to one account, a lodge held in County Cork, Ireland, by Viscount Doneraile, his sons, and his friends was reportedly disturbed by the Viscount's daughter, Miss St. Leger. She had fallen asleep in a library adjoining the lodge room and had awoken at some point during the proceedings, which she was able to view through a hole in the wall, due to some unfinished construction. She was apparently discovered by the butler, who was acting as the symbolic guard, or Tyler, for the lodge. The members of the lodge were alerted, and faced with the fact that she now knew many of the mysteries of Freemasonry, they apparently decided to make Miss St. Leger a Freemason of the lodge.

Another version of the story says that Miss St. Leger hid herself in a grandfather clock and on being discovered, or announcing herself to the lodge, was then made a Freemason. This theme is also shared by the tale of a woman supposedly made a Mason in one Royal Rosicrucian Lodge at Suffolk. Having hid herself in such a clock, the woman in question was apparently startled by the clock striking eleven, and, panicked, rushed out into the lodge, where she was immediately elected Deputy Grand-Mistress. While it may be that such stories are not in every way accurate, it seems that Miss St. Leger was made a Mason early in the eighteenth century, and other women may also have been adopted into Masonic lodges as such. It is perhaps noteworthy that the reported initiation of Viscount Doneraile's daughter predate the establishment of the Irish Grand Lodge, as does the exposé *A Letter from the Grand*

Mistress. According to the letter, a lodge of female Freemasons was "kept at Mr. Painter's Female Coffee-House every Tuesday from Nine in the Morning to Twelve, and the Tenth Day of every Month in the Year; where all Ladies of true Hearts and sound Morals shall be admitted without Swearing."

While the initiation of women at the beginning of the eighteenth century was an extremely rare occurrence, women would be increasingly accommodated by many Masonic bodies in various countries. Eventually, women would find themselves admitted to lodges as female Freemasons. (It might be pointed out that women Masons have not been subject to the same requirement of exposing the chest, for example, but rather wear a type of toga that is tied differently for each ritual, in such a way as not to expose the body.) It is interesting to note that the women first admitted to such Masonic and Masonic-like bodies were not only well educated but were also often ahead of their time and often ardent feminists. In 1882, Miss Maria Desaimes, a writer on the subject of women's suffrage, was initiated into a French lodge known as the Les Libres Penseurs, or "freethinkers," which was independent from the country's Grand Lodges. In more recent times, the risqué entertainer Josephine Baker was initiated as a Freemason into Lodge La Nouvelle Jerusalem in 1960 in Paris, under the jurisdiction of the feminine Grand Lodge of France formed in 1945.

In 1890, the French Lodge La Jerusalem Ecossais issued a circular asking lodges to debate the subject of allowing women to become Freemasons and participate in lodges alongside men. The following year a body for initiating men and women as Freemasons, called Le Droit Humain, was created from or by La Jerusalem Ecossais. The co-Masonic organization formally announced its existence circa 1894, though it appears not to have received any support from other Grand Lodges at that time. Nevertheless, it has also developed its own Scottish Rite body and bestows these degrees on its male and female members.

By the first decade of the twentieth century, universal co-Masonry, as it was then known, had thousands of members spread across the globe. Annie Bessant, feminist and student of Mme. Blavatsky, became a member at Benares, India, and later one of the leaders of one branch of Le Droit Humain, though she had initially rejected co-Masonry as bourgeois. The lodge to which she was first introduced had among its membership several aristocrats, and at that point Bessant was a socialist. Notably, an Indian or Theosophical element is present in this co-Masonic rite, and the three degrees are collectively known as the "dharma working" (*dharma* being both a Hindu and Buddhist term for "law"). There are still mixed lodges under the jurisdiction of Le Droit Humain, some of which exist outside of France, though it has not attracted women or men as might be expected and remains one of the smaller Masonic organizations.

If some French lodges began admitting women, American lodges developed their own Masonic-like degrees and rites for women that accentuated their virtues, especially as illustrated in the Bible, in a way similar to the use of the myth of Hiram Abiff (Old Testament) by Freemasonry. Prior to the middle of the nineteenth century, there existed several such rites that were available to Freemasons and their female relatives. The degree called the Mason's Daughter and the so-called Kindred degree were open only to those Masons and their wives and daughters. The ritual of the Mason's Daughter was based on the legend of Mary, the sister of Lazarus, and the latter degree was based on the Biblical story of Ruth. However, the most widespread and probably the most successful rite of its kind in America today is the Order of the Eastern Star. The Rite is open to (male) Freemasons and women in general, although the head position is only available to a woman of the chapter, and men play a somewhat subordinate role.

The Order of the Eastern Star probably began life in France or Sweden around the middle of the eighteenth century, where adoptive rites appeared and disappeared like so many other neo-Masonic bodies. How it came to enter America is unknown, but there can be little doubt that the country received a great many unorthodox Masonic rites that emanated from the European continent. The beginnings of the rite in America were rather humble. It was organized by an American Freemason by the name of Robert Morris, who imparted the rite to his wife and then later on to other Masons and their relatives. There appears to have been little in the way of ceremony, and even less drama. Nevertheless, he was able to establish a governing body called the Supreme Constellation of the American Adoptive Rite in New York City in only a short space of time (ca. 1855). The ritual of the Eastern Star is based on the stories of several female figures, largely derived from the Bible. The symbols of the ritual are an open Bible, lilies of the valley, a sun, a lamb, and a lion, while the "heroines" of the degree are represented by a sword wrapped in a veil, a broken column, and a sheaf of corn, among other symbols.

Just over ten years later, another Freemason, the Masonic scholar Robert Macoy, reorganized the rite, and jurisdiction over it essentially passed to him when Morris departed America. Typical of the history of Freemasonry, Macoy later added another mixed body called the Order of Amaranth, the first chapter of which was founded in New York in 1883. Both the Order of the Eastern Star and the Order of Amaranth remain active, and the latter may have even have enjoyed a small revival over the last century. It is interesting to note that Prince Hall Masonry still retains many more female-orientated rites, which work alongside and correspond to the regular Masonic degrees and rites. Level with the Masonic Craft Lodge is the Order of the Eastern Star; level with the Royal Arch is a rite known as the Heroines of Jericho; for the Cryptic Rite (Royal and Select Masters) is the Circle of Perfection; for the Knight Templar Degree, there is a corresponding Ladies of the Templar Crusaders; finally, the Scottish Rite is on par with the Order of the Golden Circle.

Glossary of Terms

Accepted Mason: A term for a Freemason common in the seventeenth century.

Ancient and Accepted Scottish Rite: A Masonic structure, or rite, of thirty-two degrees (including the three craft degrees) plus an honorary thirty-third degree. (In Great Britain, this is referred to as the Ancient and Accepted Rite.)

Antient Masons: Freemasons under the jurisdiction of the "Antients" (Ancients). This fraternity merged with the premier grand lodge of England in the first quarter of the nineteenth century. Antient Masonry eventually established itself in America, where most Freemasonic rituals are of the Antient type.

Blazing Star: A representation of divinity. It is usually portrayed as a star with the Eye of God at its center and rays of light pouring out of it.

Blue Lodge: The term "lodge" is usually reserved for bodies of Masons who are responsible for bestowing only the Three Degrees. Higher degrees or rites are usually given by bodies of Masons known as "chapters" or "encampments."

Catechism: A dialogue composed of questions and answers used for teaching new members the meaning of the Masonic ritual and various Masonic symbols.

Charter: 1. To charter: to establish or authorize a group of Freemasons to form themselves into a lodge. 2. A document showing the legitimacy of a lodge.

Craft (or Craft Masonry): The first three degrees of Freemasonry only, as considered derived from the craft of stonemasonry.

Degree: A ritual or grade of Freemasonry.

Entered Apprentice (sometimes Apprentice): The first, or initiatory degree into Freemasonry.

Euclid's 47th Proposition: Otherwise known as the Pythagorean theorem; used by builders to create a right angle, especially in regard to the first corner of any construction.

Fellowcraft (earlier Fellow Craft): The second degree in Freemasonry.

Fraternity: A society composed of male members, or "brotherhood." A society exclusively made up of female members is referred to as a "sorority."

Geometric Mason: A term for a Freemason common in the eighteenth century.

Geometry: The art of producing and manipulating various shapes, usually angular, such as the square, rectangle, and pentagram, as well as the circle or ellipse.

Grand Lodge: A governing body for lodges in a specific area or province composed of Freemasons of different lodges.

Grand Master: The head of a governing body of Freemasons, whose sole purpose is to oversee the Masonic lodges of its jurisdiction (e.g., Pennsylvania, England and Wales). The term as used by Benjamin Franklin's lodge in Philadelphia seems incongruent with the use of the term generally and seems in this case to indicate the Worshipful Master.

Hermetic Tradition/Hermeticism: The name of this tradition is derived from its supposed, or mythical, founder, Hermes Trismegistus. Generally speaking, the Hermetic tradition and Hermeticism refer to the tradition of alchemy, whether regarded in philosophical and spiritual or scientific terms.

Kabbalah (also Cabala): Mystical philosophy and practices drawn from earlier Jewish mysticism and developed among the Jews of Europe around the twelfth century, especially in France and Spain. Later Christianized forms appeared, generally referred to as Christian Kabbalah.

Lodge: 1. A group of Freemasons who meet regularly in their position as Freemasons and whose activities accord with those laid down by a grand lodge, or a group of stonemasons or Freemasons meeting for a common purpose (usually fraternal). 2. A lodge building or room.

Master Mason: A Freemason who has attained the third degree (not to be confused with the Master of a lodge). In English-speaking countries, this is considered the highest degree, despite their being numerous others, these being considered merely "extra" degrees.

Master of a Lodge: *see* Worshipful Master.

Moderns: Originally a disparaging term for the premier Grand Lodge of England and Freemasons under its jurisdiction. This term was employed by Freemasons of other jurisdictions, who claimed to be older than the premier Grand Lodge.

Mosaic Pavement: *see* Square Pavement.

Old Charge: One of the old texts written by builders' lodges that records a mythological history of building.

Order: A series of grades or rituals, independent or semi-independent from Freemasonry.

Past Master: A Freemason who has served a term as the Worshipful Master of a Lodge of Freemasons.

Prussia: This was one of the largest three states of the Holy Roman Empire of Germany. It is of minor symbolic importance in the Ancient and Accepted Scottish Rite.

Quasi-Masonic: A society basing its structure and/or rituals and teachings on those of Freemasonry, though not ordained by any official Masonic Grand Lodge or governing body. Such an organization is the Hermetic Order of the Golden Dawn.

Rite: A higher degree, ritual, or set of rituals additional to the three degrees and Royal Arch.

Rose Croix ("Rose Cross"): The name of the eighteenth degree of the Ancient and Accepted Scottish Rite as well as numerous other such rites, especially in eighteenth-century France.

Royal Arch: A degree higher than those of Craft Masonry. It has traditionally been regarded, erroneously, as the second half of the third degree of Craft Masonry. In America, it is given as the seventh degree.

Scots, or Scotch Mason: Usually the fourth degree of Freemasonry in some European Masonic systems.

Scottish Rite: *see* Ancient and Accepted Scottish Rite.

Speculative (or Speculative Masonry): Not of the trade of stonemasonry, but rather a philosophical Masonry, i.e., Freemasonry.

Speculative Mason: Another name for a Freemason.

Square Pavement: Probably the drawn plan of the lodge. Otherwise it is considered the "ground floor" of the lodge.

Tessellated Border: A border surrounding the lodge, symbolically. It is usually pictured as being made of rope.

Tracing Board: An architect's, or draftsman's drawing board. In Freemasonry it is said to be for the Master of a lodge to draw his symbolic or philosophical designs upon.

Tyler: The outer guard of a masonic lodge. Usually the Tyler sits outside the lodge and introduces Freemasons to the lodge once proceedings are underway.

Worshipful Master: Essentially the head and director of the lodge. The Worshipful Master is usually elected by his lodge for a period of a year.

York Rite: A structure of various Masonic degrees, including the Mark Master, Royal Arch, Cryptic Rite, and Knight Templar degrees. This is generally considered the Christian branch of the higher degrees, though not all degrees make reference to the Christian religion. The York Rite is American, though it can be found in other countries where an American influence can be felt, like Japan. This Masonic rite takes its name from the English city of York.

Notes

Introduction

1. "Architect." *The Oxford English Dictionary*, 2nd ed.
2. Coldstream, *Medieval Craftsmen*, 5.
3. Recently Trevor Stewart, the Prestonian lecturer for the United Grand Lodge of England, 2004, has come to a similar conclusion in this regard and has highlighted the importance of discussion, lectures, and the intellectual tradition especially in eighteenth-century Freemasonry in England. Where possible, see Stewart's Prestonian lecture "English Speculative Freemasonry."
4. It should be pointed out that these "higher degrees" are sometimes referred to as "rites" and at other times as "orders." To avoid confusion, I have used "degree" to mean a single ritual, "rite" to refer to a set of Masonic or Masonic-like rituals or degrees, however connected to the fraternity, and, generally speaking, "order" to mean a society and its rituals that are essentially independent from Freemasonry—the exception being the neo-Masonic Order of the Temple, though it is clear that the inventors of this body meant it to be related to the pre-Masonic chivalric order.
5. Waite, *Encyclopaedia of Freemasonry*, 1:52.

Chapter 1

1. Hislop, *Medieval Masons*, 16.
2. Mackey, *The History of Freemasonry*, 26.
3. I have slightly modernized the spelling and grammar of quotations throughout.
4. Mackey, *The History of Freemasonry*, 30.
5. Coldstream, *Medieval Craftsmen*, 20.
6. This mythology, known usually as the "York Legend," gained considerable status in the early eighteenth century when one Masonic grand lodge at York used it in an attempt to legitimize their claim to antiquity. While the said Masonic body died out somewhere close to the middle of the century after a relatively inactive existence, the legend became, and remained, of importance in America, where Freemasonic lodges or grand lodges often refer to their specific form of Masonry as "Ancient York Masonry" and where one established system of Masonic rituals or degrees is now known as the York Rite.
7. Mackey. *The History of Freemasonry*, 95–110.
8. Knoop, Jones, and Hamer. *Two Earliest Masonic MSS.*, 28.
9. Eliade, *Forge and the Crucible*, 54.
10. Coldstream, *Medieval Craftsmen*, 20.
11. Eliade, *Forge and the Crucible*, 97–108.
12. "Jes-Lei," *Encyclopedia Judaica*, vol. 10.
13. Versluis. *American Renaissance*, 16.
14. Zoroaster, or Zarathustra as he is better known in the Middle East, was the founder of the so-called Magian religion, usually known in the West as "Zoroastrianism." He had wandered as a holy man for some time and was finally patronized by a king of Persia (roughly the area that is now known as Iran). The Roman centurions took one of the Zoroastrian demigods, Mitra, as their own deity and established the religion of Mithraism. This religion spread across most of Europe, reaching Britain and further afield, and proved the main rival to Christianity at one point.

15. Knoop, Jones, and Hamer. *Two Earliest Masonic MSS.*, 35.
16. Ibid., 35–37.
17. Ibid., 38.
18. Macoy, *A Dictionary of Freemasonry*, 218–30.
19. Abiff is translated as "my father's," and this was taken to refer to King Hiram of Tyre.
20. Curl, *Art and Architecture of Freemasonry*, 31.
21. Macoy, *A Dictionary of Freemasonry*, 176.
22. Knoop, Jones and Hamer, *Two Earliest Masonic MSS.*, 47–48.
23. Gould, *The History of Freemasonry*, 1:201.
24. Ibid., 214.
25. Ibid., 212–219.

Chapter 2

1. For an overview of the life of John Dee, see Allen G. Debus's Introduction in Dee, *The Mathematical Preface*.
2. Yates, *The Rosicrucian Enlightenment*, 214–15.
3. Ibid., 214–15.
4. Gould, *The History of Freemasonry*, 284–86.
5. Dermott, *Ahiman Rezon*, xiv.
6. Ibid., xiv.
7. Ibid., xiv *n*.
8. Szpiro, *Kepler's Conjecture*, 38.
9. Ibid., 38.
10. Ibid., 38.
11. Yates, *Occult Philosophy*, 62.
12. Impens, *Masonic Emblem*, 256–62.
13. Panofsky, *Albrecht Dürer*, 168.
14. Yates, *Occult Philosophy*, 57.
15. Ibid, 355.
16. Plato, *Symposium and Phaedrus*, 59.
17. Boas, *The Hieroglyphics of Horapollo*, xvii and 33.
18. Mackey, *The History of Freemasonry*, 349.
19. Negri, "Italian Alchemical Text," 273–94.
20. Mylius's *Basilica Philosophica* (1620), the French edition of Basil Valentine's *Azoth* (1624), the *Viatorium Spagyricum*, (1625), Daniel Stolz's *Horticulus Hermeticus* (1627), the third edition of *Theatrum Chemicum* (1659–1661). Independent of Rebis, the square and compasses would appear, for example, in an etching of Albertus Magnus's *Philosophia Naturalis* (1650).
21. Szpiro, *Kepler's Conjecture*, 16–17. Kepler's mother, Katharina, who seems to have had a most unbecoming personality, was accused of witchcraft and imprisoned at Guglingen for six years until Kepler was able to secure a verdict of innocent.

Chapter 3

1. Morris, "Post Boy Sham Exposure," 9–37.

2. In 1616, another Lutheran pastor and adherent to what might be called "conservative Rosicrucianism," Daniel Cramer, published a book of Rosicrucian emblems, *The True Society of Jesus and the Rosy Cross*. Through the book's forty emblems, Cramer established the heart (the symbol missing from the rosy-cross as a reference to Luther's device) as the central figure of Christian transformation or Christian alchemy. It is not an alchemy concerned, of course, with the transformation of metals, but of the heart, the center of the Christian's experience of Jesus, as inferred by Luther and embodied in his heraldic emblem.

3. For an overview of the earliest references to Freemasonry and Rosicrucianism see Knoop, Jones, and Hamer, *Early Masonic Pamphlets*, 26–27.

4. Waite, *New Encyclopedia of Freemasonry*, 1:356.

5. The full title appeared as *Long Livers: A curious History of such Persons of both Sexes who have liv'd several Ages and grown young again: With the rare Secret of Rejuvenescency of Arnoldus de Villa Nova. And a great many approv'd and invaluable Rules to prolong Life: Also how to prepare the Universal Medicine*.

6. Mackey, *The History of Freemasonry*, 340.

7. Ibid., 340.

8. Yet, Yates compares the *Constitutions* to Dee's *Preface to Euclid*, and claims that there is a striking similarity. Her belief in the similarity of the text, however, is based on her belief that Freemasons must have known of the preface, must have read it, and must therefore have known of Dee (and his works). As I have suggested, operative masons and architects must certainly have known the text, but as Yates herself points out, long before the establishment of the Grand Lodge, and long before the writing of the *Constitutions*, Dee had been discredited and had become obscured, if not entirely removed from history. If Masons had read the preface, they may not have known who Dee was, and moreover, Dee nowhere there recommends his own writings.

9. ". . . whimsical kinsmen of the Hod and Trowel, having (on new Light received from some worthy Rosicrucians) thought fit to change their Patron and Day . . ."

10. As Knoop, Jones, and Hamer suggest, A and Z are almost certainly not the author's initials. What they may mean, if anything, is a matter of contention. Possibly they were chosen because they are, of course, the first and final letters of the Roman alphabet.

11. Knoop, Jones, and Hamer, *Early Masonic Pamphlets*, 233–36.

12. The Letter of A. Z. exhibits a history that is not only well informed but also almost certainly heavily relies on Anderson's, while the reference to the Wardens and Grand Masters would certainly seem to derive from Philalethes' address.

13. Akerman, *Rose Cross*, 149.

14. Ibid., 150.

15. Ibid., 148.

16. Ibid., 148.

17. Knoop, Jones, and Hamer, *Early Masonic Pamphlets*, 112.

Chapter 4

1. Waite, *New Encyclopaedia of Freemasonry*, 1:360.

2. Knoop, Jones, and Hamer, *The Early Masonic Catechisms*, 24.

3. Wells, *Development of Organized Freemasonry*, 6.

4. Here the use of the term "accepted" might suggest those men who were not builders but gentlemen.

5. On the persecution of Protestants in France under Louis XIV, see Mitford, *The Sun King*, 143. On the Desaguliers's emigration from France and relocation to England, see Ridley, *The Freemasons*, 34–35.

6. Fay, *Revolution and Freemasonry*, 93.

7. Ibid, 103.

8. In some Masonic traditions, the East is held as symbolic of the sacred because the teachings of Jesus were brought from the east, though such overtly sectarian religious references were not as established and were implicitly discouraged under the premier Grand Lodges.

9. Knoop, Jones, and Hamer, *The Early Masonic Catechisms*, 31–34.

10. Béresniak, *Symbols of Freemasonry*, 68.

Chapter 5

1. See *Being One of the Old Charges*.

2. White, *Isaac Newton*, 158–59

3. On Newton's interest in alchemy, see Westfall, *Sir Isaac Newton* and White, *Isaac Newton*.

4. Yates, *The Rosicrucian Enlightenment*, 125–29 and *Occult Philosophy*, 203–5.

5. Mackey, *History of Freemasonry*, 301–14.

6. Carr, *Three Distinct Knocks*, 33.

7. See the preceding chapter regarding the symbolism of the East.

8. As we have mentioned, St. John the Evangelist, the author of this gospel, is one of the patron saints of Freemasonry.

9. The King James Bible is the standard translation of Great Britain and other English-speaking countries, especially for Protestants.

10. Since Freemasonic lodges accept men of all religions, the Sacred Book is now considered that of the initiate's religion.

11. Vitruvius, *Ten Books on Architecture*, 253.

12. Iamblichus, *The Theology of Arithmetic*, 38.

13. An older term for the compasses, or compass, is "a pair of compasses."

14. Vitruvius, *Ten Books on Architecture*, 73.

15. Carr, *Three Distinct Knocks*.

16. From the "Mason's Confession" (published in *Scots Magazine*, March 1755, but probably written circa 1727). See Knoop, Jones, and Hamer, *Early Masonic Catechisms*, 99, 103.

17. It is my understanding that there are some very few Masonic lodges that still practice this drafting ritual. I am told that there is at least one lodge in Belgium, and there are probably a few others on the European continent and perhaps elsewhere.

Chapter 6

1. Gould, *The History of Freemasonry*, 3:210.
2. Piatigorsky, *Freemasonry*, 131.
3. Waite, *The Brotherhood of the Rosy Cross*, 436.
4. For example, see Wilmhurst, *The Meaning of Masonry*, 139.
5. Another popular Masonic myth states that the third degree was once a part of the second degree.
6. The address is also included in Wells, *Organized Freemasonry*, 59–60.
7. Dermott, *Ahiman Rezon*, 47.
8. Gould, *History of Freemasonry*, 3:214.
9. While congregations of Freemasons who bestow the three degrees of Craft Masonry are collectively referred to as a "lodge," Masons conferring the Royal Arch are known as a "chapter." Some of the higher degrees are bestowed by groups known as "encampments," "valleys," or "councils."
10. Wells, *Organized Freemasonry*, 154–55.
11. Gould, *The History of Freemasonry*, 3:212.
12. Ibid., 210.
13. Dermott, *Ahiman Rezon*, 43.
14. Szpiro, *Kepler's Conjecture*, 19–23.
15. Carr, *Three Distinct Knocks*, 100.
16. Dermott, *Ahiman Rezon*, 36.
17. Ibid., xxxvii.
18. See *Apologia Demonstrationem Analyticam*.
19. Huffman, *Robert Fludd*, 32.
20. Cramer's spider's web has nine supporting threads. I do not think that any numerical significance was implied by Cramer.
21. Waite, "Robert Fludd and Freemasonry," 65–80.
22. Lang, "Substance of Freemasonry," 277–94.
23. Waite, "Robert Fludd and Freemasonry," 65–80.
24. Yates, *The Rosicrucian Enlightenment*, 222–23.
25. McIntosh, *The Rosicrucians*, 22, 53–54.

Chapter 7

1. Abbott, *Fictions of Freemasonry*, 27.
2. de la Bedoyere, *Archbishop and the Lady*, 242.
3. By 1739, Thomas Crudelli of Florence was imprisoned by the Inquisition for his Masonic membership, being released only after the then rather considerable sum of twenty pounds had been secured by the premier Grand Lodge of England, upon petition by Crudelli. Similarly, John Coustos, who had been initiated as a Mason in London but had set up a Masonic lodge in Paris, where he was resident, was also imprisoned and, in this case, tortured by the Inquisition for his Masonic membership and was released in 1744. See Wells, *Organized Freemasonry*, 38.
4. Wells, *Organized Freemasonry*, 38.
5. Ibid., 151.
6. Gould, *A History of Freemasonry*, 3:338–343.
7. Seward, *The Monks of War*, 34–35.
8. Later, the Knights of St. John and Knights of Malta would be all but destroyed by the French Revolution, which would begin in 1789. In 1792, the Order of St. John was dissolved by the French Republic in a Revolutionary zeal. In 1798, Napoleon invaded the Island of Malta and evicted the knights, who had remained faithful to the French monarchy. With the amalgamation of the Priories of Aragon and Castile into the Royal Spanish Order of St. John, the only remaining priories were those of Italy and Germany. The order of Malta continues as a Roman Catholic chivalrous order, while the name of the order has also been appropriated by one of the higher degrees of Freemasonry.
9. Seward, *The Monks of War*, 199–205.
10. Mackey, *The History of Freemasonry*, 255–66.
11. Jackson, *Rose Croix*, 6–7. Jackson discusses the various interpretations of the word "Heredom."
12. Waite, *New Encyclopaedia of Freemasonry*, 1:401.
13. Gould, *The History of Freemasonry*, 3:346.
14. Macoy, *A Dictionary of Freemasonry*, 359.
15. Gould, *The History of Freemasonry*, 3:347.
16. On the Masonic adventures and life of Cagliostro see McCalman, *The Last Alchemist*.
17. Telepneff, "Society of African Builders," 299–314.
18. Faivre, *Golden Fleece and Alchemy*, 26.
19. Anderson, *Constitutions of the Free-Masons*, 5.
20. Faivre, *Golden Fleece and Alchemy*, 92.
21. Gould, *The History of Freemasonry*, 4:47–50.
22. Ibid., 51.
23. Ibid., 51.
24. McIntosh, *The Rosicrucians*, 51–61.
25. Ibid., 66.
26. Gould, *The History of Freemasonry*, 3:369.
27. Stillson and Hughan, *History of Freemasonry*, 270.
28. According to Gould, *The History of Freemasonry*, in "1777 the system [of the Golden Rosicrucians] had obtained a footing in Prussia," 3:371.
29. Bischoffswerder had been born into a noble Thuringian family, and had served in the Prussian Cavalry. He was initiated into the Strict Observance in 1764.
30. Gould and McIntosh present rather different accounts of the elixir. McIntosh, *The Rosicrucians*, 78, claims that it was

actually administered by Bicshoffswerder to the prince and that he recovered soon after (although not necessarily as a result of the elixir). Gould says that one Schroder rode from St. Petersburg to Wollner at Berlin in order to secure from him the elixir for Schwarz, also a Rosicrucian. Apparently Schwarz died before it could be administered, but Gould says that it was administered to some animals who died from its effects, and he also claims that the medicine was subsequently analyzed and found to be lethal.

31. McIntosh, *The Rosicrucians*, 77–83.
32. Ibid., 82.
33. Greiner, *German Freemasonry*, 55–80.

Chapter 8

1. According to Jackson, around 1761 a French Mason named Jean-Baptiste Willermoz corresponded with Meunier de Precourt, a master of a Masonic lodge at Metz, Germany, presumably with particular interest in this rite. At this point, de Precourt seems to have known little about the Rose Croix except simply that it existed in some form in Germany. A year later however, Precourt would, it seems, furnish Willermoz with a rite that the German Rosicrucians were said to have known as the "Order of the Temple." Jackson suggests that Willermoz would develop this degree into his own form of the Rose Croix, completing it around 1765. There are certain problems with this theory, not least of all because, as Jackson makes clear, a rite known as the Knight of the Eagle was being practiced in France by about 1761, and the Masons of the degree were known as Sovereign Prince Rose Croix. See Jackson, *Rose Croix*, 25.
2. Waite, *Rosy Cross*, 428.
3. Ibid., 430.
4. Schneider, *Still Life*, 77.
5. Similar to the aforementioned degree in terms of mythological coloring is the Masonic society known as the Royal Order of Scotland, which appeared around the middle of the eighteenth century. The Royal Order consists of two degrees: the Heredom of Kilwinning Degree and the Rosy Cross Degree. The Ritual of Heredom of Kilwinning credits Robert the Bruce of Scotland of having established the rite in 1311 after the battle of Bannockburn. While "Heredom" has been supposed a corruption of "Harodim," i.e., the mountain near Kilwinning, other interpretations have been put forward, for example, the Latin *heres domus*, meaning "house of the heir," and the Hebrew *Har Edom*, "Holy Mountain of the Earth."
6. On the Apprentice Degree of the Egyptian Rite see Evans, *Cagliostro*.
7. Originally the Masonic Knights Templar was referred to as a degree and was only later conferred as an order. See Speidel, *York Rite of Freemasonry*, 51.

8. Evans, *Little Masonic Library*, 3:11–68.
9. Ibid., 35.
10. Stillson and Hughan, *History of Freemasonry*, 755.
11. MacNulty, *Kabbalah and Freemasonry*, 145–149.
12. The full Articles of Union (1813) are reproduced in Wells, *Organized Freemasonry*, 192–96.
13. Jackson, *Rose Croix*, 203.
14. Ibid., 69–72.
15. Gould, *The History of Freemasonry*, 3:384.
16. Waite, *New Encyclopaedia of Freemasonry*, 1:288.
17. Stillson and Hughan, *History of Freemasonry*, 796–801.
18. McLenachan, *Scottish Rite of Freemasonry*, 316–22.
19. The Royal Ark Mariner Degree, which is separate from the Scottish Rite, concentrates on the tale of the flood and Noah's Ark.
20. Jackson, *Rose Croix*, 212.
21. The double-headed eagle had appeared in Hieronymus Reusser's *Pandora* (1582) and Athanasius Kircher's *Ars Magna Lucis et Umbrae* (1665) as well as the *Secret Symbols of the Rosicrucians*, issued in two parts, in 1785 and 1788. It is found in the latter work in two slight variations—representative of the red and white alchemical tinctures—and placed on either side of a pendant of the golden Rosy Cross. The work, however, is made up of various collected treatises, some of which were printed in 1621, 1625, 1678, and 1749. See Tresner, "Our Bisephalous Bird."
22. Gould, *The History of Freemasonry*, 1:202.
23. See Morrissey, *Charlemagne and France*.
24. Zamoyski, *Holy Madness*, 160.
25. Broughton, *Medieval Knighthood and Chivalry*, 248.
26. Heer, *The Holy Roman Empire*, 25.

Chapter 9

1. Wells, *Organized Freemasonry*, 60.
2. *History of the Saint George's Society*, 27.
3. As Trevor Stewart has recently shown, many Masonic lodges in England organized lectures and debates on an extraordinary range of subjects, including the natural sciences, ethics, art, history, and physiology. See Stewart, "English Speculative Freemasonry."
4. Clark, *Benjamin Franklin*, 50–51.
5. This term, usually reserved for the head of all the lodges of one country, province, or state, seems here to mean "Worshipful Master." i.e., the head of one specific lodge, in this case St. John's of Philadelphia.
6. Johnson, *The Beginnings of Freemasonry*, 125.
7. Morse, "American Revolution," 225.
8. Ibid., 233.
9. Lancaster, *The American Revolution*, 138.
10. Ibid., 8.
11. Horne, "Freemasonry Comes to America," 370–99.
12. Peters, *Masons as Makers*, 13.

13. Ibid., 15.
14. Barry, "Masonry and the Flag," 3:88–89.
15. Coil, *Coil's Masonic Encyclopedia*, 677.
16. Lang, *New York Freemasonry*, 47–48.
17. Ibid., 32.
18. Roberts and McLeod, *Freemasonry and Democracy*, 39.
19. *The Builders Laid the Foundation*, 8.
20. Bullock, *Revolutionary Brotherhood*, 147.
21. Ibid., 154.
22. Ibid., 154.
23. Sickels, *General Ahiman Rezon*, 86.
24. For example, see Sickels, *General Ahiman Rezon*, 131–138.
25. The Mark Master Degree exists in Britain and elsewhere, though not necessarily as a part of the Royal Arch Chapter.
26. Wells, *Organized Freemasonry*, 159–60.
27. The Council of Princes of Jerusalem later became a part of the Ancient and Accepted Scottish Rite and confers the 15th and 16th Degrees of that rite.
28. Stillson and Hughan, *History of Freemasonry*, 649.
29. Ibid., 336.
30. As the three degrees of Craft Masonry are prerequisites for joining any of the Masonic rites, these properly begin with a 4th Degree.
31. *Little Masonic Library*, 5:8.
32. Catton, *The Civil War*, 8.
33. Ibid., 20–21.
34. Lang, *New York Freemasonry*, 97–98.
35. *Little Masonic Library*, 5:9.
36. Lang, *New York Freemasonry*, 98.

Chapter 10
1. Wilson, *History of the S.R.I.A.*, 13.
2. Westcott, "Rosicrucians," 37.
3. Wilson, *History of the S.R.I.A.*, 13
4. Ibid., 6.
5. Ibid., 29.
6. Westcott, *Rosicrucians*, 37.
7. McIntosh, *The Rosicrucians*, 122–23.
8. Regardie, *Golden Dawn*, 11.
9. Waite, *Rosy Cross*, 583.
10. Greer, *Golden Dawn*, 52–54.
11. By this point, the Societas Rosicruciana in Scotia had almost certainly come into accord with the branches in England, who did not admit women.
12. Greer, *Golden Dawn*, 82.
13. Ibid., 83.
14. Starr, "Freemason!," 150–161.
15. Algeo, *Blavatsky*, 24.
16. Ibid., 9–10.
17. Waite, *New Encyclopaedia of Freemasonry*, 1:57–58.
18. Root, *History of the A.A.O.N.M.S.*, 18
19. Ibid., 30–31.
20. Ibid., 48–49.

Acknowledgments

During my last few years of researching the subject of the development of Freemasonry, I have been fortunate to have had the continual support of The Chancellor Robert R Livingston Library of Grand Lodge New York. The Director of the Library and Museum, Thomas Savini, has both aided me in my research and supplied a forum for me to deliver talks on my studies. The Livingston Library kindly allowed me to photograph artifacts from their extensive collection, and those photographs are reproduced in this work by permission of the Library. Similarly I would like to thank the trustees of the Library and Museum, especially Richard Eberle, as well as the staff, especially Catherine Walter for all her support, patience, and for supplying me with information on the artifacts themselves.

I would like to thank my editor, Martin Howard, for his interest in the subject, and for the time he has spent with the manuscript. My thanks must also go to Eugene Romanosky, Mark Rivers, Carla, Kyler, the L. I. College of the M.S.R.I.C.F., Katherine Lorimer at the Goethe Institute in New York, Piers, Cliff, Ted, Harvey, Bubba, Jacob Beardsley, Spiridon, Jonathon, Bob, Frank at Mensa, and, of course, my mother, father, and brother.

Bibliography

Abbot, Scott. *Fictions of Freemasonry: Freemasonry and the German Novel*. Detroit: Wayne State University Press, 1992.

Agrippa, Henry Cornelius, *Three Books of Occult Philosophy*. Edited and annoted by Donald Tyson. Trans. James Freake. St. Paul, MN: Llewellyn Publications, 1997.

Akerman, Susanna. *Rose Cross Over the Baltic*. Boston: Brill, Leiden, 1998.

Algeo, John. *Blavatsk Freemasonry, and the Western Mystery Tradition*. London: The Theosophical Society in England, 1996.

Anderson, James. *The Constitutions of the Free-Masons*. London: William Hunter, 1723.

Barry, John W. "Masonry and the Flag." *Little Masonic Library*. Vol. 3. Richmond, VA: Macoy Publishing, 1946.

Begent, Peter, and Hubert Chesshyre. *The Most Noble Order of the Garter—650 Years*. London: Spink, 1999.

Beharrell, Rev. T. G. *Odd Fellows Monitor and Guide*. Indianapolis: Robert Douglas, 1882.

Being One of the Old Charges: The Carmick Manuscript, 1727. Washington, DC: Masonic Service Association, 1953.

Béresniak, Daniel. *Symbols of Freemasonry*. Paris: Editions Asouline, 1997.

Boas, George. *The Hieroglyphics of Horapollo*. Princeton, NJ: Princeton University Press, 1993.

Broughton, Bradford B. *Dictionary of Medieval Knighthood and Chivalry: Concepts and Terms*. New York: Greenwood Press, 1986.

Builders Laid the Foundation. The. Washington, DC: Masonic Service Association, 1959.

Bullock, Steven C. *Revolutionary Brotherhood: Freemasonry and the Transformation of the American Social Order, 1730–1840*. Chapel Hill, NC: The Institute of Early American History and Culture, 1996.

Carr, Harry. *Three Distinct Knocks and Jachin and Boaz*. Bloomington, IL: The Masonic Book Club, 1981.

Catton, Bruce. *The Civil War*. Boston: Houghton Mifflin, 1988.

Clark, Ronald W. *Benjamin Franklin: A Biography*. New York: Barnes & Noble Books, 2004.

Coil, Henry Wilson. *Coil's Masonic Encyclopedia*. Richmond VA: Macoy Publishing, 1996.

Coldstream, Nicola. *Medieval Craftsmen: Masons and Sculptors*. Toronto: University of Toronto Press, 1998.

Conder, Edward. "The Hon. Miss St. Leger and Freemasonry." *Ars Quatuor Coronatorum* 8 (1895): 16-23.

Cross, Jeremy L. *Templar's Chart or Hieroglyphic Monitor*. New York: Jeremy L. Cross, 1854.

Curl, James Stevens. *The Art and Architecture of Freemasonry*. New York: The Overlook Press, 2002.

Dee, John. *The Mathematical Preface to the Elements of Geometrie of Euclid of Megara* (1570). Cambridge, UK: Science History Publications, 1975.

de la Bedoyere, Michael. *The Archbishop and the Lady*. New York: Pantheon, 1956.

———. *The Archbishop and the Lady: The Story of Fenelon and Madame Guyon*. London: Collins, 1956.

Denslow, Ray V. *Freemasonry and the Presidency: U.S.A*. Columbia, MO: Missouri Lodge of Research, 1952.

Dermott, Laurence. *Ahiman Rezon, or A Help to All That Are or Would Be Free and Accepted Masons*. 3rd ed. London: James Jones Grand Secretary, 1778.

Dobbs, Betty Jo Teeter. *The Janus Faces of Genius: The Role of Alchemy in Newton's Thought*. Cambridge, UK: Cambridge University Press, 1991.

Eisenstein, Elizabeth L. *The Printing Revolution in Early Modern Europe*. Cambridge, UK: Cambridge University Press, 1986.

Eliade, Mircea. *The Forge and the Crucible*. Trans. Stephen Corrin. Chicago: University of Chicago Press, 1978.

Encyclopaedia Judaica. Jerusalem: Encyclopaedia Judaica, 1974.

Evans, Henry Ridgely. *Cagliostro and His Egyptian Rite of Freemasonry*. New York: Macoy Publishing, 1930.

———. "A History of the York and Scottish Rites." *Little Masonic Library*. Richmond, VA: Macoy Publishing, 1946.

Faivre, Antoine. *The Golden Fleece and Alchemy*. Albany: State University of New York Press, 1993.

Fay, Bernard. *Revolution and Freemasonry, 1680–1800*. Boston: Little, Brown and Company, 1935.

Gould, Robert Freke. *The History of Freemasonry*. 4 vols. Philadelphia: John C. Yorkston & Co. Publishers, 1896.

Gray, David L. *Inside Prince Hall*. Edited by Tony Pope. Lancaster, VA: Anchor Communications LLC, 2003.

Greer, Mary K. *Women of the Golden Dawn: Rebels and Priestesses*. Rochester, VT: Park Street Press, 1995.

Greiner, Gotthelf. "German Freemasonry in the Present Era." *Ars Quatuor Coronatorum* 9 (1896): 55–80.

Hall, Manly P. *The Rosicrucians and Magister Christoph Schlegel: Hermetic Roots of America*. Los Angeles: The Philosophical Research Society Inc., 1986.

Hawkins, E. L. "Adoptive Masonry and the Order of Mopses" *Ars Quatuor Coronatorum* 24 (1911): 6–20.

Heaton, Ronald E. *Masonic Membership of the General Officers of the Continental Army*. Washington, DC: The Masonic Service Association, 1959.

Heer, Frederich. *Charlemagne and His World*. New York: Macmillan Publishing, 1975.

———. *The Holy Roman Empire*. New York: Praeger, 1968.

Henderson, Kent William. *Freemasonry Universal: A New Guide to the Masonic World*. Global Masonic Publications, Williamstown, Victoria: 1998–2000.

Hills, Gordon P. G. "Women and Freemasonry" *Ars Quatuor Coronatorum* 33 (1920): 63–70.

Hislop, Malcolm. *Medieval Masons*. London: CIT Printing Services, 2000.

History of the Saint George's Society of New York from 1770 to 1913, A. New York: Saint George's Society of New York, 1913.

Horne, Alex. "Freemasonry Comes to America." *Transactions of the American Lodge of Research*. 13.5. (1977): 370–99

Huffman, William H, ed. *Robert Fludd*. Berkeley: North Atlantic Books, 2001.

Iamblichus (attributed to). *The Theology of Arithmetic*. Trans. Robin Waterfield. Grand Rapids, MI: Phanes Press, 1988.

Impens, Chris. "A Masonic Emblem in 1522." *Ars Quatuor Coronatorum*. 115 (2002): 256–62.

Jackson, A. C. F. *Rose Croix: A History of the Ancient and Accepted Rite for England and Wales*. London: Lewis Masonic, 1987.

Johnson, Melvin M. *The Beginnings of Freemasonry in America*. Bloomington, IL: The Masonic Book Club, 1983.

Knoop, Douglas, G. P. Jones, and Douglas Hamer. *The Two Earliest Masonic MSS.*, Manchester: Manchester University Press, 1938.

———. *The Early Masonic Catechisms*. Manchester: Manchester University Press, 1963.

———. *The Early Masonic Pamphlets*. London: Q.C. Correspondence Circle Ltd., 1978.

Lancaster, Bruce. *The American Revolution*. Boston: Houghton Mifflin, 2001.

Lang, Ossian H. "Derivation of the Substance of Freemasonry and Development of the Royal Art." in the Proceedings of the Grand Lodge for the State of New York, 1918.

———. *History of Freemasonry in the State of New York*. New York: Grand Lodge of New York, 1922.

Lang, Ossian and Herbert T. Singer. *New York Freemasonry*. New York: Grand Lodge of New York, 1981.

Mackey, Albert G. *Encyclopedia of Freemasonry*. Revised and enlarged by Robert I. Clegg. Vol. 1. Chicago: The Masonic History Company, 1929.

———. *The History of Freemasonry*. New York: Random House, 1996.

MacNulty, W. Kirk. "Kabbalah and Freemasonry." *Heredom* 7 (1998): 133–205.

Macoy, Robert. *A Dictionary of Freemasonry*. New York: Gramercy Books, 1989.

McCalman, Iain. *The Last Alchemist: Count Cagliostro, Master of Magic in the Age of Reason*. New York: HarperCollins, 2004.

McIntosh, Christopher. *The Rosicrucians: The History, Mythology, and Rituals of an Esoteric Order*. York Beach, ME: Samuel Weiser Inc., 1997.

———. *The Rose Cross and the Age of Reason*. New York: E.J. Brill, 1992.

McLenachan, Charles T. *The Book of the Ancient and Accepted Scottish Rite of Freemasonry*. Revised and enlarged edition. New York: Macoy Publishing, 1914.

Mitford, Nancy. *The Sun King*. New York: Harper & Row, 1966.

Moore, William D. and John D. Hamilton. *Washington as the Master of His Lodge: History and Symbolism of a Masonic Icon*. New York: Hudson Hills Press, 1999.

Morris, Brent S. "The Post Boy Sham Exposure of 1723." *Heredom* 7 (1998): 9–37.

Morrissey, Robert. *Charlemagne and France: A Thousand Years of Mythology*. Trans. Catherine Tihanyi. Notre Dame, IN: University of Notre Dame Press, 2003.

Morse, Sidney. "Freemasonry in the American Revolution." *Little Masonic Library*. Vol. 3, Richmond, VA: Macoy Publishing, 1946.

Negri, Pietro. "An Italian Alchemical Text on Lead Tablets." In *Introduction to Magic* by Julius Evola and the UR Group. Rochester, VT: Inner Traditions, 2001.

Panosfsky, Erwin. *The Life and Art of Albrecht Durer*. Princeton, NJ: Princeton University Press, 1971.

Peters, Madison C. *The Masons as Makers of America: The True Story of the American Revolution*. Brooklyn, NY: The Patriotic League, 1917.

Piatigorsky, Alexander. *Freemasonry*. London: Harvill Press, 1997.

Pike, Albert. *Morals and Dogma of the Ancient and Accepted Scottish Rite of Freemasonry*. Charlestown, SC: Supreme Council of the Thirty-Third Degree for the Southern Jurisdiction of the United States, 1872.

Regardie, Israel. *What You Should Know About the Golden Dawn*. Phoenix, AZ: New Falcon Publications, 1993.

Ridley, Jasper. *The Freemasons: A History of the World's Most Powerful Secret Society*. New York: Arcade Publishing, 2001.

Roberts, Allen and Wallace Mcleod. *Freemasonry and Democracy: Its Evolution in North America*. Highland Springs, VA: Anchor Communications, 1997.

Root, George L. *History of the A.A.O.N.M.S.: The Ancient Arabic Order of the Mystic Shrine for North America*. Peoria, IL: B. Frank Brown Co., 1903.

Sachse, Julius Frederich. *Franklin's Account with the Lodge of Masons, 1731–1737*. Philadelphia: Lippincott Press, 1898.

Schneider, Heinrich. *Quest for Mysteries: The Masonic Background for Literature in Eighteenth-Century Germany)*. Ithaca, NY: Cornell University Press, 1947.

Schneider, Norbert. *Still Life*. Taschen, 1999.

Seward, Desmond. *The Monks of War: The Military Religious Orders*. Herts, UK: Paladin, 1974.

Sickels, Daniel. *The General Ahiman Rezon and Freemason's Guide*. New York: Masonic Publishing and Manufacturing Co., 1869.

Speidel, Frederick G. *The York Rite of Freemasonry: A History and Handbook*. Greenfield, IN: Mitchell-Fleming Printing, Inc., 1989.

Starr, Martin P. Aleister Crowley. "Freemason!" *Ars Quatuor Coronatorum* 108 (1995): 150–61.

Stewart, Trevor. "English Speculative Freemasonry: Some Possible Origins, Themes and Developments." Prestonian lecture, privately published for *UGLE*, 2004.

Stillson, Henry Leonard and William James Hughan, eds. *History of the Ancient and Honorable Fraternity of Free and Accepted Masons, and Concordant Orders*. London: The Fraternity Publishing Company, 1909.

Szpiro, George G. *Kepler's Conjecture*. Hoboken, NJ: John Wiley & Sons, 2003.

Taylor, Anne. *Annie Bessant: A Biography*. New York: Oxford University Press, 1992.

Telepneff, B. "Society of African Builders." *Ars Quatuor Coronatorum* 53 (1940): 299–314.

Tresner, Jim. "Our Bisephalous Bird." *Plumline* 8.4.

Tuckerman, W. B. "Albrecht Durer and the Freemasons." *The American Freemason* 3.1 (1911): 21–27.

Versluis, Arthur. *The Esoteric Origins of the American Renaissance*. New York: Oxford University Press, 2001.

Vitruvius. *The Ten Books on Architecture*. Trans. Morris Hicky Morgan. New York: Dover Publications, 1960.

Waite, A. E. *Brotherhood of the Rosy Cross*. New York: Barnes and Noble Books, 1993.

———. *Robert Fludd and Freemasonry: Being the Masonic and Rosicrucian Connection*. Edmonds, WA: Holmes Publishing Group, 2002.

———. *A New Encyclopaedia of Freemasonry*. New York: Weathervane Books.

———. "Robert Fludd and Freemasonry: A Speculative Excursion." *Transactions of the Manchester Association for Research* 11 (1920–1921).

———. *The Secret Tradition in Freemasonry*. New York: E. P. Dutton & Co., 1937.

Wells, Roy A. *The Rise and Development of Organized Freemasonry*. Bloomington, IL: Masonic Book Club, 1986.

Westcott, W. Wynn. *History of the Societas Rosicruciana in Anglia*. London, Privately published, 1900.

———. "Rosicrucians: Their History and Aims." *Ars Quatuor Coronatorum* 7 (1894).

Westfall, Richard S. *The Life of Sir Isaac Newton*. Cambridge, UK: Cambridge University Press, 1994.

White, Michael. *Isaac Newton: The Last Sorcerer*. London: Fourth Estate Ltd., 1998.

Williams, Loretta J. *Black Freemasonry and Middle-Class Realities*. Columbia, MO: University of Missouri Press, 1980.

Wilmhurst, C. W. *The Meaning of Masonry*. Gramercy Books, 1995.

Wilson, Henry Christopher Bruce. *Early History of the S.R.I.A.: (1937–1944)*.

Yates, Frances. *The Occult Philosophy in the Elizabethan Age*. New York: Routledge, 2001.

———. *The Rosicrucian Enlightenment*. New York: Routledge, 1972.

Zamoyski, Adam. *Holy Madness: Romantics, Patriots and Revolutionaries, 1776–1871*. London: Weidenfeld & Nicolson, 1999.

Index